BLACK SCARE

*The Racist Response to Emancipation
and Reconstruction*

by

Forrest G. Wood

*University of California Press
Berkeley and Los Angeles 1970*

UNIVERSITY OF CALIFORNIA PRESS
BERKELEY AND LOS ANGELES, CALIFORNIA

UNIVERSITY OF CALIFORNIA PRESS, LTD.
LONDON, ENGLAND

COPYRIGHT © 1968, BY
THE REGENTS OF THE UNIVERSITY OF CALIFORNIA

LIBRARY OF CONGRESS CATALOG CARD NUMBER: 68–26066

STANDARD BOOK NUMBER: 520-01664-5

FIRST PAPERBACK EDITION

PRINTED IN THE UNITED STATES OF AMERICA

Preface

"By revealing early phases of the still burning race question," Francis B. Simkins observed in 1939, the historian "arouses more attention among the reading public than is usually accorded historical works." The statement was prophetic; it has never had more meaning than it has now. In the years since the Supreme Court's desegregation decision of 1954, the United States has witnessed a variety of reactions from those who protest the government's role in guaranteeing the rights of citizens. Reactions in the southern states have ranged from "standing in the schoolhouse door," to the burying of civil rights workers in an earthen dam. Northern equalitarians, similarly, have faced de facto segregation, double standards of law enforcement, employment discrimination, and the public rejection of open housing ordinances. Indeed, following Negro marches into the all-white neighborhoods of Chicago and Cicero in the summer of 1966, Martin Luther King declared that he had never seen such hatred, not even in the most hostile sections of Alabama and Mississippi. The modern term is "backlash."

The origins of backlash go far back in human history. The thesis of this study is not that modern racism began during the Civil War, but that the war and reconstruction polarized it for the first time into a psychological force of massive national proportions. As the radicals took the initiative in reconstruction, the Black Scare became the emotional counterpart of the "bloody shirt." Emancipation had created a new class of Americans, a class that owned no land, controlled virtually none of the nation's wealth, was largely illiterate, and, most important of all, was easily distinguished by color. Humanitarians correctly recognized the government's responsibilities: to abandon the black man at this point would have been to condemn him to a state of permanent inequality. Racist demagogues, however, aware that most white Americans considered the Negro innately inferior, launched a white supremacy crusade through pamphlets, newspapers, books, leaflets, songs, pictures, and speeches, and accused the government of leading the nation down the road to ruin. It was the first white backlash.

The research for this study was facilitated by many library staffs. I am particularly grateful to the librarians of the Rare Books Room at the Library of Congress, who made available to me the vast resources in the Joseph Meredith Toner Collection, the Alfred Whital Stern Collection of Lincolniana, the broadside portfolios, and the miscellaneous pamphlet collections. The illustrations appear through the courtesy of the Library of Congress. For materials and assistance I am also indebted to the Boston Public Library, to the New York Public Library, to the Newberry Library, to the Henry E. Huntington Library, to the Western Reserve Historical Society, to the curators of the Providence Public Library's Fiske Harris Collection on the American Civil War and Slavery, and to the libraries of Bryn Mawr College, the University of California at Los Angeles, the University of Chicago, the the University of Cincinnati, Duke University, Haverford College, the University of Minnesota, the University of North Carolina, Oberlin College, Ohio State University, the University of Pennsylvania, Princeton University, the University of Texas, and, especially, the University of California at Berkeley.

This book could never have been written without the gracious assistance of many persons. I wish to thank, most of all, Kenneth M. Stampp, whose searching criticism and generous encouragement accompanied the research and writing throughout. Charles G. Sellers and Kenneth E. Bock read the entire manuscript and made many useful suggestions. My debt to Harold M. Hyman and James M. McPherson is considerable; their meticulous attention to details saved me from the embarrassment of many errors of fact and interpretation. For their editorial advice and assistance in preparing the manuscript for publication, Herbert F. Mann, Jr., Grant Barnes, Lynda Bridge, and Marlene Charyn have already received my thanks.

Portions of Chapter Six first appeared in my article, "On Revising Reconstruction History: Negro Suffrage, White Disfranchisement, and

Common Sense," published in the *Journal of Negro History* (April 1966). I wish to thank the editors for permission to reprint most of the article.

To the Committee on Research of the University of California at Berkeley and to the Woodrow Wilson Foundation, whose timely research grants were of immeasurable assistance in defraying the costs of travel, photocopying, and materials, I am grateful. The financial aid of the United States Office of Economic Opportunity in typing and proofreading is also deeply appreciated.

F. G. W.

Contents

Chapter One

THE NATURE OF NINETEENTH-
CENTURY RACE PREJUDICE:
THE ANGLO-SAXON SELF-IMAGE

"Is there no pride in your blue eyes, light hair, white faces, and intelligent brains?" former Representative Samuel Sullivan Cox asked in a speech during the presidential campaign of 1868. "If there be, let it be aroused to save your white brothers from the impending struggle."[1]

By 1868, the race issue had become probably the most decisive single factor in American political debate. The presidential campaign marked the high point of a racist crusade that had begun during the most critical months of the Civil War. In July 1862, two months before the preliminary Emancipation Proclamation was issued, the editor of the *Presbyterian Quarterly Review* made a prophetic observance: however the war should end, it was certain that "the future condition of the colored race in this country will be the question over-mastering all others for years to come. It has already pushed itself into the foremost place." The "over-mastering" question did not subside after the fighting ended, but instead grew more intense. Two months after Appomattox, the editor of a leading midwestern Democratic newspaper complained that the Negro seemed to be the only topic of discussion everywhere. From debates over the Negro's status as a slave, he concluded, the country had passed to debates over his rights as a freedman.[2]

In the postwar South, restoration and rebuilding were the most obvious concerns, but discussions about the black man reflected a profound and growing uneasiness among many whites. Writing from Orangeburg, South Carolina, in the late summer of 1865, Sidney Andrews, one of many touring northern travelers, noted that everyone "talks about the negro." Echoing certain racist members of Congress, he wrote that the people "have got nigger on the brain." No matter where the conversation started, it always ended with "Sambo."[3] This preoccupation was part of a nationwide dialogue of actions and reactions. While abolitionist propaganda and pressures had been increasing before and during the Civil War, antiabolitionist resistance had stiffened and antagonism had grown more pronounced. Similarly, every postwar attempt to give former slaves some of the rights and privileges of citizenship collided with a racist determination to thwart all efforts to improve the conditions of black people.

Although race prejudice, like most prejudices, is not usually a deliberate, conscious sentiment, in the middle of the nineteenth century the majority of white Americans believed that they were far superior to the nonwhite people of the world (and, for that matter, to most of the white people). Despite the influence of "melting pot" sentiments, Americans were extremely ethnocentric. Sometimes they called the desirable group Nordic, at other times Aryan, and occasionally Teutonic or Celtic; but whatever the name, they always meant the same people—the northern- or western-European Caucasians. Immigrants from England, Scotland, Northern Ireland, Germany, France, the Netherlands, Sweden, and Switzerland had settled the Colonies. To suggest that anyone else had a stake in the country's future was unthinkable.[4]

Some whites justified their prejudice by calling it a "God-implanted" or "natural" instinct, a tack that enabled the racists to deny responsibility for their views. In a speech before Congress, Representative John L. Dawson of Pennsylvania insisted that race prejudice was "implanted by Providence for wise purposes." Senator James R. Doolittle of Wisconsin, a renegade Republican who frequently supported the Democrats, contended that the foundations of caste lay much deeper than "mere prejudice"; he argued that it was an "instinct of our nature" to make distinctions based on race. In a widely circulated pamphlet entitled "Negrophobia 'On the Brain' " (1869), a formerly obscure writer named J. R. Hayes contrasted "prejudice" and "natural antipathy." The former, he theorized, was an "educated attribute," while the latter was a "natural manifestation" of the white man's reaction to the obvious physical, mental, and behavioral differences among races.[5] These conclusions were typical. It never occured to Hayes that what he called a "natural antipathy" was nothing more than an "educated attribute."

But many others did not indulge in such hairsplitting; prejudice, instinct, antipathy—they were all the same. One may have called the "natural revolt" of the white man a prejudice, the editor of the Philadelphia *Age* declared, but it had always existed and could not be eradicated. Arguing against both Negro and female suffrage, Thomas Hartley, a conservative Republican writer who obviously did not share his party's more equalitarian views, asserted in a long tract that racial bias was a very deep, "just, and reasonable" prejudice and not "wicked and unholy." In fact, he continued, if not carried to extremes, it was "wholesome, natural, and right." Thus some Americans readily admitted their prejudices and found no reason to be ashamed of them. The hero of Anna Dickinson's abolitionist novel *What Answer?* (1868) was Will Surrey, whose father, previously a relatively unprejudiced man, violently objected to his son's marrying a mulatto woman. Prejudice against Negroes, the elder Surrey insisted, "is a feeling that will never die out, and ought never to die out, so long as any of the race remain in America."[6] In truth, Miss Dickinson was doing little more than portraying the average American's—or at least the average Northerner's—racial view: Negro freedom, yes; Negro equality, no.

In the antebellum South, white superiority had been so taken for granted that a kind of *noblesse oblige* had developed.* Members of the planter class had long boasted of their love for the black man. They had raised him from childhood, had clothed and fed him, had cared for him in sickness and in old age, and had rewarded him for superior production. The Negro, they insisted, was happy in slavery.[7] In truth, the slave had received little more from his master than a draft horse or a prize mule would have received. Economically, the black field hand had been more akin to a domestic work animal than to a human employee. In the final analysis, the planters had been just as prejudiced as the poor whites, only in a different way. As Andrews observed, southern whites had claimed for years to be the Negro's "special friends." But after he saw how they treated the black man, he said,

---

* Some scholars have suggested that southern paternalism did not really begin until the reconstruction era was almost over, and that there were often economic kinships between blacks and poor whites that overcame the color difference. See G. G. Johnson, "Southern Paternalism toward the Negro after Emancipation," *Journal of Southern History*, XXIII (Nov. 1957), 484; W. D. Weatherford and C. S. Johnson, *Race Relations: Adjustment of Whites and Negroes in the United States* (Boston, 1934), 509; H. M. Bond, "Social and Economic Forces in Alabama Reconstruction," *Journal of Negro History*, XXIII (July 1938), 295; and W. A. Russ, Jr., "Registration and Disfranchisement under Radical Reconstruction," *Mississippi Valley Historical Review*, XXI (Sept. 1934), 163–180.

"One cannot help praying that he may be saved from his friends in the future."[8]

Benevolent paternalism was not unique, however, to the antebellum, plantation South. Northern racists frequently expressed sympathy and friendship for the Negro, sometimes condemning and praising him in the same breath. After denouncing the Negro in a speech against emancipation, Cox concluded, "I do not speak these things out of any unkindness to the negro. I speak as their friend." Early in 1866, Edgar Cowan of Pennsylvania, speaking against the Freedmen's Bureau in a sarcastic oration that provoked boisterous laughter from the House galleries, described the Negro as inferior and not entitled to political, economic, or social privileges. He then added, "I stand here the friend of the negro, just as much his friend I trust as any man on earth." Perhaps Charles Henry Smith's comical Bill Arp said it best: "I ain't agin the nigger. I like him. I'm his friend, and I want him kept jest where he belongs."[9]

Although most of these contemporary explanations of the nature of race prejudice were unenlightened, they were nonetheless revealing. The most important single determinant of white supremacy attitudes in America was time—two and one-half centuries of well-nurtured tradition and habit. In things political or economic, Americans were progressive and, by Old-World standards, radical, but not when it came to dealing with nonwhite people. Each generation of Americans had embellished the prejudices of earlier generations. Citing Manifest Destiny and national progress, white men had overrun the lands of red men and Mexicans, great planters had exhausted virgin territories, and western profiteers had unscrupulously and often cruelly exploited Orientals. As all-conquering Caucasians steamrolled across the continent into lands not their own, most white Americans reinforced their belief in the inferior status of nonwhite people.

The effort to overcome traditional myths presented the equalitarians with one of their most formidable obstacles. In a thoughtful analysis of racist ideology, a Boston clergyman named Increase N. Tarbox admitted sadly that Americans embraced, "by inheritance from our fathers, a set of ideas and opinions, which in the unquestioning period of childhood we were easily made to believe, and which have been and are still firmly held by multitudes as undoubted truths." Their accuracy mattered little because they enjoyed the most revered sanction of all— the approval of generations. They were common topics of discussion, Tarbox observed, having as their justification "everybody says so." Thus popularized, and with "such respectability as age can give," they passed with a "halo of antiquity" from father to son. By 1860 few dared to question the validity of these opinions. Tarbox spoke of many Americans who, "if you venture to disturb their faith in these old traditions, will start back instinctively as if you were trying to unsettle the foundations of everlasting truth." As the young French medical student Georges Clemenceau observed in his postwar travels through the United States, "how peculiarly difficult it is to dislodge a prejudice which has somehow succeeded in getting hold in one of the out-of-the-way corners of the tight Anglo-Saxon brain!"[10]

To support their preconceived notions of Caucasian superiority, prejudiced Americans cited two highly respected and presumably unimpeachable authorities. The first of these, the Holy Bible, was probably the staunchest bulwark of moral and historical claims to Negro inferiority in the racist arsenal. The singular fact that the Bible sanctioned something, even if only by implication, was enough to raise cries of blasphemy from anyone who found his religious assumptions challenged. Racists north and south remembered many prewar defenses of slavery, some proclaimed by Protestant clergymen, that not only had defended the institution as a "positive good," but had offered countless scriptural justifications for perpetual servitude. During the war, Copperheads and other Northerners sympathetic to the South repeated many of these statements. For example, inventor Samuel F. B. Morse, in a reply to Republican criticisms of his racist views, charged that emancipation would "remove a cornerstone which God has laid."[11]

Probably the most explicit and certainly the most sweeping religious justification for white supremacist views was the Old Testament episode of Noah and the "curse of Canaan." According to the racist version of the story, the Negroes, the so-called Hamitic peoples, were the descendants of Noah's son Ham who had been punished for watching his father sleeping in the nude by having Canaan, one of his four sons, and all of his descendants "ordained" to "servitude under the descendants of Shem and Japheth," because, as a northern racist put it, *"he judged it to be their fittest condition."*[12] Antislavery clerics, of course, challenged the biblical argument. Slavery was not God-ordained, they replied, and the curse of Canaan had no modern application. The curse had been Noah's, they insisted, not God's. Besides, the Negroes had descended from all of Ham's sons, not just Canaan. Even accepting the basic premise of the curse, Tarbox asked, how could anyone have explained the subjugation of *all* of Ham's descendants because of the curse on only *one* of his four sons? Obviously, the objections of the abolitionists were too fundamental to be resolved by quibbling over the Negro's presumed Old Testament lineage. But most Americans, especially those with strong prejudices, probably did not take the time to analyze these arguments. Since the Negro seemed so clearly inferior, they simply assumed that somehow God was at least partially responsible for his condition; thus to interfere with that condition would be to violate Holy Writ.[13]

Although racists agreed that the Negro was indeed inferior, they sometimes disagreed over the meaning of the biblical argument. In 1867, several white supremacists began debating, rather ludicrously, to just what extent God had really condemned the Negro. It all started when an obscure Nashville publisher named Buckner H. Payne wrote a pamphlet entitled "The Negro: What Is His Ethnological Status?" Writing anonymously under the pseudonym of "Ariel," Payne refuted the traditional curse-of-Canaan theory on the grounds that the Negro had not descended from Ham at all, but was a beast of the highest order and had been included among the pairs of animals in the Ark. In short, the Negro was not a mortal, had no soul, and could realize no salvation. The misunderstanding had come about, Payne argued, because biblical scholars carelessly associated Ham with the ancient Hebrew word "ham," which they had translated to mean "black." Since Ham had been named long before the curse, he added, it was obvious that there could be no relationship between his name and the color. Moreover, some of Ham's other descendants, such as Mizraim, the second son, went on to distinguish themselves as empire builders. If the Negroes were not the descendants of Ham, Payne reasoned, they must have descended from the beasts, were simply the most highly developed of the apes, and were therefore inhuman and had no immortal souls. If this were true, of course, racial amalgamation, in the eyes of most white Americans, would be nothing less than sodomy and therefore a flagrant crime against God. According to Payne, this was exactly what happened in biblical times. When certain mortals began miscegenating with soulless Negroes, God brought on the Flood to punish mankind.

In the months that followed the appearance of Payne's pamphlet, other anonymous extremists published tracts that more or less supported his thesis,[14] but most of the racist responses were unfavorable. The reason was obvious: the acceptance of Payne's theory meant the repudiation of a sacrosanct white supremacy dogma—namely, the curse-of-Canaan notion. Consequently, most racists denounced the whole idea as utter nonsense. Criticizing Payne's theology, his knowledge of zoology, and his grammar, Robert A. Young of Nashville's Shelby Female Institute zealously defended the fundamentalist interpretation of the Flood and the curse. In 1868, an unknown author who identified himself only as "M. S." criticized both Ariel and Young; and in the following year, one Harrison Berry condemned Ariel for his false and haphazard logic and erroneous conclusions. Although their reasons for challenging Payne differed, his critics agreed that Payne's basic premise—that the Negro was a beast—was absurd.[15] It should come as no surprise that none of Payne's supporters identified themselves. On the other hand, most of his critics—since they were championing what they correctly assumed was the more popular view—willingly signed their publications.

The Ariel controversy was most revealing as a reflection of the widespread belief in, and the preposterous extremes of, religious fundamentalism, at least when it involved racial matters. Indeed, despite his challenge to tradition, Payne was himself a fundamentalist. He could not view the story of the Flood as an allegory; instead, he based his whole proposition on the assumption that it was a real historical event. Payne's critics, who, unlike Payne, were apparently men of learning, displayed the same dependence on a literal interpretation of the Old Testament. What Payne actually did was force the fundamentalists either to admit their belief that God turned Canaan, a white man, black, or to acknowledge the symbolism in the writings of Moses, which they certainly were not disposed to do.

In spite of the popularity of biblical sanctions of a racial hierarchy, the vast majority of northern clergymen opposed slavery (though many churches remained segregated). The antislavery movement had owed as much to the Protestant clergy—to men like Henry Ward Beecher, Charles Grandison Finney, and Theodore Weld—as to any other occupational group. Moreover, the writings of the abolitionists had been far more enlightened than those of the proslavery school. But, as has so often been the case, it was possible to cite the Bible to support almost anything; what it all meant was that those who cited scriptures simply picked out the portions they wanted to believe and ignored the rest, a practice to which the Bible has always lent itself.

Although the Bible was a mighty force in the racist cause, there were many white supremacists who preferred less emotional and ostensibly more scientific arguments. And there were dozens of studies by anthropologists and ethnologists to support the racist view. The middle decades of the nineteenth century witnessed profound changes in man's opinions about his own origins. In classifying forms of life, some scientists constructed hierarchies based primarily on observable differences among various animals' behavior and physical development, a scheme that was remarkably adaptable to propagating the racist view of the Negro. One of the most notable American contributors to writings on Negro inferiority was Josiah C. Nott, professor of anatomy at the University of Louisiana. In 1855, in collaboration with George R. Gliddon of Mobile, Alabama, Nott published *Types of Mankind*, a manual that claimed to scientifically prove Caucasian superiority. Two years later, adding his *Indigenous Races of the Earth* to the growing but contradictory collection of scientific accounts, Nott approvingly cited the works of Gliddon, Alfred Maury, Francis Pulszky, and J. Aitken Meigs—all recognized ethnologists. In addition, he assisted in the translation of Count Joseph Arthur de Gobineau's *Essai sur l'inégalité des races humaines* (1853–1855)—a classic account of "Aryan superiority and racial determinism"[16]—which was published in this country in 1856 in a one-volume edition entitled *The Moral and Intellectual Diversity of Races*.

Important to the scientific argument because of the prestige of his name was Harvard naturalist Louis Agassiz. On various occasions following his arrival in the United States in 1846, Agassiz addressed himself to the race question, and always came to the conclusion that the Negro was naturally inferior and could never attain the same level of accomplishment as the white man. In 1850, at a meeting of the American Association for the Advancement of Science held in Charleston, South Carolina, he appeared on the same program as Nott. After the Civil War began, Agassiz, though strongly affirming his loyalty to the Union and in spite of his friendships with New England abolitionists, continued to hold his scientific racist position.[17]

It is certainly significant that while midcentury American scientists were finding a rationale for racism, the most progressive thinking in European ethnology tended to support the unity of mankind, minimized the importance of physical differences among races, and even recognized that most cultural differences could not be attributed to physical traits. Among the most advanced authorities was a German scholar named Theodor Waitz, who argued in 1858 that there were no significant differences in the "native capacities" of the races, a view endorsed by many leading American abolitionists. Favorable environmental circumstances, he wrote in the first volume of his massive *Anthropologie der Naturvölker* (Leipzig, 1858–1871), was the critical element in civilization. In the second volume, subtitled *Die Negervölker und ihre Verwandten* (1860), Waitz applied this principle directly to Negroes.[18]

American scientific thinking, on the other hand, leaned toward a belief in the diversity of racial origins, a position that arose, as William

Stanton has put it, from the "characteristic American situation of three races in uneasy conjunction."[19] The European point of view, or at least the most progressive part of it, challenged the basis of white supremacy doctrines—on which the identities of many Americans depended; thus it was essential to seek out those arguments that supported the Anglo-Saxon self-image and to reject those that contradicted it. Nor did emancipation and the Civil War do much to reconcile European-American differences. In a postwar pamphlet, "Instincts of Races" (1866), Nott clung to all of the old views. Furthermore, American racism was complicated by a scientific hostility toward the domestic one-species school of thought that based its claims on the Bible in order to advance claims of Negro inferiority.[20] Ironically, there were probably racists who cited both a biblical justification and the opinions of anti-biblical scientists to prove the validity of their positions.

The racist demagogues of the 1860's eagerly quoted the men of science. In 1861, John H. Van Evrie, a New York City author and editor who headed the publishing firm of Van Evrie, Horton & Company, published *Negroes and Negro "Slavery."* The following year, a bulky tome by Marvin T. Wheat, entitled *The Progress and Intelligence of Americans* but known popularly as "Wheat's Philosophy of Slavery," appeared, with a staggering array of scientific, historical, and sociological arguments attesting to the Negro's basic inferiority. In 1866 Van Evrie published an unsigned pamphlet accompanied by a series of drawings that illustrated Caucasian superiority through physical features. Two years later he serialized this article under his own name in the *Old Guard*, a Copperhead monthly journal. In the graphic representations, naturally, the artist depicted the white man as noble and handsome, and characterized all other races as barbaric and degenerate. In 1867 the *Southern Review* featured an African travel account that typified, in its descriptions of native habits and tribal institutions, the reports of various European ethnologists. In all of these studies, the dominant theme was the primitive savagery of life in the bush.[21]

Of course, many of the European authorities, even those who, unlike Waitz, represented the more conservative position, simply produced descriptive travel studies of African life and did not necessarily advocate the permanent subjugation of the Negro race nor insist that the black man was incapable of realizing the same level of achievement, given the same opportunities, as the white man. The political racists, however, could be expected to add the inflammatory ingredients. In 1862, an unsigned pamphlet entitled "Uncivilized Races," allegedly the "substance" of a paper read before the Anthropological Society of America, included several pages of quotations by "men of science."

Better known racist writers, like Lindley Spring and Hinton R. Helper, published books that were little more than reprints of the works of others, adding to them many critical and sometimes irrational embellishments of their own. Quoting Agassiz's description of the African, J. R. Hayes, author of "Negrophobia 'On the Brain,' " warned that under radical Republican rule the white man would be reduced to the lowest common denominator.[22]

It would be easy to misinterpret the significance of the biblical and scientific arguments, and to see them as a *cause* of widespread racism. However they were not primarily important because they gave white Americans reasons to believe that the Negro was inferior—whites did not need reasons, they could see his inferior characteristics with their own eyes. The arguments were important as feverish efforts to find authoritative support for prejudices already entrenched and to advance certain political positions. Although men like Nott, Gliddon, Agassiz, Gobineau, and some of the English anthropologists were finding biological explanations for racism, they seldom attempted to apply their theories in the practical or political realms. The men who did—Hayes, Helper, Van Evrie, Spring, Wheat, and a legion of anonymous extremists—exploited the scientific arguments in order to whip up public hostility against Republicans and Negroes. But the racism they appealed to was already there.

Thus, biblical and scientific arguments probably changed few opinions. Scholarly and theological propositions mainly lent respectability to emotions that the white man could not otherwise justify. But whatever the argument, the average white American did not need the racist anthropologist or conservative clergyman to point out the Negro's black skin, kinky hair, flat nose, large lips, narrow shins, and protruding heels. He based his assertion of his own superiority on the unscientific assumption that certain physical features were inferior to others and used the scientific argument only to document his claim.

> Blubber lips are killing sweet,
>   And kinky heads are splendid;
> And oh, it makes such bully feet
>   To have the heels extended.[23]

Herein lay one of the most crucial considerations in analyzing the nature of race prejudice: the average American was pragmatic and empirical, and, trusting in what he could see, he allowed his experiences and senses to tell him that the Negro was inferior.[24]

Other observable features, products of both the white man's culture and his imagination, were similarly contemptible. References to the Negro's speech, colloquial expressions, intellectual inertia, and body "odor," ranging from the scientific to the preposterous, were common in racist literature and oratory. The white man could "see" that the Negro was lazy; he could "see" the Negro's propensity for filth and squalor; he could "see" that the Negro was immoral, taking as his mate, without the benefit of marriage, any black woman who suited him. Most Negroes were extremely ignorant, and the white man could "see" this also. He rarely stopped to consider the political, economic, and social restrictions, imposed by himself, that accounted for the black man's ignorance. Instead, he indulged his own ignorance by assuming that the Negro's intellectual and economic backwardness was just one more characteristic of an inferior nature.

A few extremists justified their prejudices by arguing that the Negro himself was an empirical racist. In a speech in the House of Representatives in 1862, Cox suggested that the black man had enough sense to "perceive" his own inferiority. Two years later, Jeremiah S. Black, Attorney-General under Buchanan, asserted that even the black man could *see* the natural inferiority of the African race. Only the abolitionists denied it, he charged.[25] Moreover, argued the editor of the Rochester (Minnesota) *Federal Union*, the Negro's understanding of his own inferiority was instinctive; hence nothing but harm would come from trying to convince him otherwise.[26] As a black "mammy," in the words of a racist poet, remarked to her white ward:

> You sees o'd mammy's wrinkly face,
>   As black as any coal;
> And underneath her handkerchief
>   Whole heaps of knotty wool.
>
> My darlin's face is red and white,
>   Her skin is soft and fine,
> And on her pretty yallar head
>   De yallar ringlets shine.[27]

Scottish traveler David Macrae observed that the slaves had adopted the white man's code of color, so to speak, whereby a "yellow" Negro was higher on the social scale than a darker one, and the greatest insult among Negroes was to be called a "charcoal nigger." A slave allegedly told a racist writer, "we slabes is black only in dis prezzen worle; in de nex worle, we is gwine to be white fikes too! You see den dat we's not niggers."[28]

Occasionally the empirical argument wandered into the realm of complete absurdity. In *Nojoque: A Question for a Continent* (1867), his most notorious postwar book, Hinton R. Helper cited all of the traditional meanings for the colors black and white: black had always been associated with sin, evil, filth, and failure; white was the color of goodness, purity, success, and honor. See the "night-born ogre," he cried, with his "low-receding forehead; his broad depressed nose; his stammering stuttering speech." To Helper, the Negro was blubber-lipped, bow-legged, spindle-shanked, cock-heeled, and flat-footed. The Negro emitted a terrible stench, Helper insisted, largely the result of such ailments as yellow fever, fungitis, droopy breasts, hemorrhoids, goiter, tapeworm, fits, spasms, and convulsions, not to mention "moon-madness" and "mulligrubs." Graphic depictions of the Negro almost always exaggerated and distorted his physical characteristics until they were little more than grotesque caricatures. "I never heard of peepul changin their faces, nor their hair, nor their size, nor their cullor," Bill Arp remarked. "A blak Alabama nigger is just the same as his gran daddy was in Africky two thousan years ago."[29]

But equalitarianism was not without its perceptive defenders, who challenged the assumption that observable physical features indicated racial inferiority. In a brilliant parody, a Republican writer and editor named David Locke lampooned racist absurdities when, as "Petroleum V. Nasby," he compared the physique and intelligence of a Negro named Napoleon with those of Isaac, a young white man. "Issaker" had a shorted hand and a narrower foot, Nasby exclaimed, "and his heel projecks less than the nigger's by 2½ inches!" Examining Napoleon's calves, Nasby agreed that "no one kin hev intelleck whose lag isn't set in his foot better than that." In the course of his comparison, however, Nasby discovered that Napoleon could read and write, but that the "gay descendent uv the sooperior race" could do neither. Isaac must be illiterate, he concluded, because his "nigger" did his reading and writing for him. Besides, he added in a reflection embodying all of the customary racist contradiction and rationalization, "the seat of the intelleck is in the heel instead uv the brain," which is why the Negro had the most of it.[30] Though Locke's tract was a humorous burlesque of racist excesses, it underlined what was really a serious concern for both critics and defenders of racial equality—discrimination based on appearance.

The basic premises of the Anglo-Saxon self-image were the same throughout the country, but there were regional differences in intensity and mode of expression. The South, of course, has long been the favorite whipping boy of opponents of racial discrimination. However, during the middle decades of the nineteenth century, the North and West were also active breeding grounds for inflammatory racism. It should not be forgotten that the Republican party owed much of its success to Midwesterners whose chief aim had been not to eliminate slavery, but to *contain* it—for selfish reasons—within the states where it already existed. By appealing to the midwestern agrarian's economic self-interest, free soil leaders had, in fact, fostered racism. Northern white supremacy sentiments—strongest in a wide belt that stretched across the southern two-thirds of Illinois, Indiana, and Ohio, most of Pennsylvania, the lower half of New York, and almost all of New Jersey—were just as truculent as any in the country. Much of it bordering on the slave South, this was the northern area with the heaviest concentration of Negroes. Although the Negro population was not so large that the whites endorsed slavery, it was sufficient to get them excited over suggestions of racial equality. In an 1862 "petition" to President Lincoln, a reporter for the Columbus *Crisis* argued against emancipation, claiming the support of the white men of these very states.[31]

Economic and social conditions also influenced the average Northerner's thoughts and habits. Isolated on a farm or in a small town, the typical Midwesterner saw few Negroes, and on the far reaches of the western plains, the pioneer homesteader saw few people. In the urban centers of the Midwest and the East the presence of Negroes was far more obvious, but even here they generally lived in their own neighborhoods. In other words, even where they were relatively numerous, the Negroes' lack of mobility frequently obscured their presence. Working as domestics and menial laborers, they circulated in narrowly confined areas. Prominent or wealthy Negroes were conspicuous because they were rare. In fact, the typical white man was so accustomed to identifying Negroes with substandard occupations and living conditions that he probably resented the success of those who achieved economic distinction. Thus, ironically, the accomplishments of a few successful Negroes actually intensified prejudice against all of them.

Sectional differences in the nature of anti-Negro attitudes were determined by the number of Negroes in a given region, by their proportion in the total population, and by their distribution. Southerners oriented their prejudices to accommodate large numbers of black slaves, and white Northerners developed their biases within a framework of unfamiliarity and suspicion. Many abolitionists were convinced that the Northerner's hatred for the Negro was deep-rooted and unshakable. In 1853, William G. Allen, a northern Negro college professor who had fled to Europe to escape a New York City mob, published a book complaining of the "bitterness, malignity, and cruelty" that subjected northern Negroes to "social and political bondage." After the Civil War, many freedmen who had traveled through the North returned home bitter over the reception they had received from their so-called "benfactors."[32] The white North, with its relatively small Negro population, distrusted the black man. To many Northerners, he was a strange creature; thus simple ignorance was a major reason for the fear that resulted in hatred.

Even "humanitarians" who at least superficially championed the Negro cause were affected by the widespread belief in white superiority. Many Republican politicians advocated emancipation but refused to endorse complete racial equality. Speaking before the Massachusetts State Republican Convention in 1865, Ben Butler, a Union general and later a radical congressman, supported Negro suffrage, but added that when it came to any other form of equality, "my 'pride of race' teaches me that my race is superior to his." A few years later, Vice-President Schuyler Colfax proclaimed, "I believe God made us, for his own purposes, a superior race." Other Republican leaders, at one time or another, made remarks or initiated actions that reflected their belief in Caucasian superiority. To be sure, there were dedicated abolitionists, such as Samuel Gridley Howe, Theodore Tilton, and Moncure Conway, who reflected what a more enlightened generation might have called a "modified racism."[33]

So emotionally demanding was the Civil War that many leading northern intellectuals had mixed feelings. Perhaps they were disturbed by the fact that a strong government, an institution that they had traditionally distrusted, should be the most effective instrument for promoting an equalitarian cause that they espoused. Some, like Charles Eliot Norton, Francis Parkman, and Charles Francis Adams, Jr., were outspoken unionists and supported emancipation, but remained pessimistic when it came to racial equality. In 1861, apparently attempting to win public support for emancipation, Orestes Brownson reassured northern racists that southern Negroes would forever remain an "inferior element." James Russell Lowell and Ralph Waldo Emerson, shifting from earlier idealistic positions to more pragmatic ones, applauded the argument that emancipation, as a military expedient, would undermine the southern war effort by encouraging slaves to desert the plantation. Torn between his pacifist beliefs and his unequivocal abolitionism, Conway finally decided that war was justified if the cause was righteous, and that any delay in emancipation was inexcusable. When emancipation did not end the war, he resolved his dilemma by going into self-imposed exile in England. Standing almost alone in 1863 was the inexorable Wendell Phillips, convinced that the work of equalitarianism was just beginning.[34]

Ambivalence on the part of some intellectuals, however, did not necessarily serve to discredit the sincerity of abolitionist equalitarianism. The character of racism in the 1860's must be assessed in the light of prevailing conditions. Although the doubts of nineteenth-century humanitarians might disturb a modern civil libertarian, it must be remembered that the United States was still far more equalitarian than the rest of the world. Moreover, most Americans, products of their era, took Caucasian superiority for granted. To fault them for this would be to demand of them a prescience that no generation has possessed. Nonetheless, many of these same prejudiced Americans championed Negro rights, a reflection of the fact that every age has its altruists. In spite of ignorance, tradition, science, and the Bible, men of good will tried persistently to persuade their fellows to approach racial issues with more reason and less emotion. Many of the speeches and writings of moderates in both parties were pitched in this direction. The Reverend Tarbox, for example, urged Americans to put aside "small and unworthy prejudices," and "to assist in the formation of a healthy public sentiment."[35] Unfortunately, such pleas had little effect on people whose prejudice against Negroes was not small and unworthy.

It is also necessary to remember that there were (and are) degrees of racism. Broadly speaking, most white Americans in the nineteenth century, since they believed in an innate inequality among races, could be described as racist. But while they indulged the Anglo-Saxon self-image, most were not *active* racists. They had prejudices against Negroes, but they did not consciously apply those prejudices in their everyday lives. To most people, the Negro question was not, as the *Old Guard* asserted, "the most living and burning of all issues in the brains of the masses."[36] Only when race-related issues threatened to affect their lives directly did they overtly act upon their racism.

The "active" racists were those extremists who exploited the widespread public prejudice and tried, through various forms of persuasion, to associate every event with the race issue. For them, white supremacy was not merely an attitude but the yardstick against which everything else was measured. As a result, they viewed every event in terms of its racial implications and applied the race issue even when it did not make sense to do so. The number of people who openly pursued a policy of white supremacy, even in the most hostile quarters of the Democratic party, was always small. But, as with most extremist minorities, their noise drew more attention than their numbers warranted. Racists were convinced that in view of the obvious public attitude toward Negroes, 27 million white Americans would never accept the black man as an equal. To the white supremacy propagandist, the Anglo-Saxon self-image was a sleeping giant that needed only to be aroused.

Chapter Two

THE RESPONSE
TO EMANCIPATION

> Old Abraham, my jolly Abe
> What do you really mean?
> Your negro proclamation is
> A wild fanatic's dream.[1]

From the Emancipation Proclamation to the 1870's, the most vexing political issue in America was what to do about the Negro. This, the conservative New York *Journal of Commerce* declared in the fall of 1863, was the "grand question." The Democrats "organized the hatred of the negro," Horace Greeley wrote, "and they will continue to inflame the same prejudices and passions to make the government and the war unpopular by identifying both with the cause of the blacks alone." The first commandment of every Copperhead, said Montgomery Wilson, a prominent Republican writer, was, "Thou shalt hate the Nigger with all thy heart, and with all thy soul, and with all thy mind, and with all thy strength."[2]

The political exploitation of racism in the United States did not originate during the 1860's. But there was a difference between antebellum bigotry and the bigotry that followed the Emancipation Proclamation. Before the war there had been little reason for arousing hatred against Negroes because most of them had been slaves. Since, by law, they had been subordinate to whites, there had been little need to launch crusades for the purpose of keeping them in their "place." There had been sporadic outbursts of excitement, especially following incidents of slave violence. Southern state governments had prohibited teaching slaves to read and write and had encouraged the emigration of freed blacks, but these measures had been directed more against the slaveowners than against the slaves themselves. Southern lawmakers had been not racist demagogues but social and political leaders trying to preserve a cherished way of life. They had wanted to prevent agitation, not create it.

In the North, racism had occasionally led to violence, but the victim had often been the white man who championed the Negro's cause rather than the Negro himself. Although racial discrimination had been widespread, overt acts of violence against abolitionists were scattered and localized. Antislavery newspaper offices had fallen to the axe and torch, and rioters in Illinois had murdered a leading abolitionist. Speakers who had urged emancipation had been shouted down, pelted with rocks, and forcibly escorted from town. Garrison, Phillips, Weld, and the others had aggravated issues that most Americans wanted left alone. Moreover, the abolitionists, considered crank agitators by many Northerners, had spoken for a vociferous but politically impotent minority. On the other hand, the slavery interest—or men who sympathized with the slavery interest—controlled the national government during most of the years after the War for Independence. America's most revered presidents—Washington, Jefferson, Madison, Monroe, and Jackson—had been slaveowners, a fact that racists did not forget.[3] While most Northerners had not condoned slavery, neither had they been willing to risk secession or war to abolish it. Since there seemed to be little chance in the decades before the Civil War that universal emancipation would become a government policy, the exploitation of race prejudice never had become a political weapon of massive national proportions.

But there were signs of danger. The attraction of many Northerners to the Republican ranks in the 1850's had moved the Democrats to emphasize those issues that would best embarrass the new party, namely the emotional issues of the race question.[4] The designation "Black Republican" as a derogatory name for anyone who opposed the extension of slavery into the territories during the 1850's portended future Democratic strategy.* It made little difference to racist demagogues that the Republican position on the race issue had been free soil rather than abolitionist; the equalitarian implications of the Re-

---

* During the Civil War, C. Chauncey Burr, editor of the *Old Guard*, enlarged the term to "Black Republican Democrats" to include those Democrats who supported the war (vol. I, Jan. 1863, p. 23).

publican movement had made the party vulnerable. In 1860, the Democratic National Executive Committee circulated a campaign pamphlet accusing the Republican presidential candidate of advocating complete Negro equality. The Republicans demanded the elimination of "all laws which erect a barrier between you and the black man," the Committee declared. The black African "is your equal, entitled to vote, hold office, sit at the same table with you, and marry your daughter."[5]

What the growing antiabolitionist movement really demonstrated was that the antislavery cause had come a long way since the founding of the American Anti-Slavery Society in 1833. Abolitionism had achieved a substantial degree of respectability, and abolitionists had won several key federal and state government positions. The fundamental aim of the old Liberty party was about to be realized. The bitter struggle over Kansas, the ominous implications of the Dred Scott decision, and the southern intransigence at the National Democratic Convention in 1860 had all been major forces in galvanizing northern public opinion. The secession of South Carolina in December 1860 and the firing on Fort Sumter the following April were the ultimate acts of defiance. While it may have been difficult to discern a recognizable emancipationist sentiment in the disorder of secession and mobilization, Northerners generally were far more equalitarian than they had even been before. Indeed, without the war, the Emancipation Proclamation certainly would have been much longer coming.

As long as the government had a single, clear war aim—preservation of the Union—it received at least qualified support from all but the most extreme Democrats, the peace-at-any-price Copperheads. Any attack on Republican war policies could be interpreted as an attack on the cause of union. Some critics disagreed with the course of the government's military program, but since they were unwilling to risk accusations of disloyalty, few of them quarreled with its overall mission—to reunite North and South. A sizable number of Democrats sublimated almost all expressions of opposition until victory appeared secure, a course that infuriated the racists.[6] But after the Emancipation Proclamation, a growing number of Democrats were convinced that the war had become an abolitionist struggle for Negro freedom and equality.

> "De Union!" used to be de cry—
>   For dat we went it strong;
> But now de motto seems to be,
>   "De nigger, right or wrong!"[7]

At a Democratic rally in New York City, Representative Cox described Republicans and abolitionists as "two links of the same sausage made out of the same dog." "Negromaniacs" displayed a "raging madness" over the Negro, the Hartford *Times* complained. Thirty years ago the "few isolated cases" of Negromania "excited little fear or anxiety among the masses," the editor concluded, but now the lunatics were running the country. To the Copperheads, the Emancipation Proclamation was the culmination of an abolitionist drive, begun in the 1820's, to win control of the government.[8]

Eager to prove a kinship between Republicans and Negroes, racist extremists soon began an ugly campaign of name-calling. The Copperhead editor of the Columbus *Crisis* accused Theodore Tilton of seeking complete social equality for the Negro; and an anonymous writer spoke of "Horace the Greeley, who from infancy was dedicated to the work of smoothing the Woolly-headed Ethiopian and making his face shine with surpassing loveliness." The editor of the *Old Guard* insisted that both Vice-President Hannibal Hamlin and Senator Charles Sumner were part Negro and, with typical racist logic, claimed the the "peculiar lily-whiteness" of the skin of Sumner's sister indicated the presence of Negro blood. President Lincoln, the New York *Weekly Day Book* charged, planned to "elevate the negro at whatever cost to the Saxon," and the Detroit *Free Press* suggested that the President move to Haiti or Liberia, where he would certainly find a more "congenial atmosphere." Few Republicans were attacked as zealously and consistently as Abraham Lincoln.[9]

The most common racist argument was that the government was waging a war for abolitionism. But the racists knew that they had to be more specific. The people were certain to tire of a propaganda campaign based solely on unsubstantiated assertions. They would not react to a racist appeal unless a danger appeared imminent. To be effective, therefore, the extremist had to observe two cardinal rules: first, his appeal had to be emotional rather than logical, and second, he had to emphasize topics that his audience could identify with. Consequently, most racist speakers and writers concentrated on one of several "threats" that were calculated to arouse fear.

One of the most popular threats was economic. Racists everywhere predicted that emancipation would precipitate a labor crisis by encouraging mass Negro migration to the North. "A vote for [Horatio] Seymour is a vote to protect our white laborers against the association and competition of Southern negroes," the New York *World* declared during the gubernatorial campaign of 1862. Democratic newspapers such as the *World* and the Philadelphia *Age* aimed their economic argument at the uneducated and unskilled white worker. If former slaves flooded the northern labor market, they maintained, the wage earner would be the first to feel the bite of unemployment and impoverishment. Of course, this argument varied in emphasis and content according to the economy of a particular region and the composition of its population. In the industrial East, for example, the unskilled factory worker had the most to fear from mass Negro migration—or thought he did; in an overcrowded labor market, he was the most likely victim.*

The fear of Negro migration was just as intense in the Midwest, and it was more widespread. Three factors—an agricultural economy, the southern heritage of many Midwesterners, and the lower Midwest's common border with the slave South—made the residents keenly aware of the "dangers" of Negro migration. In general, the nearer the Ohio River a white Midwesterner lived, the more race sensitive he was. Many residents of the old Northwest had left their original homes in the South to escape the economic and social restrictions imposed by slavery and the plantation system. In other words, they were themselves Southerners, who had moved for many of the same reasons that the freed slaves could be expected to move. There were "poor whites" in Illinois, Indiana, and Ohio who disliked Negroes for the same reasons that the southern poor whites did. Some of them had been in the vanguard of the free soil movement, not for humanitarian reasons, but simply because they did not like Negroes, slave or free.[10]

Midwestern racists exploited this fear by accusing the government of forcing emancipated slaves to move north. Representative Clement Laird Vallandigham told a Dayton audience that the abolitionists planned to replace the white workers with cheap Negro labor in order to reduce the political and economic strength of the traditionally Democratic working people. The Detroit *Free Press* insisted that the Republican design was to compel the North to accept the indolent African "Ethiop." There was no direct evidence to support such charges, but imaginative critics had little difficulty in fabricating some.

---

* New York *World*, Oct. 18, Nov. 4, 1862; Philadelphia *Age*, Aug. 13, Sept. 8, Oct. 24, 1864.

Williston H. Lofton, "Northern Labor and the Negro during the Civil War," *Journal of Negro History*, XXXIV (July 1949), 253–256, introduces an interesting point when he shows how reduced European immigration actually created a labor shortage. Lofton contends that the industrial worker of the eastern cities had no reason to fear Negro immigration, and, indeed, that the presence of Negroes might have freed many white workers from menial occupations. The racist demagogue, of course, was not concerned with the reality of the Negro labor question, but with the fear of it.

For example, in February 1864, the Philadelphia *Presbyterian,* a radical antislavery newspaper, published an innocent statement praising
the Negro as as a worker. On March 24, the Columbus *Crisis* reprinted
the article as proof that the Lincoln administration was trying to place
the country under the domination of a radical-Negro party. The abolitionists wanted more "subservient, and less intelligent 'help,' and at
lower wages," the editor complained. Three days later, the Indianapolis
State Sentinel repeated the accusation and named the *Presbyterian* as
the prime instigator of forced Negro migration.[11]

Ohio had been a center of racism as early as 1833, when a free Negro
named M. C. Sampson wrote:

> Farewell, Ohio!
> I cannot stop in thee;
> I'll travel on to Canada,
> Where colored men are free.[12]

And nowhere was the fear of Negro migration more widespread. Racists
throughout the state exploited it at every opportunity—in political
campaigns, at party rallies, and at patriotic celebrations. In a speech
at the Catholic Institute in Cincinnati, lecturer Henry Reed insisted
that *both* races would suffer in the competition for jobs. The consequence of Negro migration, he argued, would be widespread poverty
and unemployment for all; the ex-slaves who came north would find
few jobs, but their presence would depress wages for everybody. In
1862, a week before Christmas, the *Crisis* reprinted portions of a notorious proslavery pamphlet, Van Evrie's "Free Negroism," which
emphasized the degradation of white labor under emancipation.[13] A
short time later, the Ohio legislature resolved to amend the state constitution to forbid the entry of Negroes into Ohio; at the same time
citizens of Shelby County petitioned the state government for an exclusion law on the grounds that they could never live with such a "degraded race."[14] "Ohio," the *Crisis* vowed, "shall never become the depot
for the runaway slaves and freed negroes of the South." During the
campaign for state offices in 1863, the Ohio Democratic Central Committee asked the northern soldier if he liked the idea of returning
home from battle to find his job taken by the Negro whom he had
risked his life to free. When asked to support the proposed Thirteenth
Amendment shortly before the end of the war, Representative George
Bliss of the Fourteenth District publicly refused because he feared its
passage would invite the former slaves to compete for jobs with the
returning Union veterans.[15]

Not surprisingly, Ohio had the dubious distinction of having produced two of the country's leading political racists, Clement Laird Vallandigham and Samuel Sullivan "Sunset" Cox. Cox described Vallandigham, his friend and colleague, as one of the most abused and misunderstood men in American history. "Negrophilistic fanaticism produced and encouraged an intense hatred of this statesman," he wrote in 1865. Surprisingly, Cox himself did not evoke praise from other Copperheads. Although some considered him the champion of Ohio racism, many Democrats distrusted him; and both Samuel Medary, editor of the *Crisis*, and his vitriolic successor, W. W. Webb, called Cox a "vacillating Democrat."* In truth, Cox's racism was far more strident than Vallandigham's, but he somehow never won the Copperhead admiration or the Republican censure that Vallandigham enjoyed.[16]

The economic threat was particularly effective because large numbers of European immigrants, many of whom were fleeing famine, revolutions, and political persecution in their native countries, had come to the United States during the 1840's and 1850's. The Irish, and to some extent the Germans, had crowded into the larger eastern cities, joined the Democratic party, and monopolized the unskilled labor market. By the time of the Civil War they were well represented in the Midwest and in California. This "foreign-born proletariat," fearful of social and economic equality with the emancipated slaves, was probably the demagogues' most combustible human kindling. New York City's rabid racist newspaper, the *Weekly Day Book*, made the arousal of its excitable Irish readers almost an editorial policy. Editor Van Evrie not only wrote that the Negro felt arrogant and superior to the white immigrant, but also accused the Republicans of wanting to degrade the Irishman. One hysterical racist, reminding his Irish readers of the antiforeign, anti-Catholic Know-Nothing campaigns of the 1850's, denounced the "wooly philanthropists" for "burning nunneries, mobbing Catholic priests, hanging Irishmen, and urging the passage of laws to disfranchise and degrade our adopted citizens." The Republicans' hatred for the foreigner "was just as intense as their love for the Southern black. To elevate the black and degrade the foreigner were objects which they pursued with equal intensity."[17]

Such appeals had their consequences. Angry Irishmen played leading roles in race riots in New York, Detroit, Chicago, and Cincinnati. The New York City draft riots of July 1863 were more anti-Negro than

* "Medary hates me," Cox wrote to Samuel L. M. Barlow a month before the election of 1864, "because he couldn't use me against McC[lellan]." See Barlow manuscript, Huntington Library.

antidraft, and young Irishmen were the principle antagonists. Of the
82 names of dead rioters posted by city officials, 52 were Irish and 7
were German. In the Midwest, too, foreign-born settlers were becoming increasingly hostile. Scandinavians were moving into Wisconsin
and Minnesota; and there were sizable colonies of German-Americans
in Milwaukee, St. Louis, and Chicago, and in the rural areas of Ohio,
Pennsylvania, Indiana, Illinois, Michigan, and Wisconsin.[18]

The threat of cheap labor was only one aspect of the economic argument. Many critics raised the question of caring for the slaves after
emancipation. Since the African was lazy and would not work, they
argued, white taxpayers would be forced to bear the costs of his care,
education, and job training. The Republicans planned to establish a
"Bureau of Emancipation" for the care and feeding of "contrabands,"
the Albany *Atlas and Argus* complained, but who could sustain the
cost? "Are the white working men of this country willing to bind this
heavy yoke around their necks, and entail it upon their children?"
another Democratic editor asked. Only as a slave, William B. Northend,
a highly respected Democratic lecturer, added, could the Negro contribute to the nation's economy. Van Evrie predicted that the freed
blacks would live off the labors of whites, increase local taxes by becoming welfare wards, and force staple prices up by refusing to
work. Indeed, he added, taking another approach, the emancipated
slave would no longer be a consumer of "the products of our farmers
and mechanics, and hence the demand for northern productions of
all kinds [would be] lessened." The Republicans planned to feed, house,
clothe, and educate the emancipated slave with the white man's money,
racists complained, and leave the needy whites to shift for themselves.[19]

In reality, the economic burden of emancipation—possibly excluding
the loss of the slaveowner's investment—was relatively insignificant.
Wars have always been incredibly expensive, and the Civil War was
no exception. The inflation-caused decrease in the wage earner's pur-
chasing power, the government's heavy indebtedness, the profiteering
in war contracts (which provided the capital for the great postwar industrial boom), and the indirect costs of occupational dislocation—
all of these created economic burdens that were far more profound
and immediate than the costs of emancipation.* The American tax-
payer *was* a big loser during the Civil War in terms of real income, but
the loss had little to do with the Negro.

* Economic historians are not in complete agreement about the effects of wartime
inflation on the wage earner, but the government's own reports indicate a substantial decline in the average worker's *real income*. According to one study, the average

Although white men certainly feared for their jobs and income, they were more alarmed by the threat to their physical security that the "savage African" presented. In the economic argument, critics condemned both Negroes and abolitionists, but the emphasis was frequently on the latter—the emancipated slave was just a pawn in the abolitionist's grand design to dominate the country. This was not the case when racists brought up the Negro's allegedly violent nature. Pointing to the absence of an advanced (by Western standards) African civilization, extremists described the Negroes as primitive, barbaric, and cruel. Forgotten was the old proslavery argument that the benevolent white man had "rescued" the uncivilized African from his pagan past and exposed him to the rewards of an advanced Christian society. Freedom, the white supremacist now asserted, would stimulate the black man's worst passions, leading him to crimes of arson, murder, and rape.[20] Suddenly, the Negro was back in darkest Africa.

Exaggerated and sometimes fabricated descriptions of Negro violence were frequent in the Democratic press. In February 1863, the *Free Press* reported that a white man in Detroit, trying to eject a group of Negroes from his home, was attacked by the "mob" and beaten severely. According to the editor, the Negro leader had "amalgamating desires." Two months later, the Cleveland *Plain Dealer* printed an article entitled "Negro Outrages in Detroit—A Little Girl Shot," which described how five-year-old Lizzie Massino had received an accidental leg wound in a street encounter with four black men. From August 1863 to the end of the Civil War, the Philadelphia *Age* printed more than

---

industrial wage index rose from 100 in 1860 to 155 in 1865, with the high ranging from 142 (woolen textiles) to 178 (city public works). In the same period, the consumer price index rose from 100 to 175, with an increase of 138 per cent in the price of clothing alone. The peak years for the overall index were 1863 and 1864, when prices rose 24 and 26 per cent, respectively. The average wage increases for the same two years, on the other hand, were only 14 and 19 per cent. Other studies for the five-year period show average wage increases ranging from 43.1 to 61.1 per cent, and cost-of-living increases ranging from 67 to 76 per cent. See Ralph Andreano (ed.), *The Economic Impact of the American Civil War* (Cambridge, Mass., 1962), pp. 179–181; and U. S. Bureau of the Census, *The Statistical History of the United States from Colonial Times to the Present* (Stamford, Conn., 1965), pp. 90, 127.

For another assessment of various aspects of the Civil War economy, see David T. Gilchrist and W. David Lewis (eds.), *Economic Change in the Civil War* (Greenville, Del., 1964). Some of the comments—especially those of Robert P. Sharkey (p. 30), Clarence Danhof (pp. 78–79), and Robert E. Gallman (p. 169)—suggest that income distribution discriminated against the wage earner, but that the whole question needs further study.

two dozen articles and editorials, many of them reprints from other newspapers, exploiting the white man's fear of the "savage African." The use of the word "outrage" was very common in these descriptions, and column headings such as "The Negro Outrage in Chicago," "Negro Outrages in Philadelphia," and so on, were typical. Few of these "crimes" were as serious as the reporters made them seem. Most, in fact, were minor incidents inflated far beyond their true proportions, and the stories were based largely on hearsay and secondhand evidence.[21]

Racist newsmen reporting violence blamed Negro victims as often as Negro aggressors. A Negro who injured a white man, for any reason whatsoever, was a criminal, but a white man who injured a Negro was only reacting to provocation or defending himself from a threatened attack. At times Negroes were only remotely involved in violent incidents, but racist reporters still made them the villains of the stories. Early in 1863, a Detroit judge sentenced a Negro named Faulkner to life imprisonment for the rape of a nine-year-old white girl. A handful of the city's rowdies, unhappy with what they thought was a lenient sentence, tried to kidnap and lynch the convicted rapist. Foiled, they converged on a random Negro home, burned the house, and killed the inhabitants. Their appetites only whetted, they recruited additional men and began terrorizing a Negro neighborhood. Before soldiers were able to disperse them, the rioters had set fire to 35 houses and had beaten many Negroes. The Albany *Atlas and Argus* called it "The Negro Riot in Detroit," but even in the newspaper's own description, there was no evidence that Negroes had actually rioted. Riots or near-riots against innocent Negroes also broke out in sections of Illinois and Ohio after the War Department ordered certain Union generals to find work for the "contraband"* Negroes in those states.[22]

Often Negroes were the unfortunate victims of violent outbursts for which they offered no provocation other than their skin color. During the infamous New York City riots of July 1863, angry whites killed

---

* The term "contraband" has been attributed to General Benjamin F. Butler because of his May 1861 refusal to surrender fugitive slaves who had found their way to Union lines. Since the slaves had been employed in the construction of Confederate batteries, Butler declared that they were tools of war and that " 'contraband' was the ground upon which I refused to release" them. Eventually, the term was used, unofficially, to describe all slaves that fell into Union hands, and was also a common slang term for Negroes generally, especially among the racists. See James G. Randall and David Donald, *The Civil War and Reconstruction* (Boston, 1961), pp. 371, 371n; and Mark M. Boatner (ed.), *The Civil War Dictionary* (New York, 1959), p. 172.

and injured scores of innocent and defenseless blacks. According to James D. McCabe, one of Horatio Seymour's campaign biographers in 1868, at least a dozen Negroes lost their lives in one day. Many were "driven into the river, beaten, or forced to leave the city." If a Negro had the misfortune to fall into "the hands of the mob, he was treated with the most savage cruelty," McCabe added. "The rioters seemed to lose all humanity when dealing with the blacks." Significantly, this was the account of a Democrat in an election year; Republicans were even more horrified. In an effort to illustrate the senselessness of race prejudice, Anna Dickinson devoted two chapters of her novel *What Answer?* (1868) to a description of the riots.[23] The bulk of of the evidence suggests rather strongly that Negroes were usually the victims, not the instigators, of race riots, and that they were sometimes accused of crimes committed by whites. One of the cruel ironies of racism in the 1860's was the display of violence by the enlightened, civilized white man against the barbaric, uncivilized Negro; but the demagogue, after doing his part to excite the mob, blamed the "savage African."

Though racists were alarmed over the alleged savagery of the northern Negro, they were almost hysterical when they stopped to contemplate the danger latent in the southern Negro. Northern Negroes were relatively "civilized" and accustomed to freedom; moreover, they constituted a very small proportion of the total population. But what would happen, the racist asked, in states where semicivilized Africans accounted for 30, 40, or even 50 per cent of the inhabitants, or in those isolated areas where blacks outnumbered whites by as much as nine to one? To the alarmists, the Emancipation Proclamation was an official invitation to slave uprisings.[24]

> They call for insurrection
> Among the savage blacks,
> To murder all their masters—
> To slay them in their tracks.[25]

The Republicans had two aims, the New York *World* proclaimed: the military aim of promoting slave uprisings and the political aim of flooding the North with emancipated blacks. Other newspapers feared the "savage and brutal passions" that would be unleashed on "feeble women, aged and sickly men, and young children." Would the abolitionist editor of the New York *Tribune*, the Albany *Atlas and Argus* asked, "listen at midnight for the fancied shrieks of violated women—the wailings of mangled children—the groans of tortured and powerless men?"[26]

Actual cases of slave violence during the war were hard to find, but the racist press stimulated the imaginations of its readers by citing examples of Negro barbarism in Africa and the crimes of slaves and free Negroes in Latin America, particularly on the Caribbean islands. Copperhead speeches, newspapers, and tracts were filled with stories, anecdotes, and eye-witness accounts of the grisly conditions in Latin America. "All around us are scattered the ruins of free negroism," Van Evrie wrote in one of the most popular racist pamphlets of the decade. The catastrophes in Mexico, New Granada, Haiti, Jamaica, and Central America "all testify in thunder tones to beware of the breakers of free negroism." The New York *Daily News* printed a story about West Indian Negroes who had allegedly feasted on the bodies of children, and concluded, "With millions of the same race in our land, it is well that we should ponder awhile upon the possible fruits of Abolition." Describing the eighteenth-century slave insurrections in the Caribbean, Van Evrie told how rampaging Negroes had "marched with spiked infants on their spears," then "sawed asunder" white men and raped white women "on the dead bodies of their husbands."[27] Another extremist related this same episode in verse:

> Oh, de Sangomingo darkeys had a standard which dey bore;
> 'Twas a pretty little baby's head, all dripping in its gore!
> And if we undahstand aright de President's Proclaim,
> He tells us de Dixie niggers dey may go and do de same.
>
> Oh, de Sangomingo darkies, dare old Massas took and tied,
> And den dey got de handsaw and sawed'em till dey died!
> And after dey had sawed'em till dey sawed away dare lives,
> You may bet dey had a good time a kissin' ob dare wives.[28]

In spite of the racist's alarming predictions, the southern Negro's most distressing reaction to the Emancipation Proclamation, if he knew about it, was flight. Yet even this did not dissuade some critics. In the absence of slave insurrections that they could point to as examples of the black man's barbarism, they did an about-face and criticized his inaction. By *not* rising up in revolt, they said, the slave prolonged the war. "Not a telegraph wire was cut," one Northerner complained, "not a railroad track broken—not a depot of arms and army provisions fired—through the whole course of the war." Others went further. An Englishman insisted that the slaves fought "as lustily for slavery" as northern Negroes fought for union. Helper accused the slaves of deliberately betraying Union soldiers who had lost their way behind Confederate lines. "Their highest ambition," he screamed, "was to kill Yankees."

Helper, in fact, waved his own version of the "bloody shirt" in an attempt to arouse hatred against the freedmen for allegedly undermining the northern war effort.[29]

The most curious view of emancipation and its concomitant evils was the one that feigned sympathy for the Negro. According to many critics, the black man could not cope with the practical responsibilities of freedom. Unable to endure, he would perish. The emancipated slaves were an unhappy lot, Vallandigham insisted; the southern system was "far better in every way" than the life of "poverty, degradation, and crime" that northern Negroes were driven to. In Congress, Representative Thomas L. Price of Missouri predicted widespread starvation and depopulation if a proposed bill for compensated emancipation passed. Slaves were well fed and content, racists argued, but free Negroes were undernourished and sickly; the Cleveland *Plain Dealer* and the Indianapolis *State Sentinel* charged that in the District of Columbia alone, countless "contrabands" were dying of starvation. The Negroes, with no place to go and no one to care for them, were becoming extinct under forced emancipation.[30]

> But what dey're gwine to do wid him I'd really like to know;
> It's very well to set him free—but where's he gwine to go?[31]

The New York *Journal of Commerce*, a moderate Democratic newspaper, called the Republicans "pseudo-philanthropists" who were doing the blacks a great injustice by taking them out of the "sphere of life in which God has placed them." As late as January 1866, the Omaha *Weekly Herald* accused the Republican party of trying to destroy the Negro race.[32]

Such arguments, of course, were little more than updated modifications of prewar defenses of slavery that had pointed to the "happy" slave. Addressing the Democratic National Convention in 1864, S. S. Nicholas, one of the party's leading theoreticians, summarized the benevolent racist position thus, "Of all the faults and crimes of the nation from its connection with the negro race, there is none so prominent as that which has occurred during the present war." The abolitionists had failed "in their main purpose of inciting the use of the knife and torch in negro insurrections"; but they had succeeded in luring the slaves from their "comfortable homes" with false promises, and in bringing them to the Union lines, where, faced with starvation and exposure, they were dying "like rotten sheep." The most dastardly of all abolitionist accomplishments was the willful murder of thousands of helpless blacks by fanactics who claimed to be their benefactors. Abolitionist "scrubbers" like Chase, Sumner, and Phillips were trying to "wash" the Negro white, another critic declared; but "Sambo" would surely catch cold and die from sitting in the Freedmen's Bureau.[33]

The suffering Negro, Democrats maintained, was living proof of how the Republicans really felt about the black man. Abolitionists would not sit "side by side" with Negroes "in the same pews or even in the same church," Representative James Brooks of New York remarked at a meeting of the Democratic Union Association. He pointed out that they would not intermarry with Negroes, and added, "I cannot persuade my friends of the *Tribune* to make negroes associate editors with them." The editor refused to employ "Negro reporters, compositors, or pressmen." Brooks did not identify his "friends of the *Tribune*," and it was unlikely that he had many, but his accusations probably had some substance. When Greeley said that Americans should not expect too much from the Negro, the New York *World* had presented the statement as an indication of his personal expectations. Greeley, however, was merely being realistic about the Negro's educational and economic backwardness. Most abolitionists conceded it would be some time before Negroes could attain the economic and intellectual levels that whites had taken generations to reach. The Democratic press, of course, printed such statements as examples of Republican duplicity. If the editor of the *Tribune* wanted to be a "negro Moses," why did he keep the black man "at arm's length?" the Albany *Atlas and Argus* asked. Another Democratic editor queried, "Is the Negro eligible for the Presidency?" and facetiously challenged the Republicans to put a Negro on the ticket. The truth of the matter was, he said, Republicans despised the Negro. Except for a few "crack-brained enthusiasts and harmless old women," the Philadelphia *Age* remarked, not one abolitionist "cares a rush what become of Sambo, or his posterity."[34]

Although the racists accused the Republicans of hypocrisy, it was difficult for them to do so without revealing their own inconsistencies. At a rally in Lancaster City, Pennsylvania, in September 1863, Jeremiah S. Black defined a radical Republican as a man who advocated Negro equality in order to "show the superiority of the African race over the Saxon race." A few moments later, however, he condemned the "abolition cant of humanity" as "most disgustingly hollow and false." The Republicans had no genuine interest in the Negro's welfare, he concluded; their appeal to the white man's compassion for the oppressed slave was a fraud, designed only to strengthen their control of the government.[35]

It was perhaps inescapable that Republicans who pointed out these Democratic contradictions should themselves sometimes appear to be racist demagogues. It was the Democrats, Republicans said, who were the real "nigger lovers." A political cartoonist for *Harper's Weekly* asserted in 1862 that the southern slaveowner was the greatest "Nigger worshipper" of all: he sent his son to war, but fearing financial loss he kept his field hands at home. In two 1863 leaflets first printed by the Johnstown (Pennsylvania) *Tribune*, another Republican accused the Democrats of having been the principal advocates of Negro equality ever since the days of Thomas Jefferson. They made the African a citizen in Maine and Massachusetts, gave him the ballot in New Hampshire, and passed the lenient suffrage laws in New York. The Democrats had advanced the Negro cause in America farther than anyone else, the leaflets argued, "and yet they deny being in favor of negro equality, and charge it upon the Republicans—just like the thief who cries 'stop thief' the loudest."[36]

Finally, after emancipation, Democrats and Republicans alike continued to urge that colonies be established outside the United States for the free Negroes. Before the Civil War, the free Negro population had been relatively small, and the "threat" that it had posed correspondingly insignificant. Universal emancipation, on the other hand, gave the nation four million new citizens—thus creating problems that many white Americans considered unsolvable. So colonization suddenly seemed plausible and even necessary to people who had not been attracted to it before. For example, a visionary racist calling himself "Obed Kedar" published two allegorical tracts that urged Negro deportation; if the Negroes were not deported, he insisted, the American political system was doomed. In an "open letter" to the President, one James Mitchell urged colonization on the grounds that white Southerners feared forced racial amalgamation if the Union won the war, a situation they would resist to the last man. The general acceptability of colonization could be seen in the fact that some Republicans, including a few who claimed to be sincere friends of the Negro, supported it. One of these was Hollis Read, a New York City minister, who praised the Negro for his fortitude and endurance in the face of severe adversities, but suggested that these commendable faculties be applied to the establishment of communities in Africa. Read opposed forced deportation, however, and recommended that the Negro go voluntarily and only if he had something to contribute to the new settlement.[37] This was not an unpopular view among Republicans who could see no other solution; though they viewed themselves as fundamentally equalitarian, they nonetheless hesitated to assert that the black American had just as much right to the country as the white American.

Advocates of colonization cited one authority that few other racists dared claim—President Lincoln. On August 14, 1862, the President had suggested to a delegation of Negroes visiting the White House that they might be happier in a home outside the United States. He had also investigated the possibility of locating emancipated slaves in Latin America, but never followed through on the plan. Democrats circulated Lincoln's remarks widely because, in addition to his colonization suggestion, he had declared that "not a single man of your race is made the equal of a single man of ours." A careful reading of this statement in context would have shown that Lincoln's reference was a realistic appraisal of the Negro's economic and social opportunities rather than a judgment about his innate inferiority.* But the proponents of white supremacy, spawned in the hurly-burly, could not be expected to entertain the luxury of objectivity, and they often quoted this statement out of context to show an official authority for their racism and to prove that Republicans were just as bigoted as Democrats.[38]

The Democrats leaped at every chance to exploit the obvious Republican inconsistency on colonization. In the Ohio gubernatorial campaign of 1865, General Jacob Dolson Cox, the Republican candidate, had a difficult time explaining his conservative views to the more equalitarian members of his party. When queried by the Oberlin Committee, an ad hoc group of abolitionists who had appointed themselves guardians of the Negro's interests in the pending elections, Cox stated flatly that he did not believe whites and blacks could ever live together in the South. Instead of advocating deportation, however, Cox suggested setting aside contiguous parts of South Carolina, Georgia, Alabama, and Florida, where the concentration of Negroes was already

---

* A mild controversy continues to swirl around attempts to clarify Lincoln's real feelings toward the Negro. For a perceptive review of "the task of capturing the President for the equalitarian cause," see Ludwell H. Johnson, "Lincoln and Equal Rights: The Authenticity of the Wadsworth Letter," *Journal of Southern History*, XXXII (Feb. 1966), 83–87. Johnson raises serious doubts about those portions of the letter that make Lincoln sound almost like an abolitionist. He calls one paragraph an outright fake, and questions the authenticity of two others.

heavy, as a permanent home for the freed slaves. In other words, he favored what might be called "domestic" colonization. The only solution to the present dilemma, Cox said, was the "peaceable separation of the races on the soil where they now are." The idea was not new, and it satisfied neither side. The Columbus *Crisis* and the *Old Guard* attacked Cox immediately for hypocrisy, and the Oberlin Committee, of course, rejected anything less than complete integration of the races.[39]

Before long, it became obvious that establishing Negro colonies in the 1860's was even less feasible than it had been forty years earlier. The prewar colonization societies had attracted those who had been more anti-Negro than antislavery. They had advocated emancipation followed by deportation, and had rejected all suggestions of equalitarian coexistence; so they had quickly alienated abolitionist support. By the 1860's, all of the problems left by the war and, most important, a new humanitarian spirit were added to the difficulties faced by the earlier movement. In reality, the colonization schemes of the Civil War were nothing more than expedients, usually ill advised and almost entirely speculative. By this time, most whites were willing to acknowledge that the black race was in America to stay—though that acknowledgement did not ordinarily imply that Negroes would have complete equality. Moreover, although colonization was considered by representatives of both parties, it was not an issue that aroused the emotions the racists customarily appealed to. As a result, white supremacy propagandists did not pursue the question with too much zest. The colonization proposals of the 1860's constituted a feeble last attempt to resolve racial problems by elimination.

> O! send him to his mother's care,
> That colored cuss and leave him there:
> Send him today and let him stay,
> That colored cuss from Africa.
>
> Another anthem then we'll raise,
> With louder songs of joy and praise,
> We'll celebrate the glorious day
> That moves the colored cuss away.[40]

To spread the gospel of white supremacy, racists used every means of communication. In addition to the usual printed materials and soapbox speeches, angry comments from racist congressmen—often made during debates that did not involve the Negro—reappeared in newspapers and pamphlets that were circulated among the general public.

Songs and poems exploiting race prejudice were also common: several political songbooks were published during the 1860's, and some Democratic newspapers made racist poetry and humor a regular editorial feature.

A few critics preferred pictorial forms of expression. (See Plates 1–12.) Independent publishing houses and lithographers, such as Bromley and Company, Kimmel & Forster, and A. Zenneck, produced most of the pictorial racism of the decade. In the reproduction of posters and broadsides, Bromley and Company was to the Democratic party what Currier and Ives was to the Republican party. Posters, placards, and broadsides bearing cartoons, caricatures, and slogans circulated throughout the North, especially during election campaigns. The derogatory leaflet illustration was probably racism's most crude form of expression. In the 1860's, political cartoons were naïve and awkward, sometimes bordering on the obscene. They displayed little of the sophistication—the rich mixture of wit, imagination, and cynicism— that cartoons became famous for in the 1880's. Pictures of Negroes and white abolitionists in grotesque and humiliating situations decorated occasional newspapers or tracts, notably the La Crosse (Wisconsin) *Democrat* and the Richmond *Southern Opinion*, but these were the exception rather than the rule. Most of the racist press had not yet learned the value of a visual editorial.[41]

Despite this, the Democratic press was the leading outlet for racist demagoguery. The major eastern journals—the New York *World*, the New York *Daily News*, the New York *Journal of Commerce*, the Washington *Evening Union*, the Albany *Atlas and Argus*, the Hartford *Times*, and the Philadelphia *Age*—exploited race prejudice relentlessly. The establishment of the *Age* was one of the most direct and sudden responses to the Emancipation Proclamation; its first issue was published in March 1863, and it vigorously supported the southern position on slavery throughout the Civil War.[42] Phineas Wright, head of the militant, antiwar Order of American Knights, made the *Daily News* the official organ of his organization. Ignoring the more moderate Democratic newspapers, he joined the *Daily News* editorial staff, assumed complete editorial control in January 1863, and intensified the racist policies of publisher Benjamin Wood.[43]

In the Midwest, the Columbus *Crisis*, the La Crosse *Democrat*, the Chicago *Times*, the Cincinnati *Enquirer*, the Cleveland *Plain Dealer*, the Detroit *Free Press*, the St. Louis *Times*, and the Indianapolis *State Sentinel* were among the most active racist publications. Few newspapers, East or West, were as extreme as the *Crisis* and the *Democrat*, both weeklies. Samuel Medary, founder and publisher of the *Crisis*, was one of the country's leading Copperheads.[44] The *Democrat*, one of the few racist newspapers to use political cartoons regularly, devoted most of its eight pages to editorials, articles, and letters-to-the-editor that condemned the "nigger-loving party." Editor Marcus Mills "Brick" Pomeroy called it, simply, "The White Man's Paper."

But among racist newspapers, one stood out above all others. As frantic as many of the items in the *Crisis* and the *Democrat* were, neither could approach Van Evrie's New York *Weekly Day Book*. It was almost exclusively a white supremacy newspaper. From October 1861 to October 1863, its official name was *The Caucasian*, and readers (and critics) continued to call it that long afterward. Van Evrie claimed, falsely, it had national circulation; he also claimed that it was the only publication of its kind, and it unquestionably was. The *Day Book*'s editorial policy, printed at the masthead of most of its editorial pages, read, "White Men Must Rule America." The newspaper fought every effort to improve the condition of the black race; its declared goal was "the utter rout, overthrow, and extermination of Abolitionism from American soil." Van Evrie often used most of a page to advertise his own publications. Printed in boldface at least half an inch high, his ads included such slogans as "White Men to the Rescue," "White Supremacy or Negro Amalgamation," and "White Supremacy or Social Anarchy." Examples of headlines and column headings included "White Supremacy Forever! Negro Equality, Never! Never!" "Can Niggers Conquer Americans?" "Shall the Working Classes Be Equalized with Negroes?" "Shall the Negroes Come North?" "Can We Amalgamate with Negroes?" and "Miscegenation."

Although the *Day Book* was the most vituperative of the racist journals, its influence should not be overestimated. In the first place, it did not represent the Democratic party or even a faction of the party, nor did it claim to. Van Evrie rarely supported candidates for public office, most of whom he considered too moderate. In addition, the *Day Book* was a weekly, hence it printed, all in all, fewer racist tirades than the Copperhead dailies. The Philadelphia *Age*, for example, included more anti-Negro propaganda in a week's six issues than the *Day Book* did in one issue. Moreover, Van Evrie did not enjoy a large audience (although he claimed to have one). The paper was in financial trouble throughout most of its thirty-year existence; pleas for new subscribers appeared frequently, and advertising was meager.[45] Had Van Evrie enlarged and diversified the range of topics in the *Day Book*, he might have appealed to more people. Every good newspaperman knew that variety—a little something for everybody—increased circulation. But Van Evrie, despite his pleas for new subscribers, appeared not to care about attracting them. The *Day Book* writers were so extreme and at times ridiculous that only fanatics supported them. Though it was common practice for newspapers to exchange articles, few *Day Book* items ever appeared in other publications.

Another of Van Evrie's enterprises was *The Old Guard, a Monthly Journal, Devoted to the Principles of 1776 and 1787*, published by Van Evrie, Horton & Company and edited by C. Chauncey Burr. Occasionally the journal printed articles of a literary nature, but for most of its existence, the *Old Guard*'s contributors (Burr was the most consistently racist among them) confined themselves primarily to political issues, especially white supremacy. Located originally in Hackensack, New Jersey, but moving a short time later to New York City, the *Old Guard* first appeared in June 1862.[46] Various issues in 1863 and 1864 contained handsome frontispiece portraits of such notable Democrats and Copperheads as Horatio Seymour, George Pendleton, Benjamin and Fernando Wood, Vallandigham, and Cox. Interestingly, the issues that made up Volume IV (1866) carried portraits of former Confederate generals. Late in 1869, although he reaffirmed his commitment to "state sovereignty and white supremacy," Burr sold his interest to Van Evrie.[47] Under its new editor, Thomas Dunn English, the *Old Guard* began publishing more literary and cultural articles, and racism virtually disappeared from its pages. Perhaps white supremacy was the journal's life blood; the *Old Guard* folded within a year.

In addition to racist newspapers and periodicals, a vast number of white supremacy pamphlets were published in the 1860's. Some of them enjoyed immense popularity and notoriety. Bishop John H. Hopkin's 1851 sermon defending slavery reappeared in 1863 as a pamphlet, and immediately became one of the most frequently quoted tracts in the racist's repertoire. Van Evrie's "Free Negroism," originally written in the 1850's as the introduction to a book, was published as a pamphlet in 1862, and four more editions followed between 1863 and 1866.* Por-

* Frank L. Klement, in *The Copperheads in the Middle West* (Chicago, 1960), pp. 104–105, implies that Samuel F. B. Morse, president of the Society for the Diffusion of Political Knowledge, wrote "a bulletin entitled 'Results of Emancipation.'" The "bulletin" was nothing more than Van Evrie's "Free Negroism" with its title changed to "Emancipation and Its Results." The SDPK version carried Morse's name as the president of the organization, as did all of the pamphlets published by the Society. The major bibliographical aids, including the Library of Congress Catalogue and the Depository Catalogue, list "Free Negroism" as an anonymous tract. However, in his introduction to James Hunt's "The Negro's Place in Nature" (1864), Van Evrie claimed authorship of "Free Negroism."

tions of it were reprinted in Democratic newspapers, and in 1868 it appeared again as an entire chapter in Lindley Spring's *The Negro at Home*, making it probably the most quoted white supremacy publication of the decade.[48]

Although the extremists took themselves and their cause seriously, they were not without their humorous moments. In verse, song, and allegory, several writers, most of them unknown, published satires and witty dramatizations designed to humiliate the Republicans and lampoon the Negroes. Led by J. F. Feeks of New York, a handful of publishers produced over a dozen humorous pamphlets in the year and a half following the Emancipation Proclamation. In "The Democratic Gospel of Peace, According to St. Tammany" (1863), the villains were "Wind-wall Fill-up," "Fed-ricks Dug-glass," "Henry Wore Breeches," "Gray-hit Smith," "Ho-race Greedy," and "Charles Summon-her," who sang "unto their little niggah idol." Fernando Wood, a New York City Copperhead, appeared as "Fernando, Chief of the Man-hot-ons," a peacemaker and honest statesman. To "St. Tammany," Negroes were "kangaroos or niggahs . . . whose hind legs exceeded in length their front legs, and they had lambs' wool for hair." They were "somewhat tawney in complexion," given to carrying "their fore paws in their breeches pockets," and "their heels were considerably thrust out backwards quite naturally." Similar works, all published anonymously in 1863, were "The Lincoln Catechism," "God Bless Abraham Lincoln," "The Book of the Prophet Stephen, Son of Douglas," "Abraham Africanus I," "Lincolniana," and "Revelations: A Companion to the 'New Gospel of Peace,' According to Abraham." The last pamphlet, which included material from "The Democratic Gospel of Peace," cast Wendell Phillips as "Phillip the Amalgamator," who made war on the people of the "Cottonade" and who had "taken him a wife from among the daughters of Niggero."[49]

"Revelations" was a spoof on the first and second parts of Richard Grant White's four-part *The New Gospel of Peace According to St. Benjamin* (1863–1866) a satirical attack on the peace-at-any-price Copperheads. It was perhaps characteristic that the racist spent most of his time reacting rather than innovating. It was equally characteristic that his polemics had virtually no literary merit. The "collected works" of racism during the Civil War era are a monument to bigotry's dearth of intellect and imagination, and the effectiveness of the racist literary effort remains questionable. Since the prejudiced reader already had his mind made up, the satires probably introduced a little humor into what was ordinarily a serious matter. But since so many of the pamphlets, satiric and otherwise, were of unknown authorship, the average reader must have been skeptical. Anonymous writing was not very convincing because it spoke with no authority. The most immediate reaction to an unsigned pamphlet was suspicion. Surely most Americans in the 1860's were sophisticated enough to question a writer's reasons for concealing his identity. The logical conclusion was that he was a sorehead intent only on causing trouble and determined to avoid responsibility for his remarks.

Although the racist demagogues were a vociferous and prolific group, they did not produce most of the political propaganda of the 1860's. In terms of total wartime literary output, their contribution was relatively small, and they remained a distinct and often hopeless minority. It is doubtful that America has ever witnessed an era of such vast pamphlet production. Led by the Union League movement, war supporters produced an unprecedented quantity of patriotic literature, most of which did not mention the Negro at all. Similarly, newspapers supporting the Union effort far outnumbered the Copperhead sheets. Government-sponsored mass rallies were common throughout the North, and the Republican press printed many of the speeches made at the rallies and elsewhere. Moreover, whereas there were various magazines supporting the war and the antislavery cause, the *Old Guard*, in its dedication to white supremacy, stood alone. In sheer volume, Van Evrie, Burr, Feeks, the Society for the Diffusion of Political Knowledge, and others of their ilk could not approach patriotic organizations such as the New England and New York Loyal Publication Societies. An estimate of 20 unionist lines to 1 Copperhead line in pamphlets, periodicals, and newspapers is probably conservative. Nor did the racists have a monopoly on zeal. Unionist enthusiasm for the war, though not always uniform, was no less intense than the Copperhead repudiation of it.

The outburst of frantic racism that followed emancipation came largely from a minority fringe, and no attempt was made to unify these angry expressions of prejudice into an organized drive. Democratic spokesmen usually touched on one or more aspects of the race question in their speeches and writings, but they never attempted to turn their most incendiary issue into a true movement. A few malcontents did organize into action groups—some radical, like Wright's Order of American Knights, and some moderate, like Morse's Society for the Diffusion of Political Knowledge—but the race issue never became their all-consuming passion. Van Evrie's *Weekly Day Book* and the *Old Guard*, assisted by the publishing firm of Van Evrie, Horton & Company with its *Anti-Abolitionist Tracts*, stood ready to step in as the mouthpieces of organized racism; and Copperhead politicians like Vallandigham, Cox, and Fernando Wood were willing to serve as its chief ministers had the cry gone out for any. But the white supremacists, failing to generate the unified support they had hoped for, could not, or would not, get together.

Members of the racist press even disagreed over just who was a racist. Shortly before the end of the Civil War, the *Old Guard* attacked the New York *World* for being a Republican newspaper in disguise. A few months later, Van Evrie made the same accusation in the *Day Book*. The *World*, he complained, was posing as a Copperhead newspaper for the sole purpose of embarrassing the Democrats. To Van Evrie, the *World*'s publisher, Manton Marble, was a dedicated abolitionist.[50] It was characteristic of racism that its spokesmen should fall to quarreling among themselves. Those to whom name-calling came so easily could not be expected, when provoked, to exercise restraint.

Chapter Three

NEGROES IN UNIFORM

"What we are doing now—organizing and arming negroes, forming negro Battalions, Regiments, and Brigades—is but outraging public sentiment," Representative Brooks cried at a New York City Democratic rally in December 1862. The people of Europe had previously looked at America as the model republic, he continued, but they now turned with horror from the "disgraceful exhibition" of twenty million white men calling on four million African slaves to shed the "fraternal blood" of eight million white men.[1] Probably influenced by articles like one in the London *Morning Post* condemning the spectacle of "negro soldiers fighting in support of the Federal Government,"[2] Brooks was in the vanguard of many whites who shuddered at the prospect of Negroes in uniform.

As the manpower demands of the war intensified, the reasons for using Negro volunteers in the Union army became increasingly obvious. Some Northerners endorsed the practice simply because it would tend to reduce the number of white troops required and thus the number of white casualties. Washington and Jackson had set the precedents, a Philadelphia abolitionist wrote; according to eyewitnesses, in the War of 1812 black soldiers had proved themselves able fighters. In 1863, "an officer in the 9th Army Corps" urged field commanders to recruit former slaves in conquered southern territory, in order to add 160,000 men to the army and provide an ideal "police force" in occupied areas. Racist army officers, of course, staunchly opposed such suggestions. In June 1863, General George W. Morgan, a member of General William T. Sherman's staff, resigned his commission because of the government's decision to enlist black soldiers. Four months later, Colonel William R. Morrison, who soon afterward became an outspoken racist member of the House of Representatives, facetiously remarked to a group in Edwardsville, Illinois, "With Africa for an ally we might conquer the rebels, England and France, and the other nations of the earth."[3]

The participation of Negro soldiers never reached such dimensions, of course, but by the time the war was a year old, Negroes did figure in the government's military program. In the spring of 1862, General David Hunter organized the "First South Carolina Volunteer Regiment," made up of former slaves from the southeastern states. Before the group could see service, however, confusion and mismanagement led to its dissolution. In the summer and fall other units were raised with more success, and by 1863 the idea of Negroes in uniform had gained considerable acceptance. By the end of the war, about 179,000 Negroes had served in the Union forces, most of them recruited from the southern states.[4]

In a logical reaction, northern white supremacists predicted gloomily that the Confederacy would begin recruiting its own Negro soldiers. The Albany *Atlas and Argus* voiced this fear in October 1864; and at about the same time the editor of the New York *Daily News*, after calling the Negro a cowardly fighter, declared that the South would be forced to draft its slaves, who would then be "molded into an invincible fighting machine"—a contradiction that he failed to reconcile. A few days before the election, another editor wrote that the rebels had already begun a slave-enlistment drive. Alarmed by this possibility, racist critics pointed out that the Union army enjoyed a considerable advantage in numbers so long as both sides used only white soldiers, but that the entry of slave soldiers into the rebel force would greatly reduce that advantage. The North, they argued, with less than 8 per cent of the nation's black people, could certainly not match the South in total Negro manpower, a contention that the War Democrats could endorse. The fact that Negroes in the Union forces more often than not were from the South seemed not to occur to those who voiced this argument.[5]

In truth, it was doubtful that even the Copperheads expected the South to use slave soldiers to save its cause. By the fall of 1864, two and one-half years had passed since the first Negro had been sworn into the Union army. Although some Confederate leaders, including Robert

E. Lee, had for some time advocated the use of slave soldiers, it was not until the desperate final months of the war that the southern government actually adopted such a policy. And it was less than a month before the surrender at Appomattox that rebel officials formally authorized slave "enlistments." Of course, throughout the war slaves performed numerous back-up duties, thereby freeing regular soldiers for combat, so slave manpower had always been a factor in the southern military effort.

Negro soldiers offended the racists for reasons far more fundamental than possible southern retaliation: they were convinced that the enlistment of blacks was the second step (after emancipation) to absolute racial equality. After making soldiers out of Negroes, Brooks told the Democratic Union Association, the government could try to justify making them citizens. The New York *Journal of Commerce* and the Albany *Atlas and Argus* flatly accused the government of using the Negro soldier to promote social and political equality of the races. "We see looming in the distance our new nobility," the *Atlas and Argus* jeered "Sir Sambo Shoddy, Count Cuffee Codfish and the Marquis of Mulemeat." In 1864, 43 Democratic congressmen, in a signed and published petition, condemned the use of black soldiers as part of a Republican drive to establish "the equality of the black and white races." The Republican party's ultimate aim, the petitioners declared, was to guarantee the Negroes "the right of suffrage and also of social position." In the 21 months from February 1863 to the presidential election of 1864, the Detroit *Free Press* printed almost two dozen articles and editorials criticizing the use of black soldiers.[6]

No publication was more outspoken on this point than the New York *World*, the leading Democratic newspaper in the North. Its editors exploited every incident, however minor, to magnify the social implications of Negro soldiery. In March 1864, the New York City Union League Club gave the 20th Regiment of Colored Volunteers a rousing send-off, complete with flag waving and patriotic speeches. The *Journal of Commerce*, true to its moderate philosophy, described the occasion in a small article. The *Daily News*, though extreme in its despair, nonetheless refrained from inflammatory denunciations. Not so the *World*. What a spectacle, the editor exclaimed, to see fair maidens waving white kerchiefs from Union Square and offering their love and honor "to a regiment of hypothetical Othellos, marching on their way to possible glory in bran-new [sic] uniforms, with white gaiters, beneath a spic-and-span silken banner, embroidered by . . . fair white hands!"[7] The editor of the *Old Guard*, equally outraged by the whole affair,

made several salacious allusions and actually printed the names of the
152 women who had signed the banner.* The Philadelphia *Age* also
described the incident, and on May 3, quoting the Chicago *Times*, told
of the departure of the First Illinois Colored Regiment. "White women
were there in attendance to bid farewell to black husbands, around
whose necks they clung long and fondly," the *Times* had written. "Black
women, too, and men almost white, were locked in each other's arms."[8]

Whatever the racist's reasons for these specious criticisms, his resentment was shared to some degree by many white Americans. The argument that the Negro had the right—if not the duty—to join the fight for
his own freedom had no appeal for many white people, who objected
on the grounds that the Negro was not a citizen and should therefore
not exercise the rights of one. Since he had no stake in the country's
future and could never enjoy the fruits of victory, they reasoned, he
should have no part in bringing that victory about. The debate in
Congress early in 1863 over House Bill 675, a measure calling for more
troops, clearly reflected the strength of this view. Representatives William Allen, Chilton A. White, and Samuel S. Cox of Ohio, James A.
Rollins and Elijah Norton of Missouri, Henry May of Maryland, and
Charles Wickliffe of Kentucky angrily protested the section that called
for Negro recruits. Summing up their argument, White proclaimed,
"This is a government of white men, made by white men for white men,
to be administered, protected, defended, and maintained by white
men."[9] Charles Halpine's "Miles O'Reilly" put it in a much more
comical way:

> Some tell us 'tis a burnin' shame
> To make the naygers fight;
> And that the thrade of bein' kilt
> Belongs but to the white.[10]

As Halpine implied, the insistence that only Caucasians should be permitted to die on the battlefield approached absurdity. Congressional
statements may have been more dignified and restrained than those of
the Copperhead editors and the rabid pamphleteers, but they were no
less preposterous.

The most popular and compelling arguments opposing Negro enlistments were those that somehow involved the white soldier. Who were
the better fighters, racists asked, well-disciplined whites or uncontrol-

---

* "Editor's Table," The *Old Guard*, II (Apr. 1864), 93. Included on the list were
the wife and daughter of Hamilton Fish, former Congressman, Governor of New
York, United States Senator, and later Secretary of State under Grant.

lable blacks? How would morale be affected by the presence of black comrades-in-arms? Could white troops avoid discrimination and mistreatment at the hands of abolitionist officers? What kind of commanders would be appointed to lead black battalions? These questions and others like them appeared again and again in racist literature and oratory.

In answering their own questions, critics often compared the fighting qualities of the two races, sometimes in a joking manner and always at the Negro's expense. "It is impossible to make a whistle out of a pig's tail," the Cleveland *Plain Dealer* stated. Van Evrie suggested that Negroes use their thick skulls for head banging—which was the only way they knew how to fight. A bill proposed in Congress that would have authorized equal pay for white and Negro troops was called a step "to perdition" by the New York *World*. Africans "receive the praise while the white soldiers do the fighting," Representative William Allen complained in Congress. Early in 1863, the *Old Guard* and the Albany *Atlas and Argus* attacked Henry Ward Beecher and the New York *Independent*, an ardent abolitionist newspaper, for allegedly recommending an "alliance" with the Negroes. "Only the negro can find [victory]," the *Atlas and Argus* quoted the *Independent* as having said. "Give him gun and bayonet, and let him point the way! The future is fair: God and the Negro are to save the Republic!" "God and the negro," the *Atlas and Argus* countered; "such names mingled!" "For finance, issue Greenbacks," the editor sneered, "for war, Blackbacks."[11]

Republican statements praising Negro military exploits, since they were frequently exuberant, lent themselves to racist distortion and misinterpretation. In the summer of 1863, Horace Greeley praised the First Kansas Colored Regiment as "the best disciplined and most perfectly drilled regiment in the American army." Indignant, the Philadelphia *Age* called Greeley's comment a "confirmation of the truth of the Abolitionist doctrine that the negro is as good as a white man!" Our brave white troops, the *Age* maintained, certainly did not feel very complimented by "this attempt to exalt the negro over their heads." Later, the New York *World* expressed shock at Greeley's compliments to a company of Negroes who had held their lines during a long forced march while many white men had reportedly dropped from exhaustion; and when Indiana's Governor Oliver P. Morton praised a group of Negroes who returned from a skirmish with all of their equipment, noting that some of the whites in the battle had come back empty-handed, the state's leading Democratic newspaper, the Indianapolis *State Sentinel*, accused him of implying that the whites were cowards. "Every effort is being made by the Abolitionists to disparage the white

soldiers and elevate the negro soldiers," the editor complained. Abolitionist speakers and writers had declared that the black troops were
superior, others cried; where would the campaign to elevate the African
end?[12]

No one was more lavish in praising black soldiers—and no one was
more severely condemned for it—than Pennsylvania Representative William Kelley, an outspoken abolitionist. In July 1864, the Albany *Atlas
and Argus* quoted the New York *Commercial Advertiser*, which had
printed Kelley's description of a recent expedition under General
Samuel D. Sturgis. Two hundred Negro troops "protected *sixteen hundred* demoralized white troops from the rebel cavalry, and brought
them in in safety," the congressman had remarked. "Is it possible," the
Atlas and Argus asked, "that sixteen hundred stood quietly by and let
their gallant protectors do all the work against the rebels?" On the
floor of the House of Representatives, the editor went on, Kelley had
named "the NEGRO SOLDIERS of the loyal army" as the men "of
this era of whom the poet will sing in the highest strains" and "of whom
the historian will write his most glowing panegyrics." What profane
blasphemy to discredit the white soldier in the black African's favor!
"The language of such papers as the [Albany] *Evening Journal*, the
cheers in Congress over fabulous negro exploits, the remarks of such a
member as Kell[e]y of Philadelphia exalting the black above the white
soldier, is [*sic*] rapidly filling the public mind with disgust."[13]

As the presidential election of 1864 drew close, racists intensified
their criticism. In Campaign Document No. 11, the Democratic National Committee accused Senator Henry Wilson of Massachusetts, a
militant abolitionist, of saying that the black soldier was "equal to the
white in everything, and superior to him in endurance."[14] Right up to
election eve, the Democratic press printed dozens of similar statements
and attributed them to Greeley, Kelley, Wilson, and others. Attacking
men for making such statements, whether true or fabricated, must have
seemed ironic to Americans who recalled the proslavery argument that
the Negro had a "natural" ability to perform difficult and tedious
physical tasks.*

---

* After the war, racists continued to reflect on the Negro's alleged lack of courage.
Describing his wartime experiences to a Democratic gathering in Columbus County,
Pennsylvania, Captain Charles B. Brockway called the Negro soldier the most
cowardly he had ever seen. In 1867 Hinton Rowan Helper said the Negro soldier
was "enfeebled with fear, quivering with fright, skulking with trepidation, and
otherwise behaving with the most shameless and unpardonable cowardice." See
Democratic Party, Pennsylvania, *Proceedings of the Nob Mountain Meeting* (Philadelphia, 1865), pp. 61–65; and Hinton R. Helper, *Nojoque; A Question for a Continent* (New York, 1867), pp. 200–204.

To many, the question of the Negro's fighting ability was irrelevant. The most damnable aspect of Negroes in uniform, they insisted, was the sheer insult to the white soldier who was forced to fight alongside a black man—to march, as Brooks put it, "shoulder to shoulder, with this seething, sooty negro." In fact, the very thought of accepting black help was an insufferable indignity, an affront to the white man's masculinity; and a few fanatics even said that defeat and death without Negro soldiers was better than victory and survival with them. Colonel Morrison asked a group of people if they thought that white soldiers would appreciate having their "shattered and broken columns" reinforced by "the poor debased African."[15] Most such questions, of course, were racist polemics, generated by newsmen and politicians and not by troops in the line. White soldiers in shattered and broken columns probably would have welcomed any kind of reinforcements, regardless of the color of their skins. As the witty "Miles O'Reilly" put it:

> In battle's wild commotion
>   I shouldn't at all object
> If Sambo's body should stop a ball
>   That was coming for me direct.
>
> Though Sambo's black as the ace of spades,
>   His finger a thrigger can pull
> And his eyes run sthraight on the barrel-sights
>   From under its thatch of wool.[16]

The public praise of Negro soldiers led, predictably, to charges that they, as objects of special attention of abolitionists in the government, received preferential treatment. White soldiers were being murdered as a result of exposure to unnecessary risks, a Democratic campaign orator lamented in 1864, while Abraham Lincoln petted Negroes. According to some, abolitionist officers deliberately placed white soldiers who opposed the government's Negro policies in the most hazardous positions on the battle line. But while some white supremacists were crying "favoritism," others were denouncing the government for permitting the use of untrained, inefficient, and inexperienced Negro troops in the most critical battle positions, thereby jeopardizing entire campaigns. "A breastwork is to be stormed in the face of murderous fire that a military eye must have foreseen could be withstood by none but those of the most approved and stubborn courage and perfect discipline," the New York *Daily News* cried in describing the siege of Petersburg. According to the *News*, the decision to use "inferior" Negro troops caused the northern forces to risk losing the engagement and many black soldiers died needlessly. But seven months later, in an editorial on how the Negro had "hindered and embarrassed the war," the Philadelphia *Age* criticized Union commanders for allegedly refusing to expose Negroes to danger during the Petersburg mine operation, with the result that the operation was a complete failure.[17]

In reality, although Negroes probably were less likely than whites to be killed in battle, they faced greater dangers from other sources. The records indicate that the battle-inflicted casualty rate for Negroes was substantially lower than that for whites, while the overall Negro death rate was conspicuously higher. Of course, since black troops did not join the lines until eighteen months after the war had started, a man-hour combat casualty figure—if it was possible calculate one—might be more meaningful; but it seems obvious that even after they joined the army Negroes did not face combat in the same proportions as whites. However, an extremely large number of Negroes died from diseases and other noncombat causes—ten times as many as died in battle—an emphatic indication that they did not always receive the same food and medical care that whites enjoyed. For one thing, since captured Negro soldiers were not usually treated like conventional prisoners of war, the percentage that died because of malnutrition and mistreatment in southern prison camps was greater than the percentage of whites who died that way. Until 1864, when the Confederate government agreed to recognize captured Negroes as prisoners of war, many were sold into slavery and some were murdered outright. On the other hand, a large number of black troops worked at menial tasks far from the lines and thus were not exposed to enemy fire or capture, so the fact that a far greater percentage of Negroes than whites died in the war actually incriminates the Union army as much as the Confederacy.[18]

The racist accusation of favoritism became especially heated when the perplexing and sensitive question of prisoner exchanges arose. Committed to the idea that individual black and white soldiers were equal (though they were not paid the same), the Union government refused to accept only white soldiers in exchange for southern prisoners of war, and insisted that black captives be returned on equal terms. To the southern government, however, an armed Negro was little more than an insurrectionary slave, and even white officers who commanded Negro units received harsh treatment. Understandably, the South did not wish to comply with the Union demand, for compliance would have been an implicit recognition of racial equality. Consequently, exchange negotiations bogged down, and it looked as if thousands of northern soldiers, white and black, would be condemned to prolonged confinement in

Confederate stockades. The racists, predictably, made the most of the situation.

Thousands of white boys were rotting in Andersonville, the Albany *Atlas and Argus* charged, because Lincoln and Secretary of War Edwin M. Stanton refused to "abandon their party hobby of an *equal* exchange of negroes for white men!" Two weeks before the presidential election of 1864, a campaign speaker in New Haven denounced the government for Negro favoritism, and a short time later the Democratic National Committee published his remarks in a widely circulated pamphlet.[19] The accusations of favoritism were patently false, as the casualty figures indicated. The federal government had only asked for equality in prisoner exchanges; but to the white supremacists, equality was the same thing as favoritism.

Inevitably, a problem arose over just who would command the Negro units. To enlist blacks was one thing; to assign men to lead them was quite another. Certainly, racists believed, no respectable white officer would accept such an assignment. Initially many officers, especially West Pointers, agreed. The War Department would have to search among the abolitionists for men to lead Negroes, the New York *World* predicted. An applicant for a "lieutenancy in the *Corps d'Afrique*" would have to swear to several abolitionist dogmas, the editor sarcastically remarked: he had to prove that Nero was a Negro whose color had been distorted by inferior Caucasian historians, he had to subscribe to the miscegenetic origin of Scipio, he had to prove that Hannibal's father was black, and he had to admit that the popularity of the names "Caesar" and "Pompey" among slaves was proof of "the antiquity of military genius in the race of Ham." As an incentive to those who would take the oath, the *World* continued, the Secretary of War planned to offer promotion bonuses to white officers. The white men who accepted these commissions were, in the minds of the critics, the scum of the army, and thereupon forfeited all claims to military honors.[20]

Although they were horrified by the thought of white officers commanding Negro troops, those who opposed having Negroes in the army found the idea that black officers might be allowed to lead *white* troops the most preposterous of all, although this never came close to happening. In 1863, for example, the Philadelphia *Age* accused Representative Kelley of proposing the appointment of a black general. A short time earlier, Kelley had delivered a speech to a predominantly Negro audience in which he had declared that the Negro was the "coming man" of the war. He was voicing a popular abolitionist theme based on the conviction that the war was essentially a struggle for Negro freedom.

In the course of his remarks, he echoed the common complaint that there was no outstanding Union general who could inspire his troops to win a decisive victory. If no such leader appeared, he concluded, flamboyantly and somewhat patronizingly, the cause of Negro freedom must provide that inspiration. Though the Congressman had not suggested that a Negro actually be elevated to the rank of general, the *Age* reported what the editors considered his most distasteful implications. A few months later, David G. Croly, managing editor of the New York *World*, commented sarcastically, "It will be a sad misfortune if this war should end without a battle being fought by a black general in command of a white or mixed body of troops."[21]

Although most of the racist's complaints about the evils of Negroes in uniform were largely speculative and therefore easy to dismiss, the question of what might happen when black soldiers marched into southern states was a source of genuine anxiety for more than a few Northerners. Arming ex-slaves would bring dreadful consequences, racists predicted. The sight of a black man, armed and in uniform, would incite the otherwise peaceable slaves to "arson and murder," especially if the slaves should happen to recognize him. A few extremists accused the Republicans of deliberately using Negro soldiers to "exterminate" the southern whites. S. S. Nicholas warned that Negroes were members of an "alien foreign race, bound to us by no ties of affection or sympathy as the children of a common country" would be bound, and that moreover they had the "supposed injuries" of slavery to avenge. Understandably, many Southerners shared the Northerners' anxiety. "We shall have trouble here with the negroes," a southern friend of Manton Marble, the New York *World*'s publisher, wrote from New Orleans in August 1863. "The blacks are all *to be* armed, & it is astounding that Gen. Banks shouldn't know that these blacks are as likely to kill his men as any other whites—especially when there is so much ill-feeling between black and white 'volunteers.' " Even the loyal slave states, because of their large Negro populations, feared what blacks in uniform might do, and objected to proposals for raising Negro regiments. During its 1863–64 session, the Assembly of the Commonwealth of Kentucky passed a resolution, supported by Governor Thomas E. Bramlette, protesting the enlistment of Negroes in the state.[22]

The Democratic press was particularly active in predicting and publicizing incidents of violence by Negro soldiers. The Columbus *Crisis* and Philadelphia *Age* freely quoted accounts from southern journals like the Richmond *Enquirer* and the New Orleans *Era*. To illustrate what happened when Negroes became soldiers, the *Age* even cited an abolitionist source. Quoting from the *Christian Recorder*, the official organ of the African Methodist Episcopal Church, the *Age* told how a company of black Union soldiers had freed several slave women in Virginia. With the help of their liberators, the women then turned a whip on their former master. The *Christian Recorder*, elated by the fact that northern Negroes had emancipated southern Negroes, published the article as a story of slave liberation. But the *Age*, concentrating on the flogging, printed it as an example of Negro military brutality, brutality that northern Negroes were apparently proud of. Similar articles appeared in the *Age* several times during the 1860's.[23]

The more brutal the offense, of course, the better copy it made. In August 1863, the *Crisis* featured a story about eighteen Negro soldiers who killed an elderly Tennessee white man. Afterward, they allegedly shot, stabbed, and drowned the man's son and four grandchildren. Early the following year, the same newspaper graphically described how three Negro soldiers from the 55th Massachusetts Regiment had raped a white woman. New York City's two major Democratic newspapers, the *World* and the *Daily News*, also carried many reports of cruelty and violence by Negro soldiers. In one story, a southern unionist in Johnsonville, Tennessee, who had been ostracized by his secessionist neighbors since the beginning of the war, was "bucked and gagged" by Negro soldiers, showing that even those courageous Southerners who remained loyal to the North suffered. In one month in 1866, the *Daily News* printed five articles on violence and riots ostensibly instigated by black soldiers.[24]

It is difficult to assess the extent and significance of acts of violence allegedly committed by Negro troops. It would be a mistake, obviously, to depend on Democratic newspapers, as a measure of the actual number of incidents. Descriptions of the same event were printed in many journals; in some cases, one newspaper's account was merely reprinted verbatim in several others. Thus the description of a single incident appeared in several different newspapers at different times, and this tended to magnify the frequency of Negro "outrages." In addition, the stories often wandered from the truth. Negro soldiers who had been slaves did occasionally display excessive bitterness toward white Southerners; but such incidents were, by and large, conspicuous by their infrequency. Thus, the racist had to manufacture much of his reporting of violence, a technique at which he became highly skilled.

By the end of the war, the demagogues had exhausted most of their arguments against the use of black soldiers. Their alarmist predictions had become tedious; the dangers of Negroes in the wartime army, as the white supremacists had defined them, had simply not materialized. Desperate for issues and unwilling to give up, the propagandists turned to the "threat" of a permanent black army as a last resort. The radicals have asked us to "disband our white armies, and trust to negro soldiers," the Albany *Atlas and Argus* charged as early as February 1863. Later, the 43 Democratic signers of the "Congressional Address" accused the Republicans of conspiring to organize "a considerable body of [Negroes] into a standing army." If General John C. Frémont was ever appointed governor of a conquered southern state, the Cleveland *Plain Dealer* prophesied, he would quickly raise several regiments of "Chasseurs d'Afrique." Thus, the hysterical white supremacist saw the Negro soldier as the means by which the future success of the Republican party would be ensured: he would enforce the will of an Afro-radical oligarchy. The ink on the Emancipation Proclamation had hardly dried when Representative White of Ohio accused the Lincoln administration of organizing "black battalions" in order to subvert "the supremacy of the white race in eleven States of this Union, and [make] the colored the dominant race in those States."[25]

As the end of the war approached, the fears of a permanent Negro army mounted. In the summer of 1864, the Philadelphia *Age* asked what would be done with the black soldier when the fighting stopped; his army life had been easy and pleasant compared to the life he had come from. Complicating the problem, the editor added, was the fact that military recruiters had enlisted only the worst Negroes—criminals, ruffians, vagabonds, idlers, and former slaves—who would not adapt willingly to a life of self-support. When the war was over, he concluded, Americans should not be surprised to find "a huge black mass, [with] fearful energy [for] mischief, hovering directly over us."[26]

The slowness with which black soldiers were mustered out of the army after Appomattox convinced many critics that they had been right. The Republicans obviously had a "settled policy," the elder Frank Blair charged in a speech in Memphis, of making black troops a "regular force which should give law to the country." Begging for the disbandment of Negro regiments early in 1866, the *Age* asserted that there were more black men in the army than white men.[27] Republican newsmen quickly pointed that this was not true. The New York *Times* agreed that there were more Negro volunteers than white; but when the white regulars were added, the Negroes were outnumbered by eighteen thousand.[28]

Of course, no Republican in or out of government planned to create a standing Negro army-and-police force, and even if one had, no method of implementing such a plan was available. Few extreme abolitionists had earned high military rank, and when one who had, General Frémont, took it upon himself in August 1861 to emancipate the slaves that had come under his jurisdiction in Missouri, President Lincoln quickly countermanded his orders. Furthermore, at no time were Negroes themselves in a position to exercise independent military authority. On the contrary, the black soldier's treatment at the hands of federal authorities was often little better than his treatment at the hands of the white community at large. The Union army established strict rules of racial segregation and held to them closely throughout the war and reconstruction; in fact Negroes frequently complained of discrimination in the army—in particular, of lower pay and assignments to menial, noncombat tasks. In short, it seems that the Republican approach to the use of black troops was a cautious one. To what extent, if any, racist pressures induced this caution is impossible to determine.

Chapter Four

THE MISCEGENATION
CONTROVERSY OF 1864

> Oh, give to Caesar Caesar's due,
>   A white wife if he chooses;
> His children tho' they're black and blue,
>   No more shall black folks' shoes.
> Oh grant him rights in politics,
>   Oh give us equal laws,
> . And gently, gently, let us mix,
>   White MAS with black PAPAS.[1]

Racist demagoguery in the United States came to its first climax in
1864. The presidential election was, to the racist fanatic, a national
referendum on the government's Negro policies in general and the
Emancipation Proclamation in particular. Encouraged by gains in the
elections of 1862, Democratic leaders decided to launch an all-out political offensive emphasizing nonmilitary issues: the Legal Tender Act,
excessive government spending, profiteering, conscription, and the
words and actions of the abolitionists. Although the war was the primary issue, throughout the entire campaign the race question, imposing
itself on almost every political discussion, was still a very incendiary
topic; and in 1864 it took on, briefly, a new aspect.

Late in December 1863, a 72-page booklet entitled "Miscegenation:
The Theory of the Blending of the Races, Applied to the American
White Man and Negro" appeared in a few eastern cities. At a glance,
it seemed that the anonymous author, who recommended a program

of systematic race mixing as a cure for all the nation's race problems, was an overzealous abolitionist. In reality, it was written by two racists in an effort to discredit the Republican party. The booklet attracted little attention for several weeks. In the first place, not many copies were immediately available, since most of the copies from the first printing were sent by the authors to people selected for their purposes. In the second place the title was not eyecatching—no one had ever heard of the word "miscegenation" before.

The word itself—made up from the Latin *miscere*, to mix, and *genus*, race—in a short time became a synonym for illicit interracial sexual relations. A "miscegen" was a child of mixed parentage—which meant he was the result of a union at that time considered "clandestine." The authors of "Miscegenation" actually created two more-specific words for race mixing: "melaeukation," from the Greek *melas*, black, and *leukas*, white, and "melamigleukation," which added a stem from the Greek verb *mignumi*, to mix, but meant the same thing. (It is not difficult to see why these latter terms never caught on.) After 1863, those who sought an abusive word generally abandoned "amalgamation" and used "miscegenation," which instantly acquired all sorts of salacious and derisive connotations. To amalgamate meant merely to mix; but to miscegenate meant to mix different races of human beings—it was a much more precise word and one without any possibly favorable overtones.*

The authors of "Miscegenation" were David Goodman Croly and George Wakeman, both of the New York *World*. Croly, born in Ireland, grew up in New York City, and had worked for two of the city's leading newspapers, the *Evening Post* and the *Herald*. He subsequently founded the Rockford (Illinois) *Daily News*, but later returned to New York, and in 1862 became managing editor of the *World*, a position he held for ten years.[2] Croly and Wakeman never acknowledged their roles in the creation of "Miscegenation," and there is no way of determining

* Gunnar Myrdal, in *An American Dilemma: The Negro Problem and Modern Democracy* (New York, 1962), p. 55n, says "Miscegenation is mainly an American term and is in America always used to denote only relations between Negroes and whites. Although it literally implies only mixture of genes between members of different races it has acquired a definite emotional connotation." Myrdal is only partly right. Miscegenation did not "acquire" its present undesirable meaning; it had it as soon as it was invented. Moreover, to call this meaning a "definite emotional connotation" is to understate all the ramifications of the word's origins and use. To the white supremacists of the 1860's, miscegenation was no less horrible than treason, cannibalism, or infanticide. It originated as a term of utter contempt and remained one throughout the period.

just how much each man contributed to it. Wakeman's youth, obscurity, and inferior position with the newspaper (he was a reporter) might suggest that his role was a secondary one. On the other hand, Julius Bloch has contended that Wakeman coined the new words and did the actual writing, although Croly was the principal architect of the hoax.[3]

"Miscegenation" ostensibly an abolitionist's plea for the planned mixing of races, stated, "If any fact is well established in history, it is that the miscegenetic or mixed races are much superior mentally, physically, and morally, to those pure or unmixed." It was the "melting pot" character of the American population, the authors continued, that accounted for the "greatness of our race." All that Americans needed to become "the finest race on earth" was the "negro element which providence [had] placed by our side." If we failed to mix, we would become weak and degenerate; but if we mingled we would become "powerful, prosperous, and progressive." We now had an excellent chance to complete the melting-pot process—because the Civil War was not merely a war for the Negro's physical freedom, it was "a war looking, as its final fruit, to the blending of the white and the black."[4]

According to the pamphlet, it had to be "declared in our public documents and announced in the messages of our Presidents," that the intermarriage of whites and blacks was both desirable and beneficial. After that, California should be opened "to the teeming millions of eastern Asia," because the physical and mental characteristics of the Japanese and Chinese "must be transplanted to our soil." Croly and Wakeman added Orientals to the scheme because Americans generally believed that Negroes were animalistic and childlike, Orientals were subtle and mystic, and Caucasians were intellectual and progressive; accordingly, the ideal "miscegen" would be a blend of "all that is passionate and emotional in the darker races, all that is imaginative and spiritual in the Asiatic races, and all that is intellectual and perceptive in the white races."[5]

Miscegenation, the booklet continued, would help certain groups more than others. Among those expected to "benefit" most were the Irish, who if they were ever to overcome the problems of urban poverty had to mingle with Negroes. "The fusion, whenever it takes place, will be of infinite service to the Irish," the authors said. Although the Irish hated the Negroes now, they had a great deal in common, and indeed poor Irish women were already attracted to black men.[6] As Croly well knew, few white Americans would be more enraged by the suggestion that their women breed with Negroes than the Irish immigrants.

However, it was in the South, the booklet contended, that the impact of organized interbreeding carried out on a massive scale would be most widespread and profound. The southern white woman held in her heart a secret passion to be in the arms of a black man, but prejudice, pride, and tradition had prevented their union. "The full mystery of sex—the sweet, wild dream of a perfect love, which will embrace all that is fervid and emotional in humanity—can never be generally known until men and women the world over are free to form unions with their opposites in color and race." Unaccountably, Croly and Wakeman also said that Northerners should imitate the Southerners' freedom from prejudice—which contradicted their own explanation of why interbreeding was not already widespread in the South, in addition to gainsaying common knowledge.[7]

Croly and Wakeman left few areas of human existence untouched. They argued, for example, that Christianity was intimately involved with race mixing; Adam and Christ had been not pure Caucasians but men of color—Mediterraneans with dark hair and olive complexions. Like most genuine abolitionists, they endorsed the idea of Negro soldiery, and urged their readers to share their "hearts and homes" with the fighting black man. Miscegenation would eliminate race prejudice itself, they insisted, because it would rid the country both of the objects of prejudice, the Negroes, and the bearers of prejudice, the whites. If all future generations were brown, complete brotherly love would prevail. After all, no less an abolitionist than Wendell Phillips said the same thing—the "mingling of races" was the only solution to race problem.[8]

Croly had a grand scheme to get leading abolitionists and Republicans to endorse the principle of miscegenation. He sent advance copies of the booklet to several well-known abolitionists, enclosing with each an unsigned request for a sympathetic response, to be sent to a New York post office box. These responses, which Croly planned to circulate widely in the Democratic press, were supposed to do great damage to the Republican cause and clear the way for a Democratic victory in the forthcoming presidential election.

It now seems apparent that Samuel Sullivan Cox had knowledge of Croly's plan, but there is no way of knowing to what extent he was implicated.* On February 17, in a long speech in Congress against a

* However, from November 1863 to the summer of 1864, Cox corresponded regularly with Samuel L. M. Barlow, part owner of the *World*. Though most of the fourteen letters written by Cox concern their mutual interest in George McClellan's nomination for the presidency on the Democratic ticket, they also reflect a genuine personal familiarity. (Of course, it is possible that Barlow knew nothing of Croly's scheme.) See the Barlow manuscript, Huntington Library.

proposed freedmen's bureau bill, Cox sharply attacked the Republicans
and what he alleged was their booklet. Quoting "written proof" in the
form of excerpts from the *Anti-Slavery Standard,* the *Angle-African,* and
the New York *Tribune* that were sympathetic with the principle of
racial mingling, Cox claimed that miscegenation was the doctrine "toward which the Republican party will and must advance." He held up
in his hand a circular from a recent Republican meeting at Cooper
Institute in New York City, in which he claimed direct quotes from
"Miscegenation" were approved and read into the record. Every Republican editorial, speech, and congressional action, he said, indicated
unequivocal support for both the pamphlet and its principles. Henry
Ward Beecher had "uttered the same sentiments contained in the pamphlet," he concluded, and he had been joined by Tilton, Greeley, and
Phillips.[9]

But hardly a year had passed when, in an introduction to a reprint
of the speech in his book *Eight Years in Congress,* Cox openly acknowledged the fraudulent nature of "Miscegenation," and even identified
the authors as "two young men connected with the New York press," a
really startling revelation in view of the general Democratic eagerness
to label the pamphlet legitimate.[10] It seems difficult to believe that an
outsider could have had access to this kind of information so soon.
So closely was Cox himself identified in the minds of some people with
Croly's booklet that a resident of Indiana, in July 1865, actually credited
him with coining the new word. And Edward A. Pollard of Richmond,
one of the leading southern racist writers of the period, apparently had
not read Cox's book because three years after its publication he was still
convinced that the authors of "Miscegenation" were really abolitionists.[11] Although he escaped exposure in spite of Cox, it would be
interesting to know whether Croly ever regretted taking Cox into his
confidence.*

At the end of the war, Cox moved to New York City, where he was associated
with the law firm of Charlton T. Lewis, and began to solicit favors for friends of his
in the government from both Gideon and Edgar Welles. See the Gideon Welles
manuscript, Huntington Library. The reasons for Cox's move are not fully clear;
however, his failure to be reelected in 1864 and the subsequent gerrymandering of
his former district certainly dimmed his chances for a comeback in Ohio. See David
Lindsey, *"Sunset" Cox: Irrepressible Democrat* (Detroit, 1959), pp. 95–97; and Wood
Gray, *The Hidden Civil War: The Story of the Copperheads* (New York, 1942), p. 220.

* Despite Croly's and Wakeman's refusal to claim authorship, their identities were
not a well-kept secret. As early as October 1864, the Democratic National Committee
offered to send to anyone in the country a copy of "Miscegenation" for 35 cents; orders
were to be mailed to 35 Park Row—the address of the *World.* See Democratic Party,
National Committee, Campaign Document No. 11 (New York, 1864), p. 5. And Cox,

The most direct and emphatic reply to "Miscegenation" was John H. Van Evrie's "Subjenation: The Theory of the Normal Relation of the Races: An Answer to 'Miscegenation.' " The ink on Croly's pamphlet had hardly dried when "Subjenation" appeared, imitating "Miscegenation" right down to the color of the cover, the number of pages, and the size and style of type. Just as Croly and Wakeman had introduced several new terms, Van Evrie provided his assortment of new words, beginning with "subjenation," which came "from *sub*, lower, and *generatus* and *genus*, a race born or created lower than another," and meant "the natural or normal relation of an inferior to a superior race." The real question before the country, he declared, was "subjenation vs. miscegenation." In addition, Van Evrie accused Lincoln and his Cabinet of being "tools of the cunning monarchists of the Old World," on the grounds that when the President had issued his "Miscegenation Proclamation" he had proclaimed a monarchy.[12]

Van Evrie also pointed out, in a sentence composed of magnificent tautologies, the true foundation of this country: "The equality of all who God has created equal (white men), and the inequality of those He has made unequal (negroes and other inferior races), is the cornerstone of American Democracy and the vital principle of American civilization and human progress." The author of "Miscegenation," he continued, supported the theory that all mankind had descended from one type—the notorious and confuted single-species theory. This premise

---

of course, did everything but name Croly and Wakeman in his 1865 book. Also, excerpts from Cox's speech in Congress and from the columns of the *World* were sprinkled throughout the eight pages of Campaign Document No. 11. (Nevertheless, as late as 1868, Edward A. Pollard, a prominent Virginia journalist, endorsed the abolitionist origin of "Miscegenation." See the *Lost Cause Regained* [New York, 1868], pp. 130–131n.) In 1880, Joseph Sabin's *A Dictionary of Books Relating to America, from Its Discovery to the Present Time* (New York, 1868–1936), XII, 221, named Croly, Wakeman, and one E. C. Howell as coauthors. Sidney Kaplan, "The Miscegenation Issue in the Election of 1864," *JNH*, XXXIV (July 1949), 284, citing the *Real Estate & Builders Guide* of May 4, 1889 (the year of Croly's death) as his source, points out that there is no evidence that Howell, who was the *World*'s city editor and whose initials were really "S. C.," had anything to do with the pamphlet. The most positive disclosure of the authors' identities came 36 years after "Miscegenation" was published when Mrs. Croly, in 1900, stated, "the little brochure was the joint work of Mr. D. G. Croly, my husband, and a very clever young journalist, Mr. George Wakeman." See Kaplan, pp. 284–285. (Mrs. Croly, the former Jane Cunningham, and her husband were married in 1857, and after the war she was to become active in the feminist movement which, ironically, drew much of its support from former abolitionists.)

was "the foundation of his whole argument. Demolish this and every-thing else that he [said disappeared] 'as the baseless fabric of a vision.' " Van Evrie concluded his rebuttal with a long list of biblical "facts" that he claimed disproved the single-species theory.[13]

The Democratic press was more equivocal than Van Evrie, and re-sponded to "Miscegenation" unevenly and sporadically during the spring of 1864. On February 17, the Albany *Atlas and Argus* condemned the pamphlet, but conceded that the unknown author spoke only for the extreme wing of abolitionism. Croly's New York *World*—unlike most of the Democratic newspapers, which were only mildly interested in Cox's speech—printed almost the entire speech on February 20, but waited until March 5 to print its first review of the booklet. The Detroit *Free Press* of February 24, in reporting Cox's speech, pointed to the ironic fact that only a few years earlier racial amalgamation (resulting from unions between slaves and masters) had been one of the most popular arguments against slavery, but now it was apparently advocated by abolitionists as "the great and ultimate good to result from the horrors of radical rule." On St. Patrick's Day, in a long review that may have been written by Croly himself, the *World* cited (and dis-torted) many of the same responses of "leading negrophilists" to the pamphlet that Cox had noted in his speech, but carefully avoided any discussion of its authorship.

But if Croly had feared exposure, the gullibility of Copperhead news-papers like the Philadelphia *Age* and the New York *Daily News* must have relieved him. In a hysterical editorial, the *Age* vehemently denied that "the thing was a hoax" or an attempt "to burlesque the extrava-gance of Wendell Phillips & Co." On the contrary, the editor said, there was "abundant evidence to prove that the views set forth in that pam-phlet [were] shared by a large part of the Abolition party." He did not, of course, present his abundant evidence. Reprinting a review of "Mis-cegenation" from the London *Saturday Review*, the *Age* accused Greeley, Phillips, Theodore Tilton, and Anna Dickinson of endorsing the principles set forth in the pamphlet. The editor of the *Daily News*, in two full columns of frenzied bombast, insisted that either Tilton or Miss Dickinson was the author, and accused the *Atlas and Argus* of being timid on the miscegenation issue.[14]

Although most Republicans, even the extreme abolitionists, gave "Miscegenation" an unfavorable reception or ignored it altogether, some of them unwittingly provoked racist outbursts. On March 16, Greeley reviewed the pamphlet, and without endorsing its principles suggested that if two people of different races wanted to marry, there should be no law either to encourage or prohibit it. Such matters, he said, were the personal affairs of the couple involved. But to the racist demagogues, even this was blasphemous; on the following day, the *World*, the *Daily News*, and the *Age* all accused Greeley of urging race mixing. The principle of miscegenation had become doctrine and dogma of the Republican party, the *Daily News* charged; and the *Age* asked, "Will it be a plank in Mr. Lincoln's next platform?" On March 21, the Detroit *Free Press*, though still preferring "amalgamation" to "miscegenation," also assailed Greeley for his remarks.

In the last analysis, however, Croly and Wakeman conceived their attempt to embarrass the Republicans rather sloppily. First of all, their decision to remain anonymous must have raised some doubts in the minds of many readers. Anonymous writing was popular among the racists, but not among the abolitionists, most of whom were only too proud to sign their publications. Croly and Wakeman tried to make the reader think that the author was a Republican who was afraid to identify himself, and who wanted his argument to spread on its own merits—not because he, a famous abolitionist, wrote it. However, because some of its statements were so fantastic and because it was anonymous, it is doubtful that many Americans accepted the pamphlet as legitimate. The almost immediate denial by the *Age* of any trickery indicated that there were from the outset strong suspicions about the booklet's authenticity. A few bigots, like Van Evrie, probably took "Miscegenation" for what it purported to be, but most people must have considered it either a hoax or the work of a harmless crank.

Secondly, Croly made a colossal miscalculation. Though he assumed correctly that the vast majority of white Americans considered the Negro an inferior human being, he mistakenly supposed that their prejudices were indicative of their gullibility. There had never been any indication that they would consider racial amalgamation seriously. Abolitionists had spoken occasionally of race mingling, but this never implied, and was only a rarely interpreted as implying, intermarriage. Politically, economically, socially, and intellectually, Negroes in both North and South were so far removed from the mainstream of American life that it would have taken much more than an abolitionist mandate to bring the races together—and most whites knew it.

The best way of determining the influence of "Miscegenation" and "Subjenation" on the general public is to measure the change, if any, in popular reactions to the race issue as indicated by the 1864 election results; the results show their influence to have been negligible; in fact, Cox himself was defeated.

Nonetheless, certain Democratic newspapers endeavored throughout the campaign to inflame the electorate about the miscegenation issue without bothering to exploit the pamphlets. "It is only quite recently," the New York *Daily News* warned on April 4, "that under its new name, a real, completely organized, living monster rears its horrible head in our midst and threatens to devour society itself." And the *World* was quick to make capital out of a heated dispute that arose within Republican ranks after Elizur Wright, a Boston abolitionist, in a letter to the editor of the *Anglo-African*, implied that Negroes were less virile than white men. In a caustic reply, the Negro editor insisted that the black man had always been more masculine than the white man, "Look at him: *tall, brawny, well-limbed, sound brained as God made him, a man and a brother.*" Caucasians were *"sharp-nosed, hatchet-faced, lank-haired people,"* the *World* quoted the *Anglo-African* editor as saying, italicizing what it considered the most repugnant passages. The *World*'s editor, reviewing the exchange with considerable hilarity, called it "decidedly rich" to hear the blacks claiming to be "a healthier, sounder, brighter race than their New England admirers." In the weeks that followed, other Democratic publications printed similar reports of the exchange, usually tying it to the miscegenation issue.[15]

But it would be a mistake to conclude that the Democratic press was united on the issue. The farther one moved from the Northeast, and especially from New York City, the less popular it became. Many midwestern racist editors, for example, said nothing about miscegenation during the early months of 1864; the danger of racial intermarriage was simply not a compelling concern in this region. Even in the East the reaction was not uniform. New England's leading Democratic newspaper, the Boston *Post*, situated as it was in an abolitionist stronghold, ignored the miscegenation issue and rarely mentioned the Negro at all. Since it had a conservative, fairly well educated audience, its editors realized that they would gain little by resorting to racist demagoguery.

Republicans who bothered to defend themselves against the charge that they advocated miscegenation got little relief from the racists. When the Philadelphia *Press* pointed out that Negroes had never considered miscegenation until the Democrats made an issue out of it, the *World* replied by accusing William Wells Brown and Dr. J. McCune

Smith, both Negroes, of publicly supporting race mixing long before the publication of "Miscegenation,"* and accused the *Press* of being out of step with its party. As the Louisville (Kentucky) *Courier* noted some time later, none other than Frederick Douglass had once said, "The races will blend, coalesce, and become homogeneous." Shortly after its indictment of Brown and Smith, the *World* quoted the *Press* as having said, "To solve the negro problem we must make away with the colored race by absorbing [it in] the white." Moreover, the *World* charged, the leading Negro newspaper in the North, the *Anglo-African*, had demanded a mulatto nation. Black men and women were "ready to amalgamate," the editor declared; all that was needed to guarantee a new age of "gold-colored" people was to reelect a Republican administration and Congress.[16]

Miscegenation, it is true, was the favorite campaign topic of the racists; but a dispute needs disputants, and there was very little defense of miscegenation from Republicans and abolitionists simply because there was nothing to defend. Although equalitarians did not condemn intermarriage, neither did they advocate it. To them, as to most other Americans, the controversy was pointless. Even Democratic leaders did not present a unified front in the debate over whether race mixing was a bona fide Republican policy. The average Northerner was obviously more concerned about the war and economic problems than about anything else.

Two fears underlay the racist outcry against miscegenation, fears that had usually been at the bottom of other racist campaigns—namely, the fear that the sanctity of white women would be lost, and the fear that the white race would be "mongrelized."

Few causes aroused emotions as easily as those that exploited the white man's concern for his womenfolk. The fine and delicate character of the southern white woman, Van Evrie insisted, was the result of the South's traditional attitude toward race relations. "The very conception of love—upon which all lawful intercourse of the sexes is founded— is impossible, eternally impossible, between whites and blacks." White women throughout the South feared that the Northerners' purpose in pursuing the war was the "degradation and debauchment" of their sex, he concluded. The New York *Daily News* observed in March 1864 that "delicately organized" northern white ladies, too, were repelled by physical contact with black men, because "the negro's body is dis-

* Of course what the *World* overlooked was that it was tacitly acknowledging the Democratic origin of "Miscegenation."

agreeably unctious, especially in warm weather, and when under the influence of the strong 'emotional' excitement so certainly produced on his animal nature if permitted to follow her with lascivious glances, and to lay lascivious hands upon her."[17]

The *Daily News*'s concern for white women did not, of course, extend to female abolitionists, who for years had been scoffed at for their lack of femininity. "Yes, we are induced to believe that some American women have gone, and others are going, to this shocking extremity of unnatural, legal prostitution, known as miscegenation," the editor wrote just five days after discussing the Negro's lasciviousness. They were doing this, he added, "in a self-sacrificing spirit, with the conscientious religious purpose of elevating the despised African race to its supposed deserved place on their own social level, and of preserving the effete Caucasian race in America by mixing its weak and watery blood with the warmer, purer, fresher, thicker, nobler blood of the Ethiopian." The editor asked just who these women were, and then answered himself: they were easily found "near to the center of modern civilization, the hub of the universe, Boston itself." They were, according to Van Evrie, "ladies (?) of fashion and fortune" who had pledged their "love and honor" to "burly negroes."[18]

Not surprisingly, racist editors made the most of the few interracial liaisons that came to their attention. In April 1864, quoting a letter originally written to the Philadelphia *Press*, the New York *World* told about two local society matrons who had openly consorted with Negro men. After marrying their black lovers, the ladies flaunted their new status by promenading down a busy avenue. Entitling its article "Practical Miscegenation in New York," the *World* commented that the ladies were "reducing the amalgamation theory to practice with a vengeance." It was not surprising that there were two women in all of New York City "with tastes so depraved" as to marry black men; but it was "astonishing" that they were also "women of wealth and refinement, and [that] their conduct [was] approved by their acquaintances." Such behavior, the editor declared, was proof that abolitionism had taken over the Republican party, and that "the natural repugnance of the white to the negro race" had been replaced by a "sentimental regard" for the Negro. Although the original letter made no mention of the Republican party, the *World*, assuming that Democrats would never behave this way, deduced that Republicans were responsible for the whole affair. Early in November, the Philadelphia *Age* told of a white woman who had deserted her husband and eloped with a Negro, taking her five-year-old daughter with her. The reporter spared no words to arouse sympathy and compassion for the abandoned husband.[19] A racist poet, using a term that Lincoln had coined, retold the tale:

> This, sad experience taught me;
>   To ask my love I went,
> Said she, "I prefer a man
>   Of 'African descent.' "[20]

An English visitor, William Hepworth Dixon, proposed that New England women who entertained the idea of race mixing did so only because they thought it might improve what they considered the decadent condition of the South. There were many northern ladies, Dixon stated, who believed that marriages between southern whites and Negroes would "improve the paler stock." However Dixon noted that although many a New England matron said it would be a good idea for "the fair damsels of Charleston and Savannah to wed black husbands," none would say "it would be well for her own girls to do so."[21] To Dixon, it appeared that that those who really advocated race mixing considered it appropriate only outside their own region and, for the South at least, as a form of punishment—an unconscious admission that miscegenation was really odious.*

At times, racist hysteria over miscegenation was undoubtedly provoked more by a desire to titillate than by political motives or genuine anxieties. For example, one anonymous writer—either a sick comedian or a sadist—told how the Republicans, as part of a so-called plan to change the "Ethiopian skin," were plotting to kill or castrate all the white men of the South. The southern white women would then be apportioned out among the Negro men, and any who resisted would be "flung out" for "the use of the unbridled and unbroken-in Black Ourang-Outangs," who would "deal with them according to their natural instincts." Similarly, Negro women would be saved for breeding with northern white men.[22] Later in his pamphlet, the author presented "Uncle Tom's Drama," a play in which white maidens with "quivering limbs" and "snow-white bosoms, that ever throbbed in angelic purity,"

---

* Carter G. Woodson, *The Negro in Our History* (revised, Washington, D. C., 1941), p. 412, has suggested that many white women, especially those from impoverished backgrounds, were attracted to prosperous Negro men. This argument is a little shaky. Woodson implied that there were quite a few affluent Negro men and that the practice of intermarriage was fairly common, but he offered no substantial evidence. In truth, such relationships were exceptional. For one thing, there were thousands of poor white women, mostly from immigrant families that despised the Negro, and there were only a few prosperous Negro men. Thus, large-scale intermarriage between the two groups would not have been possible.

suffered "untold outrage, woe and wrong" at the hands of "Black Ourang-Outangs," who dragged them down to "gratify their brutal instincts." After the mass murder of all southern white children, who were "strewn" on the ground with their "brains dashed out and bodies ruthlessly gashed and bleeding," the fathers, husbands, and brothers of these "Murdered Innocents" were "chained erect" to "behold the heart-rending outrages perpetrated before them." Perhaps, other racists suggested, the former slaves might prefer northern white women. After all, the Democratic National Committee lamented shortly before the election, did not a Republican speaker in Illinois say recently that after the war the "brave Othellos of the South would come North and claim their fair Desdemonas"?[23]

Actual rapes committed by Negroes were relatively uncommon, but the racist sought them out and embroidered them gleefully. In July, 1864, the *Ohio Statesman* told how a Negro named Henry Burns had kidnapped a white widow named Mary McBride. After Mrs. McBride fell ill in a strange city, Burns brought her home, confined her there against her will for an unknown length of time, committed repeated "outrages" on her, and drugged her to prevent her escape. When the police finally discovered the victim, enfeebled and near death, they also found evidence of a recent abortion, and concluded that she had become pregnant by her abductor. The experience allegedly left Mrs. McBride on the verge of insanity.[24] The story was reported in the style typical of yellow journalism. As in other such accounts, the Negro was very black, hideous, and evil, a veritable brute, and the white woman was angelic, young, beautiful, and innocent.

Thus, the Victorian racist critic, though unaware of the ways later psychologists would explain it, was very much aware of the white man's sensitivity about his women and of the feelings that words such as "virtue" and "sanctity" aroused. We must restore society to a "healthful condition," Van Evrie declared, by instituting "subjenation, which lifts woman up, as well as the entire white race, to a higher plane of virtue and purity."[25] The favorite tool in the racist's bag of tricks was the idea of a brutish black man and a delicate white maiden engaged in the unthinkable act—interracial copulation.*

* Naomi Goldstein, in *The Roots of Prejudice against the Negro in the United States* (Boston, 1948), pp. 79–93, wrote that in America the "main focus in interracial problems is placed upon sexual relations." She mentioned three reasons: the idea that the white man has an innate antipathy to "any kind of interracial sexual relations," fears of Negro superiority in sexual prowess and vigor, and the fear of "mongrelism." The racists of the 1860's openly exploited only the "innate antipathy" to interracial sexual relations and the fear of mongrelism. The secret fear of Negro sexual superior-

The white supremacist also feared that miscegenation would make the United States a nation of mulattoes or, as the alarmists called them, mongrels. Few Northerners believed that the situation would ever come to this, but there were scores of arguments to tempt the imagination of anyone who was receptive. A southern clergyman declared in 1868, "Sir, it is a matter of life and death with the Southern people to keep their blood pure." David Macrae, who quoted him, said the dread of mongrelization was "everywhere the dread that lies deepest in the Southern heart."[26]

The "scientific" critics pointed to the mule, with its reproductive sterility and its capacity for hard work, as a prime result of mongrelism. Mulattoes—the word even had the same root as the word "mule"— became sterile, they said, after a certain number of generations (they rarely agreed on how many). Miscegenation would make America a nation of degenerates incapable even of reproducing their own kind. Despite reliable scientific evidence against the hybrid-sterility theory, many racists clung to the old beliefs or invented new ones. Devoting an entire chapter of his book *Negroes and Negro "Slavery"* to "Mulattoism and Mongrelism," Van Evrie contrived an elaborate scheme to prove that mulattoes became sterile after the fourth generation. And the New York *Daily News*, first pointing to the curse of Canaan as an illustration of God's law, printed three full columns of testimony by so-called men of science on the dangers of mongrelism. The New York *World* blamed the "half-breeds" of Mexico and Brazil for the economic degradation in those two countries. The 43 congressmen who signed the pamphlet "Congressional Address" called the "corruption of race" a violation of natural law. They also concluded that the obvious decay of Latin America was the result of racial hybridity. Cox cited most of these theories and examples in his several congressional anti-Negro speeches; on the lecture circuit, S. S. Nicholas, one of the Democratic party's more conservative theorists, raved about the deleterious consequences of mulattoism; and *On the Phenomena of Hybridity*, by the French anthropologist Paul Broca, appeared only a few months after "Miscegenation."[27]

---

ity was never mentioned, and thus there was no one to reply, as John Randolph of Roanoke had replied when taunted about his lack of masculinity, "You pride yourself upon an animal faculty, in respect to which the negro is your equal and the jackass infinitely your superior." For an amusing but serious reflection on modern man's preoccupation with the Negro's virility, see Wayland Young, *Eros Denied* (London, 1965), pp. 271–273. A candid discussion of the Negro's view is Calvin C. Hernton's *Sex and Racism in America* (New York, 1965).

Critics also "proved" that mongrelism had ruined past civilizations. The Egyptians had been a fine and noble Caucasian race until they began mixing with the inferior races among them, Van Evrie claimed. Similarly, there was much in the history of Carthaginians that resembled "the rule of the Yankee dynasty" in the United States; but the Carthaginians had become miscegenationists, mingling with the Negro tribes on their borders, and this had hastened their destruction. Destruction was just punishment for the "unnatural and beastly crime" of miscegenation. In Jamaica a white woman would not "desecrate her womanhood by mating with a negro," Van Evrie wrote in another publication, but she would marry an octoroon or a quadroon without hesitation, and the quadroon woman readily mates "with a mulatto, and the latter with a typical negro." Thus did society move toward the "preponderating element," he concluded, though pure whites and pure blacks might mix rarely. The same thing would happen in the South, where Negroes were so numerous.[28]

On the mongrelism question, as on so many others, racist critics soon found themselves mired in contradictions. Van Evrie insisted that a mulatto population had "less powers of virility" and a "greater tendency to disease," but at the same time he intimated that interracial breeding would result in the "extinction of the weaker [Negro] element" and a return to the stronger. By implying that white blood would eventually overcome Negro blood, he called into question his original statement that miscegenation would lead to mongrelization. Others expressed a belief in mulatto degeneracy, but pointed to the mulatto as the most intelligent and successful of all Negroes. Indeed, many racists used this argument to prove the fundamental superiority of the Caucasian race, saying that Negroes who had achieved success—President Roberts of Liberia and Frederick Douglass, for example—had done so only because of generous infusions of white blood. This view received additional authority when Richard F. Burton, a prominent English traveler and anthropologist, described the "darker and dingier" African tribe as the most degraded. Van Evrie himself had declared that never had a pure black African attained a position of eminence in anything.[29] Yet no critic thought it important to explain how race mixing reduced the offspring to the lowest common denominator on the one hand and raised the mulatto to a level approaching the white man's on the other.

A more confusing but actually more meaningful controversy concerned the part-Negro population that already existed. In 1860, the United States Bureau of the Census had tabulated the mulatto population at 13.2 per cent of the total Negro population. Ten years later, the national figure was 12 per cent; Michigan's 45.7 was the highest, and Nebraska's 6.5 the lowest. Both states, of course, had few Negroes to begin with. High among the former slave states was Kentucky with 20.1 per cent of its total Negro population listed as mulatto.[30]

Unfortunately, these figures were virtually worthless. They were nonetheless used, and were almost completely misinterpreted by those who used them when they were issued; they have misled many others who have used them since. The major difficulty arose from the method used to determine just who was a mulatto and who was not. The Census Bureau simply instructed its canvassers to classify as a mulatto any Negro who had a "perceptible" trace of white blood. This left the entire decision up to the individual census taker, and excluded from the mulatto figures many people who were white but had "imperceptible" traces of Negro blood and many who were Negro but had "imperceptible" traces of white blood. Some racists who disagreed with the tabulations came up with their own figures. In 1864, Van Evrie estimated that more than 50 per cent of the Negro population of Ohio was mulatto, although in 1870 the Census Bureau set the figure at 28.2 per cent.[31]

In any case, white blood meant very little when it came to making distinctions between Negroes. If a man looked as if he had Negro blood—even the smallest amount—he was considered a Negro, an example of the Anglo-Saxon's total indifference to mathematical logic when it came to matters of race. Moreover, most Americans, like the Census Bureau, used the word "mulatto" to identify anyone who had white and Negro blood, whatever the ratio. In short, they agreed with Will Surrey's Aunt Augusta in Anna Dickinson's *What Answer?*: "Quadroon, mulatto, or negro, it is all one. I have no desire to split hairs of definition. You could not be more obnoxious were you black as Erebus."[32] Yet to rely on such an inaccurate and slipshod method of determining racial status, and then to make that status the basis of a citizen's rights and privileges, was indeed a cruel injustice.

The confusion grew worse, and the language grew angrier, when abolitionists and racists began to look for the sources of the existing mulatto population. For decades, antislavery spokesmen had pointed to the southern slaveowner. The master and his white sons were responsible for the half-breeds of the nation, they said; they had taken advantage of the dependent, defenseless black woman. There were several hundred thousand mulattoes in the United States, Greeley pointed out, and there was little doubt that the fathers of at least nine-

tenths of them were southern Democrats. The least that these Democrats could do, he concluded, was to treat the mothers of their children
as "respectfully as wives." Using far stronger language, Macrae attributed the vast number of mixed bloods in the South to the "im-
moralities perpetrated by unscrupulous men under the temptations
offered by slavery."[33]

However, according to Myrta Lockett Avary, a southern white woman who wrote her memoirs in 1906, the responsibility for antebellum
miscegenation did not belong to the morally weak white man but rather
to the slave woman, who presented him with an irresistable temptation.
The female Negro, of "strong sexual instincts and devoid of sexual
conscience, at the white man's door, and in the white man's dwelling,"
had on her master a hypnotic effect that was more than he could withstand, Mrs. Avary suggested. Macrae, conceding that Negro women, in
order to win favors, might have often become "unresisting and even
willing slaves to the basest desires of those who owned them," nonetheless saw the total destruction of black womanhood as the most
terrible injustice of slavery.[34]

The racists, of course, denied that the slaveowners had any responsibility, and made countercharges of their own. According to Nicholas,
the Republican party planned to "exterminate the whole white population of the South and supply it with a better race of people, meaning
probably an amalgamation cross of the abolitionist with the negro."
The anonymous author of the "Democratic Gospel of Peace" went
further—attributing the existing mulattoes to occasional excursions into
the South by roving bands of radicals from New England. It was quite
obvious, he thought, that the color and general features of the "kangaroos" varied considerably, and that their variations had been "caused
my migratory visits of certain tribes of drummers, inhabitants of the
countries of Cannot-i-cut, and Massa-shoot-its." In "Subjenation," Van
Evrie, too, claimed that the nation's mulattoes had been whelped
largely by northern abolitionists, and accused the author of "Miscegenation," who had said that most of the mulattoes were in the
South, of committing a "glaring offense against the truth." The depraved practice of miscegenation, the New York *Daily News* maintained, was most common in New England, the citadel of abolitionism.[35]

Although the mulatto percentage of the total Negro population was
indeed higher in the North than in the South, racist critics who cited
admittedly imperfect census figures also conveniently ignored a number
of other factors. Over 92 per cent (in 1860) of all Negroes in America
lived in the slave states. This fact alone would tend to keep a visible

mulatto percentage substantially lower in the South because of the vast number of Negroes in which the mulattoes would be absorbed.* On the other hand, northern mulattoes, many of whom had escaped slavery because of their lighter skin, were seen as part of a much smaller Negro population. In addition, the differences in the circumstances of southern and northern mulattoes had a sharp influence on their visibility. Most of the mulattoes in the South were results of unions between slaves and slaveowners or between mulatto and black slaves who lived on the same plantation. Often the master had a "favorite" slave woman, usually a light-skinned mulatto, on whom he bestowed most of his clandestine attentions. Thus, the growth of the mulatto population was fairly confined, since the opportunities for intermingling were minimized; indeed, even free Negroes in the South had their movements restricted by state laws. Northern mulattoes, however, concentrated in Negro neighborhoods in the cities rather than spread all over the countryside on farms, and much more mobile than slaves, had many more chances to meet. Most white supremacy propagandists overlooked the fact that two mulatto parents produced mulatto children just as easily as white and Negro parents did, although they made much of the small group of northern equalitarians who mingled socially with Negroes.

The argument against mongrelism had two exponents: the emotional racist who actually feared it, and the pragmatic racist whose main purpose was to embarrass and discredit the Republicans. There were many more pragmatic racists, but they were not always easy to identify because they would assume any poses that were expedient and persuasive. Significantly, both kinds of racists ignored the hard fact that slavery had done far more to "mongrelize" the United States than all the words and deeds of the abolitionists. Mrs. Avary's painfully contrived explanation, for example, was nothing more than a manifestation of the agony southern white women had long endured in silence while their husbands were philandering. "Yellow" Negroes, some of them very fair, had been common sights throughout the South for decades— and no one ever wondered where they came from.

---

* Mathematically, this principle can be explained by the probability density function, as represented by a probability, or frequency, curve. Excluding all of the other factors that influenced the incidence of race mixing, a probability curve would show that as the total number of principals increased, the extreme variations would be relatively less significant. In this way, the smaller number of Negroes in the North would result in a more conspicuous reflection of a radical influence, such as miscegenation.

The most urgent objective of the pragmatic racists was, of course, to secure the defeat of Abraham Lincoln and as many other Republican candidates as possible. Conditions seemed encouraging for the Democrats. The Union armies had suffered some setbacks in the summer of 1864, and more than a few Republicans were growing pessimistic about the party's chances for success. As gloom descended over Washington, the miscegenation propagandists must have believed that their hour had arrived. Determined to give the Democratic candidates that extra nudge needed for victory, they pushed their cause with renewed vigor.

After a temporary lull in the early summer, when Negrophobic propaganda had tapered off somewhat, the white supremacy crusade, with miscegenation as the central theme, began to regain momentum. At the Democratic National Convention in Chicago, speakers attacked the "flat-nosed, woolly-headed, long-heeled, cursed of God and damned of man descendants of Africa," and the "negro-loving, negro-hugging worshippers of old Abe Lincoln." Many of the delegates to the regular Democratic convention were, in fact, more extreme in their racism than the Copperheads who gathered at Cincinnati less than a month before the election. The Cincinnati convention, which assembled to protest the candidacy of General McClellan, made no nomination of its own and ignored the race issue except to plead that Negroes be returned to slavery. But Democrats in the bosom of the party maintained their attacks right up to election eve. Two weeks before the election, for example, Judge Black accused the Republican leadership of preferring the company of Negroes to whites and of practicing miscegenation.[36]

The Democratic press, with the eastern Copperhead journals leading the way, renewed its miscegenation campaign against the Republican party and did not relax until the voting was over. The Philadelphia *Age* attacked any and every group or individual associated with the Republicans. The New York *World* declared that there were "only four solutions to the Negro question": subordination, colonization, extermination, and miscegenation. Since the Republicans opposed colonization and subordination and did not even consider extermination, it was obvious that they had to favor miscegenation. After General Nathaniel Banks, as commander of the Department of the Gulf in occupied Louisiana, had ordered the public schools in New Orleans to admit Negroes, the Columbus *Crisis* accused the federal government of trying to instill "miscegenation principles" in the children of that city. Commenting on Banks's order, the Democratic National Committee recalled that the general, while a member of the House of Representatives from Massachusetts, had speculated on the question of racial superiority by proposing that the country "wait until time should develop whether the white race should absorb the black, or the black the white." Banks had apparently decided that the white should absorb the black, the Committee implied. According to the Democratic campaign propagandists, Banks's order, by "compelling white and black children to mingle together," was part of a deliberate abolitionist attempt to mongrelize the nation.[37]

At this point, any overt Republican display of equalitarianism would bring an immediate and vociferous racist reaction. Copperhead newsmen charged that a rally and social hour at New York City's Central Lincoln Club, attended by both whites and Negroes, was a practical application of the miscegenation theory. In a first-page article entitled "Miscegenation in Earnest," the *World* described the affair as a "negro ball" where white men and "colored belles" took liberties with each other. Some of the ladies were octoroon, a reporter observed, "to suit, we suppose, the love sick glances of the Republicans." There were also quadroons and mulattoes, not to mention a few who were of the "pure Congo or Bozoo character, black as the ace of spades, and ready for any work." Quoting a host of innocent but easily distorted statements by abolitionists (none of whom were at the affair) made in previous years, the editor concluded that the social hour was just another example of the "orgies of leading Republican politicians."[38] A week later, the New York *Weekly Day Book* reprinted in its entirety the *World* article. Subsequently, Van Evrie reproduced the plagiarized account in a leaflet entitled "Campaign Document No. 1" (which bore no relationship to the official "Campaign Documents" published by the Democratic National Committee) and concluded it with these lines:

> Full a hundred and fifty of coal black wenches
> Tripped gracefully on the fantastic light toe;
> Some on the platform and more on the benches,
> Each damsel squeezed tightly her Republican beau.
> On the rostrum they sat, both ogling and teasing,
> And some waddled lazily around the hall;
> The smell was so strong that it set us a sneezing
> So we started away from the Miscegen Ball.[39]

Like the *World*, the Albany *Atlas and Argus* called the affair a "negro ball," and said that after "leading Republicans" danced with "ebony damsels" they spent the remainder of the evening "miscegenating with the copper faces."[40] Bromley and Company, the leading northern publisher of racist prints and posters, capped the entire incident with a broadside cartoon—"Political Caricature No. 4"—that depicted interracial couples petting. (See Plate 3.)

Although racists were always ready to castigate Republicans in general, they often balked when it came to naming individuals. One of the boldest was Cox, who compiled a long list of alleged abolitionist race mixers, among whom were Phillips, Greeley, Tilton, Banks, Parker Pillsbury, Lucretia Mott, Albert Brisbane, William Wells Brown, J. McCune Smith, Angelina and Sarah Grimké, Theodore Weld, Cassius Clay, and Harriet Beecher Stowe. To this role the Democratic National Committee added Beecher, Kelley, Sumner, Henry Wilson, and John Forney. These identifications, of course, were just as specious as the allusions to "leading Republicans" found in the *World* and *Atlas and Argus*. The newspapers claimed to describe examples of miscegenation without naming the principals, and Cox and the Committee named individuals without citing actual instances of race mixing.[41]

Furthermore, none of the persons named by Cox and the Democratic National Committee even endorsed miscegenation. Some, like Phillips, pleaded for the economic, social, and political "amalgamation" of the black race—that is, urged whites to give Negroes equal citizenship and absorb them in the community. Greeley, similarly, advocated "subjecting merely material differences to the ameliorating influence of an honest and unlimited recognition of one common nature."[42] In other words, both were concerned with the elimination of economic and cultural differences, not color differences. If the white man could accept the Negro as just another person, they believed, conflicts between the races would cease to exist. Differences of color and physical appearance would remain, but they would be immaterial. This view, widely accepted today, was radically libertarian in the 1860's; many Americans simply could not accept any suggestion of equality.

Since the object of the miscegenation scare was to discredit the Republicans, the closer critics could tie Abraham Lincoln to race mixing, the more effective, they thought, their campaign would be. A few months before the publication of "Miscegenation," Van Evrie's *Old Guard* implied that the President himself might be the product of a mixed marriage; and in March 1864, the Indianapolis *State Sentinel* accused Lincoln of "openly and publicly" endorsing intermarriage. In September, after Lincoln had received Frederick Douglass at the White House, the *World* reported that Douglass had said the President welcomed him with praiseworthy cordiality; the editor then went on to accuse the President of supporting the viewpoint elaborated in "Miscegenation." The Philadelphia *Age* also printed Douglass's remark, and claimed that white people seeking White House audiences were often forced to wait several hours. As the editor put it, "It looks as if Mr. Lincoln was like the conscientious actor who, when he played Othello, insisted on *blacking himself all over*."[43] The Democratic National Committee went so far as to find evidence of the President's miscegenation designs in the New York draft riots of the previous summer. After the deaths of several Negroes, Lincoln expressed sorrow because "some working people" had been killed by "other working people." From this statement, the Committee inferred that the President wanted every white workingman to love his black fellow workingman who "might possibly, in time, become a relative." Van Evrie declared that every man who voted for "Old Abe" would also be a "miscegenator or negro mixer";[44] and, for those whose tastes ran to graphic representations, Bromley and Company provided another crude broadside, "Political Caricature No. 2—Miscegenation or the Millenium of Abolitionism," which depicted the incredulous Irish and German immigrants watching as Lincoln entertained several interracial couples. (See Plate 1.)

Although the race issue may have been the most critical question for a handful of extremists, for overall appeal it still could not compete with military success. Union victories on the battlefield, highlighted by Sherman's occupation of Atlanta on September 2 and General Philip H. Sheridan's devastation of the Shenandoah Valley in October, lifted the spirits of northern voters and renewed their confidence in the Lincoln administration. One military achievement could undo six months of racist efforts. Moreover, as election day approached, Northerners were especially cheered by reports that Confederate morale seemed to be disintegrating at every level. It was highly probable that the racist demagogues had put more faith in the miscegenation issue than it deserved, and consequently miscalculated its influence. But whatever impact the issue might have had, the timely military victories were more than enough to offset it.

Thus, to the majority of Americans, miscegenation was not the most important campaign issue, although it was probably the most emotional. The election provided the voters with an opportunity to approve or disapprove a wide variety of issues, many of them raised by radical Republicans and war Democrats, as well as by the Copperheads. Economic and military matters, naturally, invited much of the voters' attention. As far as the race issue was concerned, the election of 1864 was, broadly speaking, a referendum on emancipation with the miscegenation controversy playing only a small and bizarre part. But it was not in the nature of the racist to concern himself with broad questions or with questions only distantly related to the race issue. In every political contest, his interest focused on his narrow area of interest. And he was often hopelessly outnumbered, even within his own party. It is significant that the Democratic National Committee itself did not officially sustain the miscegenation issue, although the convention speeches might have led one to believe the contrary. Of the 26 campaign pamphlets published by the Committee, only one—"Campaign Document No. 11"—dealt directly with alleged Republican endorsements of race mixing (though others, of course, made both direct and oblique references to other aspects of the race issue). Coming as it did, "Campaign Document No. 11" was the party's pathetic last gasp on the miscegenation issue. In a futile eleventh hour gesture, the Committee offered to send anyone in the country a copy of "Miscegenation" for thirty-five cents—ten cents more than the original price. But for the vast majority of the voting public, the whole miscegenation issue was just too fantastic.

In spite of the Anglo-Saxon self-image, the white supremacist of the Civil War had had a difficult time. He could never escape the fact that when he criticized the government's Negro policies, he was, in a sense, opposing the war effort, thereby exposing himself to charges of disloyalty and sometimes even of treason—a situation that the Republicans exploited fully. Northerners with only modest race prejudices—and they were certainly in the majority—restrained their hostilities at least until victory appeared certain. In addition, the racist was handicapped by the physical separation of white man from black. The vast majority of Negroes were in the South, and most Northerners were not easily excited over an "enemy" they seldom saw, especially when the *real* enemy was a rebel army.

The miscegenation controversy did not end with the election. Shortly afterward an epilogue was published by one L. Seaman, in the form of a short pamphlet entitled "What Miscegenation Is! and What We Are to Expect Now that Mr. Lincoln Is Re-elected." Assuming, like Croly, the pose of an abolitionist, Seaman dedicated his pamphlet to Henry Ward Beecher and praised the New England abolitionists for organizing the "Modern Order of Miscegenationists." The Order could claim full credit, he wrote, for Lincoln's victory at the polls. The pamphlet's most striking feature was its cover, which, like the title page, was decorated with the picture of an ogreish black man and a young white girl, their lips touching. (See Plate 5.) Seaman identified the Negro as "an 'intelligent gentleman ob color' affectionately saluting a pretty white girl of sixteen," and pointed out the "thick tufts of wool of the one" and the "long, waving auburn hair of the other." Notice, he wrote, how the "sweet, delicate little Roman nose of the one does not detract from the beauty of the broad, flat nose, with expanded nostrils, of the other—while the intellectual, bold majestic forehead of the one forms an unique, through beautiful contrast to the round, flat head, resembling a huge gutter mop, of the other." The entire pamphlet was an essay of spite—the fulminations of a poor loser.

However, with the exception of Seaman's effort, the first phase of the anti-Negro crusade came to a close after the election. Racist demagoguery, on a national level, passed into a temporary eclipse and did not emerge again for almost two years. Most of the reasons are not hard to identify. First, most public offices were in Republican hands for another two to six years. Second, the war ended, bringing an emotional letdown and denying the peace-at-any-price Copperheads their main argument; it was difficult to argue with success. Even before Appomattox, while Lincoln and the radicals were debating the reconstruction issue, the Democrats had remained relatively quiet. Third, most white Northerners strongly supported the freedmen throughout most of 1865. This support, generally unchallenged by the racists, even extended to civil rights, and it was strongest for Negroes who had fought in the Union army. Fourth, Lincoln's assassination stirred the public conscience. Americans, some of whom no doubt felt a twinge of guilt because of their attacks on him, were not as easily aroused against a people freed by the Great Emancipator as they had been. The Philadelphia *Age* mourned Lincoln's death with a grief matched by few other publications, Republican or Democrat; testimonies of sympathy and eulogies of tribute filled its pages for days. And Editor Burr of the *Old Guard* printed a stark, black-bordered, full-page memorial.[45]

Fifth, the drive for the ratification of the Thirteenth Amendment was gaining momentum; by December 1865, emancipation would be part of the Constitution. If anyone needed a chill reminder of the full meaning of this, he had only to recall that during the secession crisis both houses of a lame-duck Congress had passed a proposed constitutional amendment that would have prohibited any future congressional interference with the "domestic institutions" of the states. Had the state legislatures ratified it, the Constitution would have had a Thirteenth Amendment protecting slavery instead of one abolishing it. The ratification of the eventual Thirteenth Amendment underlined the real progress made in just a few years in attitudes toward the Negro. Finally, Lincoln's death put a Democrat in the White House, so the racists had no Republican to attack. It did not matter to them that Andrew Johnson had little in common with the Copperhead faction and even hoped to maintain the Union coalition of 1864; he was a Democrat, that was enough.

By the middle of 1865, with most of the causes of the early 1860's won or lost, Americans were anxious to resume the routines of everyday life. Demobilization, the return of thousands of veterans to the labor market, and the need for readjustment in the North and rebuilding in the South brought the realities of living to the forefront of most people's minds. They had tired of controversial propaganda, both from racists and from abolitionists. Congress passed the Freedmen's Bureau bill early in 1865, but little else was done on the Negro's behalf for the next year. In the South, white conservatives began to reestablish their state governments and set up their black codes; and in Pulaski, Tennessee, a handful of bored farmers organized a social club called the Ku Klux Klan.

The end of the war was a momentous turning point for the race issue in the United States. Although racism would continue to exist in the North, the fuel for the racists' fires would come mainly from the South. The racists began by asking questions. What would the long-range results of emancipation be? What would the Congress do under the leadership of radicals like Charles Sumner and Thaddeus Stevens? Perhaps most important of all, how would the southern whites react to whatever course Washington followed?

To get some answers to these questions, various northern writers and journalists traveled south in the months following the war, and returned with accounts of what they saw and heard. Whitelaw Reid, ace reporter for the New York *Tribune* (he was later its editor), reported that most Southerners, with no desire to renew old hates, had resigned themselves to the outcome of the war. Though he said a few "violent and malignant Rebels" might cause some trouble, Reid concluded that the South was passing through a period of supreme despair and would accept almost anything the government imposed. On the other hand, Sidney Andrews spent fourteen weeks in the South and found what he considered extremely strong and widespread hatred of Negroes. The South was willing to accept emancipation as a peace term, he observed, but at no time did southern whites consider extending civil rights or social privileges to the former slaves. Most Southerners simply assumed that the Negroes would become a class of "paid" slaves. Though the institution of slavery had ceased to exist, the whites believed that all the other rules of race relations would prevail.[46]

The official Democratic position was unclear at this point. Generally, the party was in a very bad position. It had the odious stigma of disloyalty to overcome—although most Democrats had supported the war effort, and some of them had voted for Lincoln in 1864. By the summer of 1865, "Copperhead" and "Democrat" were synonymous to many Americans, and the Republicans thoroughly exploited the situation. In addition, the number of elected Democrats in Congress was far too small to constitute an effective opposition. Out of power and out of favor in the North, they remained for the most part a suspected minority. How it must have saddened the elder Frank P. Blair to see the party of Andrew Jackson so humbled.

Moreover, those Democrats who held office had little to recommend them. "In mental calibre and political acumen," Benjamin B. Kendrick observed in his *Journal of the Joint Committee of Fifteen on Reconstruction,* "the Democrats were even more woefully weak than they were in numbers." The *Old Guard* complained that the Democratic party "split and went to pieces upon the negro." Democratic leaders in the House of Representatives included Fernando Wood, Abram S. Hewitt, and James Brooks, all from New York, Daniel W. Voorhees, William E. Niblack, and Michael Kerr from Indiana, George Pendleton from Ohio, Samuel J. Randall from Pennsylvania, Charles Eldredge from Wisconsin, and William Morrison from Illinois. In the Senate, Thomas A. Hendricks of Indiana, Garrett Davis of Kentucky, and Willard Saulsbury of Delaware could be counted on for optimistic but uninspiring leadership.[47] Among these men were some of the country's most extreme racists—so it was clear that Democratic leadership lay in poor hands.

For a year and a half after the war, racist demagoguery was confined primarily to state and local politics. An interesting campaign developed in Ohio, where two former Union generals—George W. Morgan, an ardent racist, and Jacob Dolson Cox, a conservative Republican—competed for the governor's chair. Though he was running for a state office, Morgan campaigned largely on national issues and delivered two speeches in Pennsylvania. Anticipating that the Democratic nomination would go to the man with the strongest views on the race issue, he launched a scathing attack on the Republican party. At the nominating convention he accused the federal government of trying to trample six million southern white people into the earth, "in order that an aristocracy of four million negroes shall be established upon their graves." He told a subsequent gathering that Henry Ward Beecher was, beyond a doubt, the author of "Miscegenation." In another speech, he described an abolitionist parade in Cleveland in which a Negro "queen" had been attended by white "princesses"; and he followed this with a description of a Boston parade that included a "huge negro, side by side in the same carriage with a bright and blooming daughter of Massachusetts." The racist press in Ohio echoed many of Morgan's accusations; in fact, the Columbus *Crisis* pointed out that Cox had graduated from Oberlin College, "where negro equality is taught in theory and in practice."[48]

Unfortunately for the Democrats, the results of the Ohio elections were a testimony to the northern white man's emerging, or in some cases continuing, apathy toward the race issue. In what had been one of the most race-sensitive northern states, the white supremacy candidates lost most of the contests to moderate Republicans. In the face of these defeats, racists in Ohio withdrew into temporary obscurity. In a speech on January 6, 1866, Morgan barely mentioned the Negro. Two days later, the leading lights of the Ohio party—including Thurman, Morgan, Vallandigham, and Pendleton—met at Columbus. The affair was billed as a party celebration, but the participants hardly seemed in a festive mood and the speakers made few racist remarks.[49]

Democratic hopefuls in Pennsylvania also tried to resurrect the miscegenation issue, but with little success. In September 1865, the Democratic State Central Committee met in Philadelphia, and, quoting statements of Greeley, Phillips, Kelley, and Beecher, claimed that miscegenation was the "final goal" of the Republican party.[50] In the gubernatorial contest between John W. Geary and Hiester Clymer the following year, white supremacists in the Clymer camp produced in their posters and leaflets some of the most virulent graphic racism of the decade. Emphasizing national issues, they accused Geary of supporting the congressional radicals, Negro suffrage, and the Freedmen's Bureau. "White Men and White Women—Are You Ready for This?" they demanded.

On the national level, the white supremacy crusade was only dormant, not dead. In the summer of 1866, a group of moderate Democrats, with a sprinkling of conservative Republicans and a few Copperheads, met in Philadelphia at the National Union Convention to discuss plans for political action, express support for President Johnson, and perhaps even form a new party. In the same city, and at almost the same time, radical Republicans held their own rally. Comparing the two, editor James Gordon Bennett of the New York *Herald* called the former dignified, statesmanlike, peace-loving, and Union-loving; he branded the latter the "Nigger-Worshipper's Convention" and described its participants as violent, vulgar, war-seeking, and disunionist.[51] Emancipation and war had opened a pandora's box of problems for postwar America; and the status of the Negro remained the most emotional and sensitive of them all.

Chapter Five

THE SUFFRAGE ISSUE IN THE NORTH AND WEST

"The vital question just now in American politics is that of Negro suffrage," Clemenceau wrote a few months after the end of the war. In November 1867 he repeated this assessment in even stronger terms, writing, "Any Democrat who did not manage to hint that the negro is a degenerate gorilla would be considered lacking in enthusiasm." The Democrats spoke continually about how unthinkable it was that the government should extend the franchise to "a lot of wild men." In the words of the *Old Guard*, "On the most living and burning of all issues in the brains of the masses, viz.: *negro equality* or *negro voting*, the Democratic party alone can win." In the editor's view, this was the "greatest question of all."[1]

But who was to decide which course to follow? "Johnson declares that he will allow each state to settle it independently," Clemenceau wrote, "whereas the radicals would like to have him assert his authority and settle it once for all." Mistakenly assuming that the reconstructed states would have to comply with the general rules for the admission of new states, Clemenceau concluded that to leave the disposition of the suffrage issue in the hands of southern whites would only delay a solution because the radicals in Congress would certainly reject state governments dominated by "former slave owners and rebels."[2] In an attempt to circumvent the expected opposition of Republican militants like Sumner and Stevens, the President took advantage of the long congressional recess from April to December 1865, and by executive order speedily directed the reestablishment of civil governments in every former Confederate state but Texas. But, though Clemenceau erred as to the procedures to be followed, he was correct in his prediction of the congressional reaction. Reconvening in December, the Republican-led Congress exercised its privilege of refusing to seat the members-elect from the seceded states and thereby effectively nullified Johnson's attempt to take the initiative in reconstruction.

The congressional battle lines over Negro suffrage had been drawn more than a year before the end of the war. In March 1864, while Congress was debating a bill concerning the governing of the proposed Territory of Montana, Senator Morton S. Wilkinson of Minnesota introduced an amendment to strike the word "white" from the section on voter qualifications. Speaking out sharply against the Wilkinson proposal, Senator Doolittle of Wisconsin pointed out that there were no Negroes in the territory, and that the proposed amendment was thus meaningless. Furthermore, he said, the pending bill was for a temporary government only and thus did not bind any future territorial or state government. Senator Sumner replied to Doolittle, and, though conceding that they were debating an abstraction, insisted on the change as a matter of principle. Most of his colleagues agreed, and the bill carried with the Wilkinson amendment.[3]

The issue was one of principle for the racists as well, and many of them exaggerated the significance of the Montana debate. Shortly after the bill's passage, the editor of the Detroit *Free Press* called the Wilkinson amendment an unequivocal Republican commitment to Negro suffrage. A year and a half later, the Democratic State Central Committee of Pennsylvania charged that those who voted "to place the black man on an equality with the white man in one of the richest territories of the Union will readily be recognized as the leaders of the Republican party in the Senate."[4]

Basic to the argument against Negro suffrage was the widespread conviction that the founding fathers, because they were white men, had formed a country exclusively for white men. Although in the 1860's most Americans might have agreed that all men were created equal, the notion that some were "more equal than others," which had been popular among compromising constitutional apologists seventy years earlier, was still commonly held. Washington, Jefferson, Madison, and Hamilton would never have agreed, critics argued, to put the "root digger" and the Hottentot on the same level as the Anglo-Saxon; this had always been a white man's country. The African race was not fit "to enter the political community with the white people of the country," they insisted.[5]

Since Americans had long believed that the regulation of suffrage was the prerogative of the state alone, the old issue of states' rights was a key element in the racist position. In the summer of 1864, attempts in both houses of Congress to add a Negro suffrage provision to the Wade-Davis reconstruction bill lost by large majorities, and the omission of the provision weakened the bill in the eyes of many abolitionists. However, it was widely felt that any congressional attempt to outline voting rules would violate the constitutional rights of the states. The suffrage problem was one that the state legislatures alone had to solve, the New York *World* insisted in 1867. Although the *World* did not necessarily oppose the principle of impartial suffrage, the editor said, the resolution of the question was not a national matter. Two years later, Gideon Welles, Secretary of the Navy under Lincoln, charged that if the federal government extended suffrage to "negroes and fools" it would be showing its "total disregard for the rights of the States"; and three months before the states had completed ratification of the Fifteenth Amendment, Governor Henry H. Haight of California asked his state's legislature to reject the amendment on these same grounds.[6]

By 1865, all the New England states except Connecticut had granted all males, regardless of race, full equality at the polls. Not surprisingly, however, few of the other states showed much inclination to extend the ballot to Negroes and other nonwhites. New York had granted Negro suffrage, but with certain property and tax qualifications. Although a state constitutional convention in 1868 approved an amendment that called for the removal of the property qualifications, the State Senate defeated a bill that would have put it on the ballot, and the issue died. Like New York, Wisconsin had granted qualified suffrage to Negroes, but its law, passed in 1849, was so ambiguous that it was not until 1865, after the State Supreme Court had ruled in favor of a black plaintiff, that Wisconsin Negroes actually voted. Of course, the Negro population of both of these states was relatively small. The first state with a sizable Negro population to enfranchise its black citizens was Tennessee, where the machine of unionist Governor William G. "Parson" Brownlow won Negro suffrage in 1867, although Negroes in Chattanooga had voted in municipal elections the previous year.[7] Every other northern state government displayed an unbending opposition to impartial suffrage proposals. When Republicans in the Ohio State Senate recommended the removal of the word "white" from the voting provision of the state constitution, the Columbus *Crisis* accused them of trying to make the state "a negro colony, controlled by negro votes." A few months later, bills to place the matter before the voters failed in both houses of the legislature. Other states that took similar actions with the same results included Maryland in 1867 and New Jersey in 1868.[8]

In the North, as resistance to Negro suffrage grew, several states contrived arbitrary and rather bizarre definitions of the word "white" as it appeared in their voting laws. In 1866, the Michigan State Supreme Court ruled that a man less than one-fourth Negro could vote under the "white only" restriction of the state constitution. In other words, a quadroon was a Negro, an octoroon was not. Two years later, the Ohio State Legislature passed its notorious "Visible Admixture Law," which required election officials to challenge the ballot of any person who displayed a "visible admixture" of Negro and white blood. In order to have his vote count, the accused, with two corroborating witnesses, had to swear that his parents had no Negro blood. Even after he had taken the oath confirming his all-white ancestry, the registration roster was to carry a permanent note that his pedigree had been challenged.[9]

While such laws were being passed, Democratic leaders in almost every state were denouncing the idea of equality at the polls. Pennsylvania Democrats, meeting at Nob Mountain in August 1865, made Negro suffrage the subject of songs and poems, and the following month the State Central Committee accused the Republican party of advocating racial equality and Negro suffrage. The Committee considered this a disaster; "Give the black man equal political rights in our country and you give him equal social rights," it declared. In 1866, party leaders in both Harrisburg and Reading resolved that "the white race alone is entitled to the control of the government," a view that other Pennsylvania Democrats echoed until the Fifteenth Amendment had been ratified.[10]

Similarly, Democrats in Vermont, Connecticut, New York, Delaware, West Virginia, and New Jersey spun out a series of indignant statements against equality at the polls. Each year from 1865 to 1870, delegates to the annual state convention in Ohio passed a resolution condemning Negro suffrage. "The effort now being made to confer the right of suffrage upon negroes," they protested in 1865, "is an insidious attempt to overthrow popular institutions by bringing the right to vote into disgrace." To Democrats in Wisconsin, Illinois, Minnesota, Missouri, California, Nevada, and the Nebraska Territory, the question of Negro suffrage frequently overshadowed all others. In August 1865, the Democratic party in Iowa endorsed General Thomas H. Benton, who was running for governor as the nominee of an ad hoc white-supremacy veterans' convention. The group that held the convention had originally organized during the war as "The Anti-Negro Suffrage Party," and was the only quasi-legitimate political party in the country formed exclusively to oppose Negro suffrage.[11]

In the South, few dared to suggest Negro suffrage immediately after the war. A notable exception was Judge John H. Reagan of Texas, former Confederate Postmaster-General. In November 1866, the Chicago *Times* published a letter that Judge Reagan had written on October 12 to the Governor of Texas, J. W. Throckmorton. Reagan urged the Governor and other southern leaders to grant suffrage to Negroes who could meet educational and tax-paying requirements, the rule to be applied impartially to both races. Of course, since very few Negroes could have met the requirements, the law would still have been highly discriminatory. The alternative to qualified Negro suffrage under white conservative control, Reagan argued, was universal suffrage guaranteed by federal bayonets, a situation that would invite Negro domination and racial violence. On the following day, the *Times*, in two separate editorials, applauded Reagan's recommendations as moderate and sensible. Basing his estimates on an informal census taken earlier in the year, editor Wilbur Storey said that since Negroes were apparently declining in numbers, whatever strength they would gain from the vote would only be temporary. Agreeing that federal authorities might impose universal Negro suffrage under military reconstruction if the South denied all Negroes the ballot, he concluded that southern whites, in order to guarantee white supremacy, had no other choice.[12]

But the racists of the 1860's were no more willing to concede token Negro suffrage than racists of a later generation were willing to concede token school integration; if Negro suffrage of any kind were to come, it would have to be forced upon them. Quoting the New York *Freeman's Journal*, an obscure racist newspaper catering to immigrants, the Columbus *Crisis* accused Storey of "bending to the negro suffrage storm that has been sweeping the North."[13] The Detroit *Free Press* and the Cincinnati *Enquirer* responded similarly. In fact, of the major Democratic journals in the North, only the Boston *Post* and the New York *World* expressed qualified agreement.* The very idea that a few Ne-

---

* Eric L. McKitrick, *Andrew Johnson and Reconstruction* (Chicago, 1960), p. 463, 463n. McKitrick cites the November 19 and 20 issues of the *World* as opposing the *Times*. Both issues show the contrary. In one the *World* described the suffrage suggestion as "sagacious and prudent," while the other issue barely mentioned the *Times*. Despite its conduct during the miscegenation controversy of 1864, conduct that aimed to influence the presidential election of that year, the *World*'s support of Reagan and the *Times* was indicative of the journal's consistently realistic pragmatism and of its acknowledgement of the inherent racism in Reagan's suggestion. Recognizing that the inflexible racism of the fanatics was often a handicap for the Democrats, in 1868 the *World* published an article cautioning the Democratic National Convention to refrain from writing a platform which stipulated that this was exclusively a white man's government, an article described by the Cincinnati *Enquirer* of July 6, 1868, as "a cool piece of impudence."

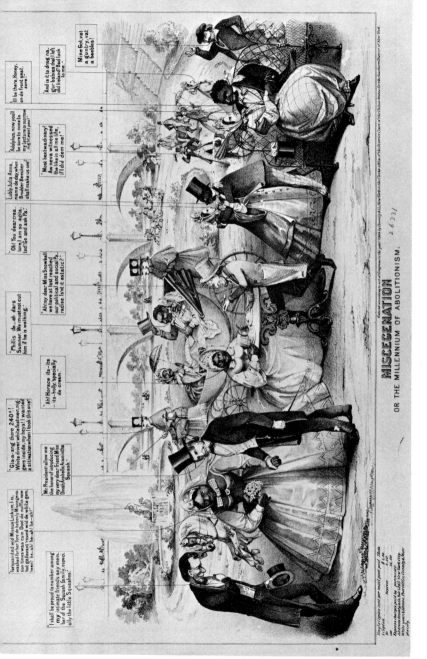

Plate 1. A campaign print designed to influence the election of 1864. (New York: Bromley & Co., 1864.)

POLITICAL CARICATURE Nº 3.

Plate 2. A campaign print designed to influence the election of 1864. (New York: Bromley & Co., 1864.)

Plate 3. A campaign print designed to influence the election of 1864. (New York: Bromley & Co., 1864.)

UNIVERSAL FREEDUM

ONE CONSTITUTION

ONE DESTINY

ABRAHAM LINCOLN PRES:

THE MISCEGENATION BALL

at the Headquarters of the Lincoln Central Campaign Club, Corner of Broadway and Twenty Third Street New York Sept. 22.ᵈ 1864 being a perfect fac simile of the room &c. &c. [from the New York World Sept. 23.ᵈ 1864.] No sooner were the formal proceedings and speeches hurried through with, than the room was cleared for a negro ball, which then and there took place. Some members of the Central Lincoln Club 'left the room before the mystical and circling rites of languishing glance and many dance commenced. But that MANY remained is also true. This fact WE CERTIFY, that we saw during the progress of the ball, were many of the accredited leaders of the Black Republican party, thus testifying their faith by their works in the hall and headquarters of their political gathering. There were Republican OFFICE-HOLDERS and prominent men of various degrees, and at least one PRESIDENTIAL ELECTOR ON THE REPUBLICAN TICKET.

BLACK REPUBLICAN PRAYER.

ABRAM LINCOLN, who art in the White House at Washington — glorified be thy name; thy Presidency has come, thy will must be done, as set forth in the Chicago Platform. Give us daily the delight of thy counsel, and lead us not into trouble, but deliver us from Jeff. Davis and the Confederate army. And O, Abram, we beseech thee to regard not the Constitution, but prosecute the war against our Southern brethren, and free dear Sambo, so that he may become white and equal with ourselves. And we implore thy Royal highness to gag the Democrats and their press, that they may not speak evil of thee or of the Republican party. Disregard all State rights, — the decisions of the Supreme Court, — and suspend the *habeas corpus* — for it becomes necessary, that we may carry out our holy cause of emancipation. Arrest every Democratic offender who sayeth ought of thee or thy administration; throw them into prison; brand him with the name of traitor and tory, that we may be avenged for thy sake. And we sincerely implore thy imperial Majesty to oppose all compromises for peace, for it will be dangerous to our cause, will arrest the " irrepressible conflict," and restore the old Union as it was.

O, centralize thy power, that we may become a strong government, — that the people will kneel before thy Royal Highness, and worship thee in spirit and in truth, — that thou art the Patriarch Abraham, sent on the earth for the salvation of mankind, and poor Sambo in particular. Remove all Democrats from office, and remember thy faithful servants who put their trust in thee.

And O, we humbly pray that thou wilt carry on the war with vigor, lay waste the Southern States, murder the inhabitants, confiscate their property, ravish their women, and burn their cities and towns.

And O, Father Abraham, when the cry of the widow and the orphan ascendeth to heaven, and the wrath of the Great Jehovah descendeth upon us for our wickedness and cruelty, and our grand armies are defeated, do thou open thy balmy bosom and hide us from that vile rebel, Jeff. Davis, and his army; for thou art to rule with power and with glory, for ever and ever. Amen.

BENEDICTION.

May the blessings of Emancipation extend throughout our unhappy land, and the illustrious, sweet-scented Sambo nestle in the bosom of every Abolition woman, that she may be quickened by the pure blood of the majestic African, and the spirit of amalgamation shine forth in all its splendor and glory, that we may become a regenerated nation of half-breeds, and mongrels, and the distinction of color be forever consigned to oblivion, and that we may live in bonds of fraternal love, union, and equality with the Almighty Nigger, henceforward, now and forever. Amen.

Plate 4. A racist parody of the Lord's Prayer, probably printed as a leaflet. (N.p., [1864?].)

WHAT MISCEGENATION IS!

WHAT WE ARE TO EXPECT

Now that Mr. Lincoln is Re-elected.

By L. SEAMAN, LL. D.

WALLER & WILLETTS, Publishers,

NEW YORK.

Plate 5. Title page of a racist pamphlet. The picture also appears on the cover. (New York: Waller & Willetts, [1864].)

Plate 6. Racist supporters of the Democratic candidate for governor of Pennsylvania in 1866 produced a series of very large campaign posters. Plates 6, 7, and 8 are three examples. (N.p. [1866].)

Plate 7.

THE CONSTITUTIONAL AMENDMENT!

GEARY
Is for Negro Suffrage.

STEVENS
Advocates it.

FORNEY
Howls for it.

McCLURE
Speaks for it.

CAMERON
Wants it.

The LEAGUE
Sustains it.

They are rich, and want to make

The Negro the Equal
OF THE POOR WHITE MAN,
and then rule them both.

The BLACK Roll
CANDIDATES FOR CONGRESS
WHO VOTED FOR THIS BILL.

THAD. STEVENS
WM. D. KELLEY
CHAS. O'NEILL
LEONARD MYERS
JNO. M. BROOMALL
GEORGE F. MILLER
STEPHEN F. WILSON
ULYSSES MERCUR
GEO. V. LAWRENCE
GLENNI W. SCHOFIELD
J. K. MOORHEAD
THOMAS WILLIAMS

THE RADICAL PLATFORM--"NEGRO SUFFRAGE THE ONLY ISSUE!"

Every man who votes for Geary or for a Radical Candidate for Congress, votes as surely for Negro Suffrage and Negro Equality, as if they were printed on his ballot.

Plate 8.

THE FREEDMAN'S BUREAU!

AN AGENCY TO KEEP THE NEGRO IN IDLENESS AT THE EXPENSE OF THE WHITE MAN.

TWICE VETOED BY THE PRESIDENT, AND MADE A LAW BY CONGRESS.

SUPPORT CONGRESS & YOU SUPPORT THE NEGRO. SUSTAIN THE PRESIDENT & YOU PROTECT THE WHITE MAN

IN THE SWEAT OF THY FACE SHALT THOU EAT THY BREAD

Negro Estimate of Freedom!

Freedman's Bureau!

FREEDOM AND NO WORK.

GOODS TO EAT & DRINK

PIES

STEWS

CLAMS

FISH BALLS

UNCLE SAM WILL HAVE TO KEEP ME.

IDLENESS

WHITE SUGAR

APATHY

WHITE WOMEN

INDOLENCE

SUGAR PLUMS

RUM GIN

WHISKY

CANDY

LIBERTY

— What is de use for free to work as long as we day make dese appropriations.

CONGRESS, IN JULY, 1866, VOTES THE
NEGRO TROOPS
$300
Each as a Bounty

The same CONGRESS IN JUNE, 1866, VOTES THE
WHITE Veterans
$100
Each as a Bounty

THE NEGRO GETS $300 ; the WHITE SOLDIER, $200 in all—at at the WHITE Soldiers served THREE Years, none of the NEGROES over TWO Years.

THE WHITE MAN MUST WORK TO KEEP HIS CHILDREN AND PAY HIS TAXES.

APPROPRIATED BY CONGRESS, JULY 1866.
To Support the Freedman's Bureau
$6,944,500

Commissioners and Clerks for Negroes,	$230,000
...ting for Negroes,	63,000
House and Wood for Negroes,	15,900
Clothing for Negroes,	1,750,000
Food for Negroes,	3,530,250
Medicine for Negroes,	500,000
Railroad Fare for Negroes,	1,320,000
School Matters & School Houses for Negroes,	535,000
TOTAL	$6,944,450

APPROPRIATED BY CONGRESS, FOR THE WHITE MAN.
HEAVY TAXES, HARD LABOR

For 1864 and 1865, the FREEDMAN'S BUREAU cost the Tax-payers of the Nation, at least, TWENTY-FIVE MILLIONS OF DOLLARS. For 1866, THE SHARE of the Tax-payers of Pennsylvania will be about ONE ...ION OF DOLLARS. GEARY is FOR the Freedman's Bureau CLYMER is OPPOSED to it.

THE BLACK VOMIT;

Or, The Bottom Rail on Top.

A new Farce composed by a Committee appointed from De-league, was played ~~cess~~fully for two days in Lynchburg. The principal characters were sustained ~~by~~ Kelso, Williams'-son and other Black and White vultures specially imported the purpose. ☞ This play is taken from scenes in Pandemonium, and has ~~bee~~n arranged and put on the Stage for the purpose of inaugurating "HELL IN ~~VIR~~GINIA."

"Two heads without a single thought."
"Two black hearts that beat as one."

~~D~~arkies of all stamp and occupations were there; one could only hear such expressions as, 'How d'ye, Mr. Jones?' 'How did you leave de family?' 'Well, I ~~hop~~e.' 'Say gents', how de ting gwine?' 'Well I hope.' 'You see dat reporter dar.' 'Yes I does.' 'Well, does you know him.' 'Yes I does.' He's spotted, ~~'~~Is any Conservatin niggers boat' 'Say Johnson, gi'me chaw tobaccer and vote de Hunnicut ticket.' ~~'He~~llo, Jim, votin' Hunnicut ticket?' 'I am dat, ole hoss.' 'Well, grab a root, den.' 'I wonder if all de nickers is all votin' on der Honeygud diget?'

The Camels Are Coming

First Step of the Mongrels before Organizing.

Mongrels on their way to C. C. H.

Will be Needed at the Richmond Treasury.

Charge of the Leaguers upon NED HORTON, who Voted the Conservative Ticket.

The Liberties of the Country " going up" on the 22d day of Oct. 1867.

The lordly Foul fearing that he might be appropriated, takes his Flight.

The Representative Man from Lynchburg.
☞ LOOKOUT SUKEY! ☜

The Representative from Lynchburg makes a Speech.

Gent'emen ob de Convenshun,—I'se a man an a brudder. I'se a membur of dis spectable body. I endos de speech dat Mr. Pompey Smash hab made. We's on de wave of dis grate rebolushun whar ders no stincshun on count ob color. Three chairs for de grate Republican party. Wid dese ~~a f~~ew remarks, gemmen of de Convenshun, I takes my seet; I does.

~~Pe~~rforming Black and ~~Bir~~ds Entering the Ark ~~Po~~nd.

When Shall we THREE Meet Again ?
In de Convenshun.

HAIR DRESSED, BOOTS BLACKED, COWS MILKED AND SKINNED!! APPLY AT THE CAPITOL.

Plate 10. A campaign print designed to influence the election of 1868. (New York: Bromley & Co., 1868.)

Negro the Only Issue!

HAVE THE PEOPLE NO OTHER INTEREST WORTH LOOKING AFTER?

STATUS OF POLITICAL PARTIES.

Republican Party in the Field.　　　　　*Democratic Party Looking for a Candidate.*

Spectacular Entertainment to attract the attention of the People while Politicians pick their pockets by means of National Banks and Treasury Rings.

Past, Present and Future of Greenbacks:

A Pamphlet of 50 pages, including the NATIONAL BANK LAW, shows how it is done.

For sale by Newsdealers, and will be mailed to any address, free of postage, on receipt of Twenty-Five Cents.

Address C. ALVORD, P. O. Drawer 381, Milwaukee, Wis.

Plate 11. A leaflet criticizing both parties for their concern with the Negro. (N.p., [1868].)

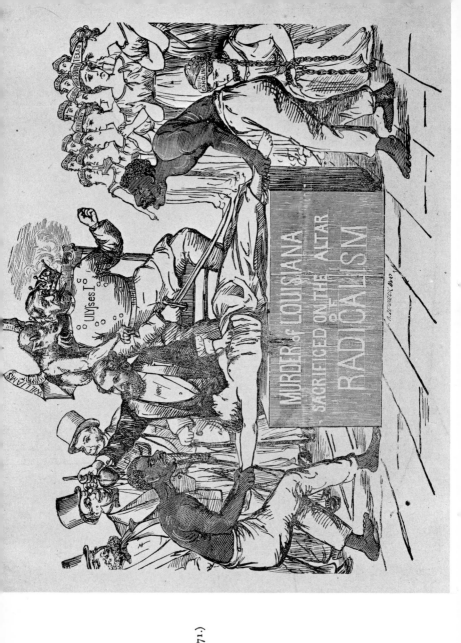

Plate 12. A racist leaflet condemning radical reconstruction.
(N.p.: A. Zenneck, 1871.)

groes might be allowed to vote caused most racists to ignore the references to the Negro's "inherent" inferiority and the superiority of "Gothic" blood in both Reagan's letter and the *Times* editorials, and to miss Reagan's purpose completely, which was to ensure Negro subordination (by keeping federal authorities out of the picture), not to eliminate it.

Judge Reagan, of course, spoke only for himself. Actually, in view of Andrew Johnson's growing leniency in the immediate postwar months, it seemed highly unlikely that federal troops would be used to enforce Negro suffrage, and most southern states, with the President growing increasingly congenial, instituted black codes that went much farther than denying the freedmen the ballot. Nevertheless, some southern whites remained fearful. Less than six months after the end of the war, a Democratic convention in New Orleans passed a resolution unequivocally denying the black race any equality, political or otherwise, and reaffirming its belief that the government was established "for the exclusive benefit of the white race." A few days later, another group, calling itself the National Conservative Union Party, met in the same city. Though they claimed to be less extreme than either the "Conservative Democrats" or the "National Democrats," the National Conservatives publicly condemned impartial suffrage.[14] However, conservative control of the South was brief, and military reconstruction soon eliminated whatever gains racists had made. It was not until October 1869, when white conservatives in Tennessee and Virginia regained control of their state governments, that southern racists were again to dictate the terms of suffrage.

In all the racists' declarations against Negro suffrage, there was an element of futility and desperation that came in part from their refusal to acknowledge what they subconsciously knew was inevitable. As Clemenceau observed late in 1868: "the panic inspired by this scarecrow [Negro suffrage] overpowers them, and the councils of the wisest among them can do nothing against it. Hence their idiotic desperation in the face of a destiny which they cannot escape. They are behaving like the savage, who, wielding his tomahawk and shouting his warcry, dashes at an approaching steam engine with the hope of stopping it."[15] To the frantic white supremacist, of course, Negro suffrage was no "scarecrow." For him the evils of equality at the polls were real; his task was to convey this reality to the public conscience.

In this task, the racist had some success, for northern antipathy to Negro suffrage was widespread. At the end of the Civil War, eighteen of the twenty-five Union states (including West Virginia) did not allow their black residents to vote. By March 1870, when the Fifteenth Amendment was ratified, thirteen of twenty-six states—California, Connecticut, Delaware, Indiana, Kansas, Kentucky, Maryland, Michigan, Nevada, New Jersey, Ohio, Oregon, and Pennsylvania—and the Territory of Colorado still denied the ballot to the Negro.[16] Obviously, the progress of impartial suffrage during these five years was painfully slow. The failure of state legislatures to act on behalf of the Negro and the opposition of various political organizations were partially responsible for this; most responsible, however, was the general public, which given the opportunity did not hesitate to vote against Negro suffrage. The record of impartial suffrage proposals which reached the ballot was dismal, a reflection not only of the prejudice of the voter but also of the success of the racist propagandist in exploiting that prejudice.

In referendums held during 1867, for example, voters in Kansas, Ohio, and Minnesota rejected impartial suffrage. Although Republican leaders in each state spoke out in support of the measure, many rank-and-file party members obviously voted against it. In Kansas, where the suffrage amendment stood alone on the ballot unencumbered by a slate of state or national candidates, it failed by a two-to-one vote, although the Republican party enjoyed a comfortable registered majority. Minnesota elected a Republican governor, and Republicans won majorities in both chambers of the legislature by sizable margins; but in the same election, the suffrage proposal was defeated. In April 1868, 61 per cent of the Michigan voters rejected a new state constitution, which provided for impartial suffrage, in spite of the fact that in an earlier election the Republican candidate for governor had won by thirty thousand votes.[17]

The most overwhelming defeat came in Ohio, where, despite a slim Republican majority in the overall voter turn-out (243,605 to 240,622), the Democrats won control of both houses of the legislature by narrow margins and an impartial suffrage amendment failed by over fifty thousand votes. "The wolf is at your door," Vallandigham had warned during the campaign; and Thurman, Morgan, and Pendleton had made the amendment the main topic of most of their speeches. A year later, Democratic leaders in New York City pleaded for the nomination of one Colonel Dan Rice of Pennsylvania for President of the United States on the grounds that he more than anyone else had secured the defeat of the suffrage amendment in Ohio; the New York leaders claimed that he had spoken to more than half a million people. Even when an amendment won, public resentment was obvious. In Iowa, where there were twice as many registered Republicans as Democrats, an impartial suffrage measure won only 56 per cent of the votes.[18] Evidently, many Midwesterners agreed with the Illinois farmer who, rejoicing over

President Johnson's veto of the second Freedmen's Bureau bill in 1866, had written, "By god, I will di before a negro shal put a ballet in the box of mine."[19]

However, the defeat of the various suffrage proposals in the North was not solely a result of racist efforts. The evidence indicates that most white voters were opposed to impartial suffrage from the very beginning. It is possible, nevertheless, that racists convinced people who might otherwise have stayed home to go out and vote against Negro suffrage, and where the vote was close this may have been decisive. In any event, the results of these elections were very encouraging to southern whites. The obvious northern hostility to voter equality, they believed, would force the radicals in Congress to modify drastically or perhaps even abandon their plans to enfranchise the freedmen. But southern optimism was short-lived. In 1867 Congress passed the Reconstruction Acts, and in the following year the national Republican platform endorsed federal enforcement of universal suffrage in the South, but asked that in the North the states retain the right to determine who could vote. The radicals defended their double standard on the grounds that universal suffrage in the South was the only way to guarantee its loyalty to the Union and prevent a virtual reenslavement of the Negroes, and that such an expedient was not necessary in the North. The argument was an open invitation to charges of hypocrisy.[20]

Nor were such charges unfounded. For one thing, though abolitionists and radicals were vocal in their endorsement of Negro suffrage, they frequently did not have a majority of their own party behind them; for another, Republican leadership was hesitant, inconsistent, and equivocal at best. Examples of its ambiguous stand on Negro suffrage were as common as examples of the Democratic party's manifest stand against it. Governor J. D. Cox of Ohio, reflecting a fairly popular view, endorsed the enfranchisement of those northern Negroes who were educated and economically independent and who had fought in the Union army; he suggested that other Negroes wait until they could prove they were qualified. In fact, before he won the formal Republican gubernatorial nomination, Cox had ordered his campaign manager to withdraw his name from consideration if the party officially declared for Negro suffrage. In February 1865, a Republican-dominated constitutional convention in Missouri defeated by one vote a motion to strike the word "white" from the suffrage article of the new constitution. Four months later, New Jersey Republicans met in Trenton and passed a strong anti-Negro-suffrage resolution. And in Maryland, delegates to the Republican-organized Unconditional Union Convention opposed Negro suffrage on the grounds that the former slaveowners would control the Negro vote and turn it to their own use.[21]

Even the abolitionists and the radicals did not always appear wholly consistent. On July 1, 15, and 22, 1864, William Lloyd Garrison replied in the *Liberator* to a letter from London University Professor Francis W. Newman, who had been highly critical of Lincoln's moderate stance on Negro suffrage. Garrison, realizing that the Negro's best interests lay with Lincoln's reelection, hoped to minimize the effect of recent attacks on the President, made by disgruntled American abolitionists who thought the government should have granted suffrage to Negroes in Louisiana. In his reply, Garrison defended the President's go-slow approach to Negro suffrage by pointing to the practical difficulties that would be brought about by giving the ballot to a people so recently freed from bondage. Moreover, Garrison expressed doubt that a constitutional amendment for universal manhood suffrage could be ratified without the support of the southern states. But he was also optimistic. "With the abolition of slavery in the South," he predicted, "prejudice or 'colorphobia,' the natural product of the system, will gradually disappear." Garrison, of course, was committed to the principle of equality at the polls, and his sanguine view of future southern race relations was a reflection of his excessive optimism; but political expediency forced him to temper his comments somewhat, thus they were easily misinterpreted both by equalitarians who were looking for support in their endorsement of Negro suffrage, and by racists who were looking both for reasons to oppose it and for examples of Republican duplicity.[22]

Because they were open to misinterpretation, statements like Garrison's tended to confuse the public about the Republican position on the question of Negro suffrage. A few months after the end of the war, in a speech that received wide circulation in the press, Governor Morton of Indiana asked why the vote should be given to the ex-slaves when Indiana's far more literate Negro population did not enjoy a similar right. Though he supported the principle of impartial suffrage, the Governor, recognizing the inconsistency in the Republican position and unable to persuade the legislature and voters of Indiana to extend the ballot to the black men in his state, did not think it right to grant suffrage to southern Negroes. Greeley, Sumner, and General O. O. Howard, at one time or another, had recommended an educational requirement for all voters, white and black; and in a speech before the Massachusetts State Legislature, Governor John A. Andrew suggested a reading test, applied to both races, as a requirement for enfranchisement. Even Thaddeus Stevens expressed doubts.[23] Afraid that the exslave's vote might be controlled by his former master, Stevens was for a time somewhat unsure whether impartial suffrage was a wise thing.* Indeed, the voice of caution was heard from Negroes themselves. At a convention of Negro men in Leavenworth, Kansas, one Reverend Twine of Atchison, convinced that the white people of America wanted what was best for the Negro, urged the delegates to adopt a resolution supporting educational suffrage requirements. The ballot would come quicker for all, he argued, if the black man did not push too hard for immediate enfranchisement.[24]

Not surprisingly, the suffrage double standard and the ambivalence of some of the leading radicals became targets for racist attacks. In the fall of 1865, Democratic leaders in Pennsylvania warned the state's residents not to be fooled by Republican spokesmen who "seek to obtain by double dealing your support [for] sentiments they do not avow." In a speech at Mansfield, Ohio, Thurman reminded his hearers that they had voted Negro suffrage down for their state, and that now what they refused to permit there they were asked by Republicans to "impose" on the South through congressional reconstruction. Pointing to the various northern referendums, Edward A. Pollard maintained that "on no modern question of politics have the people of the North shown more sensitiveness than on that of entertaining the Negro as an equal at the polls."[25]

In Congress, Democrats accused Republicans of trying to ride two horses in opposite directions. Republican senators and representatives, racists complained, advocated Negro suffrage in the South to satisfy their abolitionist leaders, but did not support similar proposals for the northern states for fear of antagonizing their prejudiced constituents. Senator Thomas A. Hendricks of Indiana asked the Republican members of the Senate how they could reconcile their support for proposals to force Negro suffrage on the South with the fact that most of the Republican-controlled northern state legislatures refused to grant the ballot to northern Negroes who were unquestionably more qualified intellectually and economically than the freedmen. The argument that Negro suffrage in the South was necessary to guarantee that section's loyalty and that no such action was required in the North, Hendricks concluded, was nothing but a fraud, designed to conceal the abolitionist drive for national political power.[26] In an exchange in the Senate with

* Nathaniel Weyl, on p. 86 of *The Negro in American Civilization* (Washington, D. C., 1960), quotes Stevens as saying that if the ex-slaves were anything like the runaway slaves he had seen around his home, they were not entitled to the ballot. Weyl cites *Memoirs of W. W. Holden* (Durham, N. C., 1911), pp. 85 and 144, as his source, but these pages show no such statement. Holden's only mention of Stevens concerns Stevens's speculation about how long military reconstruction would continue.

Republican George H. Williams of Oregon, Delaware's Willard Saulsbury also called attention to this obvious inconsistency. Saulsbury asked
Williams how many Negroes lived in Oregon, and whether they were
enfranchised. There were very few, Williams replied, and they did not
vote. How then, Saulsbury asked, did Williams justify universal suffrage for an area that was one-fourth or one-third Negro? Williams answered that he was only agreeing with the majority opinion in Congress.
When Saulsbury then pointed out that Williams had voted against a
Negro suffrage resolution in a state convention and accused him of
hypocrisy, Williams conceded that he had been compelled by public
pressures in his home state to vote that way.[27]

The racist exploitation of Republican inconsistency took on an additional dimension when Negro senators and representatives, elected
largely by the Negro voters of the reconstructed states, presented themselves to the Congress. Since the Congress established its own rules for
seating members-elect, racists said that it would be interesting to see
how Republicans received the black legislators. When the lame-duck
third session of the Fortieth Congress convened in December 1868, wait-
ing to be seated was John Willis Menard of Louisiana, the first Negro
ever elected to the House of Representatives. Speculating on the reception Menard could expect, the New York *Herald* sarcastically challenged the radicals "to extend to him the hand of fellowship or to con-
tradict their lying professions of regard for his claims as man, brother,
and citizen." Chosen to serve the remaining three months of a de-
ceased representative's term, Menard was challenged immediately by
racist members, and was never seated. In the following spring, however,
Jefferson P. Long of Georgia, one of three Negroes elected to the Forty-
First Congress, became, with the membership reconstituted in a more
equalitarian vein, the first black man to take his seat in the House.
In February 1870, during the second session, Hiram Revels of Mississippi, welcomed enthusiastically by Republican leaders, took Jefferson
Davis's old desk when he became the first Negro to serve in the Senate.
Frustrated by the absence of radical hypocrisy, Senator Garrett Davis
of Kentucky tried to embarrass the Republicans by pointing out, erroneously, that no Negro had ever been seated in the House because
the representatives had to face the voters every two years and thus were
more responsive to the wishes—and the prejudices—of the public. The
senators, on the other hand, only had to account for themselves every
six years to the state legislatures that had selected them, Davis concluded, and therefore could defy public opinion with relative im-
punity.[28] But Davis and the other Democratic critics were grasping at
straws. From 1869 to 1876, fourteen Negro representatives and two

Negro senators, encountering resistance only from the Democrats, served in the Congress.

Although the racist critics were firm and consistent in accusing the Republican party of hypocrisy and vacillation, they themselves were often confused and uncertain about exactly how to convert their ideas into programs that would have the results they desired. The most popular targets for charges of hypocrisy, for example, were the New England radicals, but criticisms of them were little more than acknowledgments that New England had long been in the vanguard of the Negro suffrage movement. The Boston *Post*, recognizing over a year before the war ended that scare tactics would not influence its readership, tried a different approach. Negroes were so few in New England, the editor declared, that their strength at the polls was negligible. Thus Negro suffrage in the Northeast was not going to change anything there, and it was easy for the radicals to legislate Negro suffrage at home and to advocate it elsewhere without arousing the wrath of their constituents.[29]

Probably the most conspicuous example of the critic's desperation was his exploitation of the fears of the less fortunate whites—particularly the recent European immigrants, most of whom had come to the United States to escape political oppression or economic deprivation and now cherished their new citizenship and their right to vote. Maintaining that the abolitionists were motivated more by hatred for the white Europeans than by regard for the blacks, the racists accused the radicals of planning to use the Negro vote to suppress the white immigrant. Today's abolitionists, Democratic writer and lecturer William D. Northend told an audience in Manchester, New Hampshire, in January 1868, were yesterday's anti-foreign, anti-Catholic Know-Nothings.[30] Most Europeans, Representative Andrew Jackson Rogers of New Jersey proclaimed, had come to America because they had heard that there was social, economic, and political equality for white men. They would have been better off staying in Germany, France, Ireland, or England, he said, than coming to this country to be "degraded" and "placed on a social position where equally with themselves negroes shall be allowed to exercise the great right of suffrage at the ballot box." And Samuel Tilden even asked if the Irish* and the Germans believed that

---

* The Irish hostility to the Negro may have been partly responsible for the futility of Catholic pleas for missionary aid to the freedmen. See John C. Murphy, *An Analysis of the Attitudes of American Catholics toward the Immigrant and the Negro, 1825–1925* (Vol. I of Catholic University of America Studies in Sociology, 1940). The title is misleading. There is almost no treatment of Irish attitudes toward the Negro in the nineteenth century, attitudes that were generally extremely hostile.

the radical Republicans "would not assert the superior rights of the negroes born in this country over foreigners?" According to the Philadelphia *Age*, a radical plan to disfranchise white immigrants was already part of the Republican program.[31]

Although many Republicans were indeed frequently inconsistent and equivocal on the issue, their resistance to universal suffrage would not compare to that of most Democrats. In the first place, Republican resistance never became a sustained crusade, with racism an essential ingredient of the party's national campaigns or platforms. In the second place, Republican anti-Negro-suffrage actions were, chronologically and geographically, uneven and sporadic. Radical suggestions that educational requirements be adopted, for example, did not usually refer to the northern Negro. Finally, after the passage of the Reconstruction Acts in 1867 and the ratification of the Fourteenth Amendment in 1868, most Republicans said very little against Negro suffrage, although they may still have been opposed to it personally.

Despite the occasional faltering of the Republican party, the fact remains that two of the greatest monuments to human rights—the Fourteenth and Fifteenth Amendments—were the achievements of a government under radical Republican leadership. In retrospect, it is difficult to imagine that they might have been passed at any other time in American history, and their passage becomes even more significant when viewed against the obvious displeasure of the state governments and the general public. It would have been much safer politically to compromise the Negro's civil rights. But the radicals did not compromise. And in the face of blistering criticisms that have echoed for a century, the Constitution was enlarged to guarantee "equal protection of the laws" to all men in all sections, a guarantee that, ironically, more white men than Negroes have probably availed themselves of.

Furthermore—and this is a point that may have been more important than most historians have realized—there were Republican leaders who recognized their prejudice for what it was and did not let it get in the way of their desire to see justice done. One scholar has identified Benjamin F. Wade, an Ohio radical, as such a person. On many occasions, Wade made no secret of his dislike for Negroes, especially his distaste for social contacts with them; but this did not blind him to the cause of human rights. Indeed, Wade "acted in accordance not with what his baser emotions influenced him to do, but with what his intelligence taught him to be true."[32] If such an explanation had merit for one person, it may well have applied to others in similar positions. Many of the others, however, lacked the strength to ignore their prejudices and support serious impartial suffrage drives. Local Republican leaders helped defeat the impartial suffrage proposals in referendums not by speaking against them but by failing to take a strong stand for them.*

Nevertheless, when the time came, most Republicans followed their leaders forward. In the early months of the postwar period, the radical faction of the Republican party was still a small minority; but it counted among its members some of the most aggressive and resolute members of Congress, including Senators Sumner, Wade, Richard Yates of Illinois, and Zachariah Chandler of Michigan, and Representatives James M. Ashley of Ohio, George S. Boutwell of Massachusetts, George W. Julian of Indiana, and, most important of all, Thaddeus Stevens of Pennsylvania. The radicals took the initiative on reconstruction, and by 1867 controlled the program. Though the radicals had their differences, they clearly shared at least two fundamental beliefs: that the Congress—not the President—had to formulate and implement reconstruction policies, and that the defeated South should not be let off lightly.

To test their strength in Congress as well as to squelch the complaint that the federal government was encroaching on state prerogatives, the radicals decided to urge passage of an impartial suffrage law for the District of Columbia. They represented a minority view and they knew it, but they also knew that a successful fight here would considerably brighten their hopes for the future. The drive to give the ballot to the District's Negroes was surprisingly long and arduous. At every step of the way it met strenuous opposition—which ranged from furious criticism in the racist press to a presidential veto. The District suffrage bill, H. R. No. 1, was introduced in the fall of 1865, in the opening session of the Thirty-Ninth Congress, but the real fight over it did not begin until the following January. In the debate, the opponents resurrected virtually every white supremacy argument ever used against the Negro. In a speech on the House floor, Rogers asked if thousands of white soldiers had died in order to "inflict" upon the residents of the Capital the "monstrous doctrine" of equality at the ballot box.[33]

On January 7, 1867, well over a year after the measure was first introduced, Johnson vetoed the bill. In his veto message, the President

---

* John H. and Lawanda Cox have suggested that much of the criticism of Republican hypocrisy is unjustified, and that many of the northern Negro suffrage referendums that failed did so despite serious Republican efforts on their behalf, not because of a Republican unwillingness to act. See "Negro Suffrage and Republican Politics: The Problem of Motivation in Reconstruction Historiography," *JSH*, XXXIII (Aug. 1967), 328–329.

forcefully but vainly argued that the Negroes of the District were not ready for the ballot. Giving it to them now, he contended, would only degrade and eventually destroy the privilege of voting. Moreover, since one-third of the city's population already was black and since impartial suffrage would attract the thousands who lived in its outskirts, the District would soon come under the control and domination of the Negro race. "It is within their power, in one year," the President concluded, "to come into the District in such numbers as to have the supreme control of the white race, and to govern [it] by their own officers." Van Evrie or Cox could not have said it better. The following day, while the New York *World* and the Philadelphia *Age* were praising the President for his courage and integrity, both houses of Congress voted to override his veto. Exactly one year later in a rousing speech before the Indiana State Democratic Convention, Senator Hendricks tried to show that the President's morose predictions were coming true; he blamed the District's suffrage law for forcing white people visiting the Capital to "transact their district business with negro officials, and if brought into court, to be tried by negro jurors."[34] There was, of course, no Negro control in the District of Columbia, and Hendricks knew it. He also knew that the governing body of the National Capital was the Congress, in which the voters of the District had no representation, and that the vast majority of his listeners in Indianapolis would never get to Washington to see for themselves; hence it mattered little if his remarks were untrue.

One development in the debate over Negro suffrage that many equalitarians had probably not anticipated was the emergence of the women's suffrage issue as a racist theme. For the two or three decades preceding the Civil War, the issue of women's rights had had to compete for attention with the antislavery movement—not to mention several lesser causes. Though they supported the principle of women's suffrage, many abolitionists had believed that the drive to emancipate the slaves would be weakened by attention to other matters and thus had discouraged feminist actions. The result was that the few equalitarians who had continued to carry the banner for women's rights were mostly the women themselves—Elizabeth Cady Stanton, Lucretia Mott, Antoinette Brown Blackwell, and others—who, recognizing that they were the largest group of non-voting second-class Americans with "masters," refused to accept the Negro-first approach of most reformers.

With emancipation finally accomplished, then, it should not have been surprising to see a resurgence of interest in feminism—and the racists, exploiting the widespread male belief that women also had their "place," made every effort to capitalize on it. However, in their effort to find another way to embarrass the radicals, they usually disagreed on just how to exploit feminism. Some held that a member of an inferior race—a Negro—should not have a right that a member of a superior race—a white woman—did not enjoy. Others pointed out that the white woman and the Negro were both dependent on white men for home, security, and happiness, and that their providers had the right to speak for them. A few racists argued that if Negroes received the ballot, then so too should the white women, thereby trying to link the two issues in the minds of those already opposed to female suffrage (who, except for that small coterie of hard-core reformers, were virtually all of the white men in America), and thus add to their own ranks. For example, the Detroit *Free Press* lampooned the Philadelphia Women's League, whose members, "in pantaloons and otherwise," cried for universal suffrage. If "Alabama Joe" was good enough to vote, the editor said, "Miss Dinah" was good enough too; and in the Senate, Garrett Davis asked how the advocates of Negro suffrage could say that black men would be more competent voters than "their mothers, their wives, their sisters, and their daughters?"[35]

The racist's linking of the two suffrage issues was also a peculiar modification of his exaltation of white womanhood. "Why place the ballot in the hands of the ignorant negro," the Indianapolis *State Sentinel* asked, "and prohibit the intelligent white woman from exercising the same privilege?" The Philadelphia *Age* and the Chicago *Times* agreed that it certainly would be more "manly and chivalrous" to work for female suffrage than for the "stalwart, greasy negro." Stumping in West Virginia during the summer of 1868, Thurman claimed that Negro suffrage would place black men on a higher political plane than the white wives, mothers, and daughters of the North.[36] It was not so much the content of the critic's remarks that revealed his desire to arouse his male listeners as it was his style and choice of words—his frequent allusions to "wife," "mother," "daughter," "sister," or "sweetheart." Thus the white womanhood symbol, the extremist's ultimate weapon in the miscegenation and social equality controversies, found a place, however feeble, in the resistance to Negro suffrage.

Although expressions like Thurman's implied an endorsement of female suffrage, most racists explicitly opposed giving the ballot to women. They simply took the position that since the white woman was obviously not worthy of the ballot, neither was the black man. In 1867, Thomas Hartley, a conservative Republican, published a long but relatively dispassionate pamphlet, "Universal Suffrage—Female Suffrage," which gave the rationale for this general view. Hartley based his argument on the assumption that female vanity would prevent most women from exercising mature judgment on political matters; and that to give them or Negroes the vote would be to invite corrupt demagogues into office by putting political power in the hands of people—children, as it were—who would be influenced by emotions and caprice, rather than by serious intellectual reflection. In agreeing with Hartley, racists cited as evidence of the female's lack of political acumen the fact that the most active feminists had also been in the extreme wing of the antislavery movement. To the white supremacy fanatics, of course, there was no more despicable recommendation.[37]

The vulgarity of some racist criticism of the feminists revealed the superior attitudes of many white men toward women generally. In the conventional nineteenth-century order of things, the woman's "place" was in the home. Accordingly, female reformers, outspoken and aggressive, did not conform to the typical white man's idea of feminine domesticity. To the Detroit *Free Press*, such women were "spiritualists, bloomers, amalgamationists, free lovers, and other worshippers of latter-dayisms." Helper called them "white hermaphrodites who personate [sic] women"; in his view, they, like Indians, Negroes, and other "swarthy numbskulls," were "utterly unfit" to participate in political affairs. Implying that they were often lesbians, Helper lamented the "public notoriety, scandal, and disgrace" of the "amazonian interference" that "has its home in the breasts of those (if, indeed, they have breasts at all) who are destitute of all the finer and purer qualities of true ladyship."[38]

Aware that an endorsement of female suffrage would probably hurt their cause more than help it, Republican supporters of Negro suffrage generally discouraged, and at times openly disapproved, any such action. In Kansas the Republican party controlled the state government, but in 1867 the voters defeated by a two-to-one margin amendments to remove the words "white" and "male only" from the suffrage article of the state constitution. In the actual voting, the Republicans split their vote on each amendment, and the Democrats voted solidly against both. Zealous suffragettes occasionally gave even the radicals an uncomfortable moment. In 1866, Elizabeth Cady Stanton asked why intelligent white women of property were not considered as worthy of the ballot as semibarbarous ex-slaves. The Democrats, watching the radicals squirm, were amused. In general, the merits of female suffrage were regarded so lightly that, according to the *Free Press*, even Negroes disapproved. "Poor Susannah," the editor wrote, "what will become of her if Sambo and Cuffee turn against her?"[39]

More significant than the female suffrage issue, and certainly more expected, was the thorny question of the status of the Orientals in the Far West. If the Negroes in the North and South received the ballot, then the Chinese in the West could expect it also. Though western racists frequently included in their complaints the Japanese (whose numbers were negligible) and the Indians (who were not Orientals, but were still classed as "pagans" or "heathens"), it was the Chinese in California who presented the major "threat." "At length," a California state senator exclaimed after hearing that President Ulysses S. Grant had acknowledged the Chinese problem, "our master in the White House has spared one moment from the contemplation of his Black Agony on the Gulf to a consideration of our Yellow Agony on the Slope!"[40]

The Negro population of the Far West was insignificant. Moreover, none of the western states bordered on an area with a sizable Negro population. Yet some of the most vulgar racist expressions of the 1860's came from western critics. Westerners were, in a sense, the most "complete" white supremacists in the nation, because they were against everyone—Chinese, Japanese, Indians, Mexicans, and, largely for the sake of agreement with eastern racists, Negroes. "We not only have the negro," California State Senator John S. Hager said in arguing against the ratification of the Fifteenth Amendment, "but the digger Indian, the Kanaka, the New Zealander, the Lascar, and the Chinese." If the radicals in Washington, D. C., "who see so much that is sublime and beautiful in the African, could only see our greater variety here," the beauty and sublimity of it would overwhelm them, he said.[41]

California's population was indeed a mixture. An 1867 state census counted 478,000 whites, 5,000 Negroes (including mulattoes), 60,000 Chinese, and 7,000 "domestic and wild" Indians. The Chinese minority was not large—about 11 per cent of the total—but it was concentrated in a few locations: San Francisco, the Sacramento–San Joaquin delta region, and some of the northeastern mining areas. In addition, by clustering together in their own little communities, the Chinese aroused particular suspicion. A sizable minority of European immigrants strengthened the general anti-Chinese attitude. Lured to California during the gold-rush period, the immigrants included Germans, Swedes,

Britons, Scots, Irish, Welsh, French, Danes, Russians, Italians, Australians, and Spaniards. Though they had no more "right"to the country than the Chinese, they nonetheless shared the common Anglo-Saxon notion that the New World and all its riches belonged exclusively to the conquering Caucasians. Nowhere was this notion more vividly recorded than in a conversation in the early 1870's between English traveler William Hepworth Dixon and an unskilled Irish immigrant in San Francisco.

> "Tell me, Pat, have you any rows with these Chinese?" I ask the servant in my room at the Grand Hotel.
> "No, Captain," says Pat; "would you have me demane meeself by jumping on a dirty thing in a pig-tail?"
> "But he lowers the rate of the wages in the docks and yards."
> "Bad lick to him—the skunk! Before he showed his dirty face in Market-street, a man could earn his six dollars a day. Now he gets no more nor two. . . . If it were not for soiling one's hands, I'd like to squash them head and heels into the bay—just there by Hunter's Point."
> "You don't say, Live and let live, eh, Pat?"
> "Live! Why, Captain, he's a heathen Chinee; a real heathen Chinee! What business has the loikes of him over here? Is not Chinay big enough for him?"
> "Come, Pat, haven't you come over from County Cork?"
> "That's thrue, Captain; but then the country's ours. We conquered it from the Injuns and the Mexicans. Let the Chinese try to conquer it from us!"[42]

Anti-Chinese prejudice also cut sharply across party lines in the West. In 1869, the California Republican State Convention passed a resolution simultaneously supporting the proposed Fifteenth Amendment, belittling the significance of the Negro issue in politics, pledging full protection of the law to "inoffensive immigrants from China," and emphatically opposing suffrage for the Chinese "in any form." Between 1868 and 1870, other protests against Oriental suffrage came from Republicans and Democrats in Nevada, Oregon, and the Territory of Washington; and racists in the Territory of Nebraska included Indians in their pleas against universal suffrage.[43] In 1871, the California Supreme Court upheld a state law that prohibited Chinese from testifying in trials involving whites. Justice Jackson Temple ruled that the law was not a violation of the equal protection clause of the Fourteenth Amendment as the appellant had contended, and stated that there even seemed to be some question whether the federal government had jurisdiction in such matters.[44]

In cases that got as far as the federal government, the Chinese in California received somewhat better treatment. United States Supreme

Court Justice Stephen J. Field, serving on the Circuit Court in September 1874, ruled that the State of California had violated the Fourteenth Amendment in its order to deny entry to and deport a Chinese woman named Ah Fong. The state may have had the right to exclude individuals of questionable moral background, he pointed out, but the case against Ah Fong was patently discriminatory. According to Field's decision, since the Fourteenth Amendment referred to "persons" without distinguishing between citizens and aliens, the state had denied a "person" within its jurisdiction due process and equal protection of the laws.[45] But the justice was simply interpreting the letter of the law; his personal views on the question of the Orientals in California were clearly racist. In a letter to the editor of the San Francisco *Morning Call*, Field agreed with an article charging that the Chinese presence was a menace to the security of all Californians and that some means had to be found to restrict it.[46]

Obviously, the Westerner had an aversion to the Chinese that existed long before there was any question of sharing political rights. Feelings against Orientals had been strong since the 1850's. Many discouraged and frustrated miners abandoned their low-yield diggings and afterward watched Chinese come in and extract riches that they themselves had been too impatient to sweat over. In addition, the Chinese prospector's frugality exasperated many merchants and traders who made their fortunes by "mining the miners." Later, when the Central Pacific Railroad Company imported thousands of new Chinese, their presence aggravated an already festering sore.

Without a political voice, these quiet foreigners, aloof and unobtrusive, were at the mercy of their white neighbors and the white courts. The possibility and then the probability of equality at the polls suddenly threatened to change all that. In June 1869, delegates to the California State Democratic Convention angrily denounced the proposed Fifteenth Amendment on the grounds that it would enable Negroes and Chinese to hold public office. Southern whites could be represented by men with such "high sounding names as Senator Caesar and Congressman Pompey," State Senator Hager sarcastically complained, but Californians would have to be content to elect men "with less illustrious but no less euphonious names, such as Senator Chy Lung and Congressman Tong Achick." Dixon gloomily observed that the Chinese, with their enormous capacity for reproduction, would soon number six hundred thousand. If they got the ballot they could easily hold the balance of power, he said. "In some districts they will make a majority, selecting the judges, forming the juries, interpreting the laws." The consequence, he concluded, would be a war of races between those who "feed on beef" and those who "thrive on rice."[47] Although most critics were less pessimistic, they made similar predictions in order to frighten their audiences. The fear of race war was therefore not exclusively southern nor did it always refer to Negroes.

For mixed reasons, many Easterners and Midwesterners were similarly fearful of the Chinese "threat." In a speech in Philadelphia, Jeremiah S. Black included "Tartars, Mongols, [and] Chinese" in his racist remarks. The New York *World*, in an article entitled "John Chinaman Next," speculated that since the slaves were now free, the abolitionists would soon turn their attention to the Chinese in the West, and other Democrats shared this expectation. At the New York Democratic State Convention in 1868, Samuel J. Tilden warned against the dangers of mixed races from Mexico, of Chinese swarming all over the Pacific slopes, and even of Indians demanding political rights. After the election, Henry Clay Dean, predicting a "great flood" of African and Mongolian races "to be let in upon us to destroy the country and scandalize the right to vote," echoed Tilden's view. Speaking at Terre Haute, Representative Daniel W. Voorhees of Indiana predicted that the "Chinaman," the Japanese, and the "Gipsey" would follow the Negro to the polls. If the Chinese got the vote, the Columbus *Crisis* warned, they would "overthrow the civilization of the Pacific Coast with the barbarism of the oldest and worst countries [*sic*] on the globe." Sambo's " 'wool' will give way to the pig-tail," said the *Crisis*.[48]

Anti-Chinese propaganda, like most racist propaganda, soon grew muddled and contradictory. Some critics, to illustrate the Negroes' "degradation," actually praised the Chinese. The Detroit *Free Press* extolled the Chinese for their family loyalty, their industriousness, their advanced civilization, and their self-reliance. They were not not "barbarians like the subjects of the King of Dahomey," the *Free Press* declared. Even Hager asked, "If we extend suffrage to the African, how can we refuse it to the Chinese? They are superior as a race to the African; [and] have maintained a government and attained a civilization superior to [that of] the negro." "Such a race could *fully* blend with our own," another anti-Negro writer stated in 1869. "Here is where the true sense of the expression, 'unity of the races,' is made clear," he continued, "but with the negro it is not 'unity' in any sense, nor can it ever be." In an attack on the Republican senators from California, Oregon, and Nevada, Hendricks spoke glowingly of the highly developed culture of the Chinese people. But in spite of this, he said, "Nevada does not want the Chinaman, and she does want the

colored man to vote. She has no colored people, but she has Chinamen."
It suited the purposes of western Republicans to extend the ballot to
Negroes, he concluded; it did not suit their purposes to extend it to
other races.[49]

Aware of the strong western hostility to the Chinese, eastern Republicans tried hard to avoid a controversy that might divide the party.
Groups like the National Labor Union, the Settlers' League, and the
National Labor Congress pressured the government to oppose Chinese
immigration; the Republicans found it easier to justify this opposition
after southern planters began to recruit Oriental field hands. For these
and other reasons, and knowing that they did not need the Chinese vote
to ensure a Republican "ascendancy," Congress passed a law that denied
naturalization to foreign-born Chinese. Since citizenship was a requirement for the ballot, and since almost all of the Chinese were foreign-
born, the western racists were among the most successful in American
history. T. Thomas Fortune, the Negro editor of the New York *Globe*,
wrote sadly in 1884 that in the United States shelter and protection
were given to people from all over the world—except the African and
"the industrious Chinaman, who was barred out by the over-
obsequiousness of the Congress of the nation, in deference to the sand-
lot demagogues of the Pacific Coast, headed by Dennis Kearney, because
it was desirable to conciliate their votes, even at the expense of consistency and the unity of the Constitution."[50]

It was five years from the introduction of the District of Columbia
suffrage bill in 1865 to the ratification of the Fifteenth Amendment in
1870. In view of the aggressiveness of the radical Republicans on most
other matters, it is not unreasonable to ask why it took them so long
to win the fight for a constitutional amendment to give the vote to the
black men of America. The answer to this question is entangled in the
whole complex issue of congressional reconstruction policies. The reconstructed state governments of the South, with the enforcement of
federal bayonets, had been extending the ballot to the freedmen without
a constitutional mandate; while the radicals, at least through the election of 1868, preferred to sidestep the issue of impartial suffrage on a
nationwide basis in order to avoid antagonizing northern voters. Thus,
the delay was the result of both the success of Negro suffrage in the
South and political expediency in the North. It should not be forgotten
that if it had not been for the votes of the southern Negroes, Ulysses S.
Grant might have lost the presidential election of 1868.

When the resolution proposing an amendment was finally introduced

in 1869, white supremacists both inside and outside the Congress re-
doubled their efforts. The Columbus *Crisis* denounced the measure as
a "bogus amendment" and a "nigger superiority bill" that would bring
Ohio face to face with mongrelism. Senator Saulsbury of Delaware led
the antiamendment forces in Congress, and Democratic spokesmen
across the country predicted all sorts of calamities if the states ratified
the measure. Likewise, in approving or rejecting the amendment, state
legislatures followed party lines closely—Republicans voted for it,
Democrats against. In fact, shortly after ratification, following elections
that shifted control of state legislatures from Republicans to Democrats,
a few legislatures attempted, unsuccessfully, to rescind or withdraw
earlier ratifications; New York tried it in 1870, and Indiana in 1871.[51]

"With the ratification of the Fifteenth Amendment," Clemenceau
wrote in the spring of 1870, "the American revolution is over." He
was convinced that the "heart" of reconstruction had been the question
of suffrage, and now the issue was settled for the entire nation. If the
two parties would get together on this "capital question," he had
written two years earlier, "one important cause of disagreement will
have been removed," and the revolution would be "theoretically accomplished."[52] But Clemenceau was an optimist. With the ratification
of the Fifteenth Amendment, the "capital question" was resolved, and
the revolution was "theoretically accomplished"; but the parties had
not gotten together and the "important cause of disagreement" remained. There were debates over bills for enforcing the amendment,
and as late as 1879 spokesmen for both parties were still arguing whether
the Negro should have been enfranchised.[53]

But many years later, one eloquent ex-slave made all the arguments
seem foolish: "The ballot is the citadel of the colored man's safety,
the guarantor of his liberty, the protector of his rights, the defender of
his immunities and privileges, the savior of the fruits of his toil, his
weapon of offense and defense, his peacemaker, his Nemesis that watches
and guards over him with sleepless eye by day and by night."[54] Unfortunately, his picture of the ballot was a dream. Through a variety of
both insidious and overt devices, American white supremacists continued to deny the black man de facto what he had been granted de
jure; and the general public was largely indifferent. The racists reacted
to the Fifteenth Amendment in essentially the same way they had
reacted to the Thirteenth and Fourteenth Amendments—they found
ways to circumvent the law. Literacy tests, poll taxes, "grandfather
clauses," and eventually intimidation and social and economic pressures were to succeed where legislation had failed.

Chapter Six

RADICAL RECONSTRUCTION
AND THE AFRICANIZATION
OF THE SOUTH

> Oh! if I was a nigger,
> I'd do just as I please,
> And when I took a pinch of snuff,
> All Yankeedom would sneeze.
> Then Congress too would worship me,
> And bow down at my feet,
> And swear that since the world began,
> There was nothing half so sweet.[1]

The debate over the status of the postwar South began long before the first Reconstruction Act, which was passed on March 2, 1867. Louisiana, for example, had been under military occupation since the spring of 1862; and two years later its loyal white citizens had approved a new state constitution under Lincoln's "ten per cent" plan. With the primary purpose of restoring the seceded states to their proper place in the Union as quickly as possible, Lincoln stipulated that whenever in any state a total number of voters equal to one-tenth of the votes cast in that state in the presidential election of 1860 should take an oath of allegiance to the United States and establish a state government with the abolition of slavery, the state would receive immediate presidential recognition. (Whether the radicals in Congress would go along with this was another question; but it was a collision with the Congress that the President wanted to avoid, hence his willingness to forgo majority rule for the sake of speed.)

As the war progressed, speculation over the course that reconstruction would follow increased. In February 1863, Representative James A. Rollins of Missouri, reflecting the view of many northern conservatives who believed that the South should be allowed to reestablish its own state and local governments without federal interference, complained that there was "a great deal of talk [in the Congress] about the reconstruction of southern society, of infusing into the minds of the people there northern ideas and sentiments, of giving them the basis of a new population." A few months later, barely two weeks after he had commanded the Union Army's V Corps at Gettysburg, Major-General George Sykes, claiming to represent the "conservative portion of the Army," insisted that whatever reconstruction took place, slavery would "remain as it was."[2] But the following year congressional radicals expressed their displeasure with the President's leniency by passing the Wade-Davis bill with its "iron-clad" test oath. This plan provided that a majority of white male citizens enrolled by a provisional governor had to take an oath to support the Constitution of the United States, and that in order to vote for delegates to the state constitutional convention, the voters had to swear that they had never held state or Confederate office during the rebellion, and had never borne arms against the United States or aided its enemies. Fundamentally, the Lincoln plan was based on a minority promise of future allegiance, while the Wade-Davis proposal called for a majority recognition of past loyalty.

Although the President pocket-vetoed the Wade-Davis bill, the debate over reconstruction intensified. What did all northern "thinking men" propose to do with "millions of homeless negroes?" Representative George Bliss of Ohio asked three months before the end of the war. Surely the government could not encourage them to move north, he added, or "enfranchise them with political equality." Speaking in Ohio, William M. Dickson, a Republican, maintained that "the votes of the black men will be too valuable to be slighted." Moreover, he argued, since the white man eventually had to yield "to power and interest," the practical realties of political life would compel him to overcome his personal emotions.[3]

Surprisingly, Southerners often appeared the least concerned of all. Acting under President Johnson's Proclamation of Amnesty and Reconstruction, conservative state governments set up sweeping black codes during the summer and fall of 1865, and found their own way of dealing with the race problem. "It remains for the people" through their legislatures and at their conventions "to define the status of the emancipated slaves," William W. Holden announced in Raleigh, North

Carolina, before accepting an appointment as provisional governor. "I, for one, have no fear in this regard," he stated. "I am willing to see the alphabet, the Bible, and the school book placed in their hands, and to recognize among them the marriage relations heretofore so culpably disregarded. The extent of their further elevation belongs legitimately to the governing race."[4]

The vast majority of southern whites simply took it for granted that the black race would remain subordinate to the white in every respect, and thus it is not surprising that the extent of its "further elevation" was not very great. Dealing with almost every aspect of the freedman's existence, the black codes in some states confined Negro land ownership to the country, and in other states to the towns. The Negro's rights in court varied from state to state, but generally he was not entitled to the same treatment as a white defendant or witness and in some states he could testify only in cases exclusively involving Negroes. To ensure individual responsibility, the codes outlined apprenticeship and work regulations and the terms of contracts, marriages, and family relations. A law in Mississippi that allowed sheriffs to hire out the labor of vagrant Negroes who could not pay their fines became especially controversial in the North because it appeared to be a step toward the re-enslavement of the blacks. The fact that virtually any Negro could be classified as a vagrant—including gamblers, peddlers, entertainers, beggars, prostitutes, panderers, and unemployed persons—gave local authorities broad powers for controlling and suppressing the undesirable members of the black population.

According to benevolent (and optimistic) white Southerners, these laws were also for the Negro's protection because they forced him to fulfill agreements, to maintain a home for his family, and to seek and secure employment. Discouraging vagrancy and idleness by restricting his mobility, they were supposed to fortify his sense of responsibility to both his family and his neighbors. To keep masses of indigent ex-slaves from flooding the towns, some states required the former slave-owners to continue caring for Negroes who were unable to work; and there were also codes that provided some welfare for orphans, the sick, and the aged. Of course, white Southerners often added as an after-thought, the black codes also protected innocent whites from lawless Negroes.[5]

In practice, however, the codes were designed primarily to benefit and protect the whites. The provisions designed to safeguard the freed-men were more nominal than real. For example, in some states a servant whose rights were not respected by his master could leave the master's service voluntarily. But if the master decided to take advantage of the law that prohibited a servant from being absent from the premises without permission, who would the local magistrate most likely believe? In other states planters were prohibited from evicting helpless former slaves, but there were also laws against trespassing and laws requiring Negro occupants to have leases. What was to prevent a planter from calling a helpless former slave a trespasser, or from challenging an occupant's lease? Masters of Negro apprentices were required to provide food, clothing, and training, but the apprenticeship was often compulsory. If the master did not fulfill his obligation, to whom could an unwilling apprentice complain? Indeed, if any state or local agency decided to ignore the laws that were ostensibly for the Negro's benefit, to whom could an impoverished, ignorant, illiterate black man appeal? The Negroes of the South, in economic and political limbo, were barely one step away from chattel slavery. Though freedmen gathered in several places to protest, the outlook for relief was grim. The only agency they could appeal to was the Freedmen's Bureau, but this was a temporary, wartime organization, created to last for a year after the war's end; in February 1866, the President vetoed a bill to extend its services indefinitely.

All of this had a profound influence on the attitudes of northern whites, both in and out of the government. Though many Republicans had opposed the extreme proposals of Stevens and Sumner, and the majority opinion had been, for a while, with the racists, the severity of the black codes, the incorrigibility of southern militants, Johnson's almost obsequious leniency toward former rebel leaders, and his intransigence in the face of modest congressional proposals for alleviating the Negroes' suffering soon alienated many northern conservatives. Republicans in general did not object so much to the President's veto of the Freedmen's Bureau bill as to the "tone and reasoning" of his veto message, George L. Prentiss, a New York clergyman, observed. Furthermore, Prentiss pointed out, the moderate Republicans were angered, and the old proslavery and Copperhead leaders were delighted, when it looked as if "the negro was going to be abandoned by the President and handed over, before long, to the unchecked control of his former masters." Moreover, as David Macrae, a European traveler, noted, it was only when the southern states began to select as their local and federal officials men who represented the old "secesh" element that Northerners said "this will never do." According to Macrae, Republicans finally decided that the former rebel states had to divest themselves of all disloyal interests, and came to believe that since "the white people will not elect loyal men, we must allow the negroes to do it." In the end, moderate Republicans such as Lyman Trumbull of Illinois, at first unwilling to endorse drastic measures and then confused and angered by the President's lack of cooperation, felt compelled to cast their lot with the radicals.[6]

There were many reasons for the extremity of the radical program, not the least of which was retribution. Many Northerners wanted to avenge the deaths of sons, husbands, fathers, and brothers; thus the bloody shirt became a symbol of vengeance and a banner for political action. There were, of course, less emotional motives behind the radical program: one was to secure the political expatriation of the secessionist leaders in the South, another was to consolidate the gains of a centralized, industrialized economy by giving northern entrepreneurs the inside track to southern resources, especially coal, iron, and transportation, and a third was to mobilize the black vote in order to guarantee what Stevens is said to have called the "perpetual ascendancy" of the Republican party. In addition, the party was by this time committed to some kind of equality for the Negro—it had to go beyond emancipation. The black man, first as a slave and then as a convenient war symbol, had been part of the Republican image since the days of the Kansas-Nebraska Act. The party could not abandon the Negroes, Clemenceau observed, and retain its primary reason for existing. "So it will have to make a plea that the freedmen of the South be given the right to vote." And Macrae corroborated Clemenceau's view, saying, "Events have only pushed Republicanism forward to consistency." Finally, it should not be forgotten that there were Northerners who wanted to win for the ex-slave all the rights and privileges of citizenship, as well as the ordinary comforts and pleasures of human existence. Unfortunately, this motive—the humanitarian one—sometimes was given as a reason for actions that were not humanitarian at all.[7]

The racists, however, were not interested in what motivated the radicals; all they knew was that the nation was "plunging into madness and folly." To them, the most alarming aspect of the radicals' program was the proposal to enfranchise the ex-slaves. According to the 1860 census, two southern states, South Carolina and Mississippi, had black majorities. By 1870, Louisiana had probably become the third; the census taken in that year showed a slight Negro majority in Louisiana, but the census was known to be inaccurate for both races. The Negro populations of the other southern states in 1870 ranged from 48.8 per cent in Florida to 25.2 per cent in Arkansas. Three states—Alabama,

Georgia, and Virginia—had, like Florida, populations that were more than 40 per cent Negro.[8] It was obvious from the outset, then, that any plans to enfranchise the freedmen in the fifteen former slave states, unlike similar plans in the North, would involve vast numbers of blacks. For the first time, the racist demagogue had an issue that was both colossal and real. Estimating the number of eligible Negro voters of the South at eight hundred thousand, which was roughly one-fifth of the southern black population, Thomas W. Hartley argued that when so many ex-slaves were involved "considerations of mere temporary expediency, of mere party advantage, fall paralyzed to the ground." Northerners who refused to grant impartial suffrage in their own states, he continued, were now forcing it upon others "by the bushel." "A little retail negro suffrage here, where it can do little harm, is denied," remarked Samuel S. Cox in Brooklyn; "wholesale negro suffrage there is enforced where it is supreme."[9]

According to most critics, if the freedmen were given the ballot, their appalling ignorance would ultimately destroy the democratic process in the South. Many ex-slaves, they complained, had never heard of the candidates they were asked to support. Others allegedly could not identify their home county or give their exact ages. A few critics went so far as to claim that some of the blacks were of such low intelligence that they had trouble remembering their own names. After interviewing an illiterate field hand in Georgia, Whitelaw Reid said it was regrettable that the vote would be given to men of such low intelligence. And in October 1865, only a few months after his own election, Tennessee's noisy Governor William G. Brownlow claimed that impartial suffrage would "open the ballot-box to the uninformed and exceedingly stupid slaves of the Southern cotton, rice, and sugar fields."[10] Although Brownlow was obviously referring to those Negroes in the black-belt states, he did not exclude his own state. Brownlow's opposition to Negro suffrage was based primarily on his fear that the freedmen's ignorance would make it easy for the hated planters to control them, especially in the deep South.* Unquestionably, there was staggering ignorance among the vast majority of the freedmen, but this was also true of the southern poor whites, most of whom had the right to vote.

---

* Although Brownlow supported slavery as late as 1861, he was also rabidly anti-secessionist, and for this reason his eastern Tennessee newspaper was suppressed by Confederate authorities and he was even imprisoned for several months for suspected complicity in bridge burnings. These experiences evidently embittered Brownlow so much that he became a militant supporter of radical Republican reconstruction policies.

White Southerners were almost naïvely confident that northern public opinion would not permit Congress to force Negro suffrage on the South. They based their confidence in part on the truculent words of northern racists like Hartley who said, "judging by myself, and comparing the limited extent of my prejudice against the colored race with that of the generality of the Northern people, I do not believe that the people of the North will allow large armies to be raised for any such unfair and oppressive purpose." More significant than declarations like Hartley's were the returns from the state elections in the North, which seemed to justify southern optimism; and the Democratic party's surprising show of strength in such Republican strongholds as Maine, New Hampshire, and Minnesota was especially encouraging. A month after the election of 1867, white conservatives in Little Rock pledged that they would "preserve the principles of the national Constitution by co-operating with the Democratic party of the Union." The "astonishing results" of the recent elections throughout the North, they added, gave Southerners a public mandate to help Democrats and conservatives everywhere defeat the radical drive "to destroy our old constitutional government and set up in its place one in which others than white men shall have the controlling influence." Democrats in Louisiana met in 1868, and on the basis of the same elections expressed confidence that northern Democrats would not let them down.[11]

Nevertheless, other southern whites were not as optimistic as their neighbors. Refusing to take heart from northern elections, they displayed genuine fear over possible Negro enfranchisement. In fact, there were signs during the early months of radical reconstruction that some southern whites, sensing the inevitable, hoped to capitalize on the black vote and recruit it for their own purposes. For example, in February 1866 racial moderates at the Texas Reconstruction Convention proposed a sweeping plan that included three alternative means for extending the ballot to the freedmen. Although such moves never amounted to much, they proved that not all southern whites thought impartial suffrage impossible. In 1879, Wade Hampton, a former Confederate general and later both Governor of South Carolina and a United States Senator, boasted that during the 1860's he had been the first white man in the South to recommend Negro suffrage, and that many "intelligent and reflecting whites" had agreed with him.[12]

Such endorsements of Negro suffrage by southern whites were, of course, examples of political expediency. The opportunity to control a large bloc of Negro votes and thereby continue the planter's domination of southern economic and political life appealed to more than a few former slaveowners, and many people were well aware of it. Hartley said that if Negroes were granted the ballot he would be "not at all surprised to see the great majority of them voting the ticket of their masters." Governor Brownlow recommended that all the Negroes in Tennessee be removed to a separate territory, arguing that if this were not done, they "would be influenced by leading secessionists to vote against the Government, as they would be largely under the influence of this class of men for years to come, having to reside on and cultivate their lands." Both Thaddeus Stevens and the New York *World*, representatives of opposite ends of the political spectrum, had expressed similar apprehensions, and President Johnson at one time insisted that this was a major reason for his opposition to Negro suffrage.[13]

Though they rarely endorsed impartial suffrage, southern whites did occasionally express sympathy for the freedmen. In December 1867, delegates to a convention of a new Conservative party, meeting in Richmond, resolved to do all they could for the Negroes, but insisted that the ballot belonged in the hands of whites only. In April 1868, Democrats at their annual state convention in South Carolina, where Negroes outnumbered whites three to two, were much more generous and expressed a willingness, "when we have the power," to grant the Negroes, "under proper qualifications as to property and intelligence, the right of suffrage."* Even containing these vague conditions, the statement was surprising. Three months later, Democrats in Texas announced their desire to see all of the freedmen protected by the laws of the state. In Louisiana, the Democratic State Central Committee, pleading for the restoration of white rule, even asked the Negro leaders of the state for support, assuring them that they would be treated fairly under an all-white Democratic state government.[14]

In spite of these moves, it was highly unlikely that a Negro-supported white conservative oligarchy would evolve; nevertheless, northern Negro leaders were frightened because they expected Republicans to back down in their demands for Negro suffrage when it looked as if their political power might be threatened by it. In July 1865, delegates to a convention of black men in Philadelphia insisted that there was absolutely no basis for the suspicion that former slaveowners would control the freedman's vote. The Negro could not be made to do, "now that he is free, what he could not be forced to do when a slave," the convention proclaimed. In response to the charge that the Negro's

---

* T. Harry Williams, in "An Analysis of Some Reconstruction Attitudes," *Journal of Southern History*, XII (Nov. 1946), 474, 476–479, has argued that this view has been exaggerated and that the planter class, as a whole, opposed Negro suffrage under any conditions.

ignorance would make him the willing tool of the white Southerner, the delegates pointed scornfully to the class of people the racists themselves appealed to. One needed only to glance at the kind of whites "urged to the polls at every election" by fearful racists, they declared, to realize that the conservative anxiety over the corruption and degradation of the ballot by an ignorant Negro electorate was a "hypocritical and malignant subterfuge." That is, those who claimed to fear a white-planter oligarchy based on a manipulated black vote betrayed themselves by their own appeal to the most ignorant and rowdy whites.[15]

In analyzing the politcial effects of radical reconstruction, there is probably no issue that evokes more criticism, and for which there is less documentary evidence, than that of white disfranchisement. From the moment that Republicans in Congress proposed, as part of the Wade-Davis bill, severe terms for the restoration of political rights for southern whites, critics of the government began to fear that the radicals would try to guarantee Negro rule by denying the ballot to thousands of whites. The Wade-Davis bill, if interpreted strictly, could have conceivably disfranchised every Southern white man, from general to private, who had served in the Confederate army, a number that probably exceeded one million—not to mention additional thousands who had supported the southern cause. One had only to look at the states where the ex-slaves constituted over 40 per cent of the population to see what this could mean—Negro voting majorities in seven of the eleven former Confederate states.

Under the terms of the Reconstruction Act passed on March 2, 1867, all former Confederate officials who were disqualified from holding office by the third section of the Fourteenth Amendment were denied the right to vote, and this provision had to be written into the new state constitutions. The federal commanders of the five military districts established by the law were given sweeping civil powers and authorized to arrange for the calling of constitutional conventions. But the law was vague, left a great deal unsaid as far as the status of the existing state governments was concerned, and ended up doing little more than creating confusion in the South. Thus Congress passed a supplemental act on March 23 that specifically gave federal officials the authority to take the initiative in a number of matters; and a third law passed in July gave them the right to deny registration to anybody who they did not think was taking the required loyalty oath in good faith. At the same time, the provisions for determining just who was ineligible by virtue of service to the Confederacy were modified so as to require less evidence in order to deny registration. Anyone already registered who could not qualify under the new rules was to be removed from the roles.

Unfortunately, the facts of disfranchisement are so incomplete and the statistics so scarce as to almost defy analysis. To begin with, there are no valid figures to show just who was disfranchised or how many were disfranchised under the section of the Fourteenth Amendment imposing political disabilities on former Confederate officials, though the guesses run as high as two hundred thousand.[16] Secondly, in establishing the military districts, Congress did not create an administrative office to coordinate operations, thus there was no central agency to compile data. Consequently, of the ten states that were subject to the terms of the Reconstruction Acts (Tennessee having been restored earlier for ratifying the Fourteenth Amendment), recorded disfranchisements— ranging from 350 in Florida to 16,343 in Virginia, and totalling 47,125— only exist for five, and even they are somewhat suspect. Since there was no standard procedure for keeping the records straight, most of these statistics were submitted in reports by federal officers who had supervised voter registration: the fact that some of them were given in round numbers increases skepticism.[17]

Moreover, the existing figures pertain only to those registered and disfranchised for the purpose of selecting delegates to the several state constitutional conventions. There were many opportunities in later state and local elections for radical officials to deny additional whites the right to vote. Only an exhaustive combing of the registration and election records in all ten states for the years in which the white conservatives did not have control will enable the historian to determine the extent of disfranchisement. Finally, for the five states where only registration figures are available, the student of reconstruction history simply cannot draw any conclusions. Throughout the South except in Alabama, Negro majorities were registered under the Reconstruction Acts only where they outnumbered whites in the general population, which suggests that disfranchisements were not decisive.*

---

* Students of reconstruction history have rarely challenged the traditional argument on disfranchisements. Two articles by William A. Russ, Jr., "The Negro and White Disfranchisement during Radical Reconstruction," *Journal of Negro History*, XIX (Apr. 1934), 171–192, and "Registration and Disfranchisement under Radical Reconstruction," *Mississippi Valley Historical Review*, XXI (Sept. 1934), 163–180, are typical examples. In one, Russ states that "white majorities were cut down or wiped out entirely," a view that has been repeated so many times that few have dared to question it. That such universal opinion could be based on such tenuous and fragmentary evidence is one of the enigmas of reconstruction historiography. A more

But the absence of evidence never restrained the racist. On April 15, 1865, a few hours after Lincoln's death, Van Evrie savagely denounced an alleged abolitionist plot to secure "nigger supremacy" by disfranchising southern whites. It was not just a matter of a few thousand, he insisted; Frederick Douglass and Horace Greeley were determined to enfranchise *all* blacks and disfranchise *all* whites. By 1868, when several of the southern states were well on their way to restoration under radical rule, many racists were convinced that their earlier fears had been justified. The venomous La Crosse (Wisconsin) *Democrat* attacked "black niggers from the cotton fields and the white niggers from New England" for stealing the ballot from respectable southern whites and giving it to illiterate blacks. And in July 1868 the Chicago *Times* stated, "the hideous villainy of the reconstruction infamy lies not in giving the negroes suffrage, but in disfranchising white men and so legislating as to give the negro party ascendancy." A few alarmists even predicted that *northern* whites would lose the vote. On July 23 Samuel S. Cox rhetorically asked a Brooklyn audience: "If Congress can overturn white suffrage South, can it not establish black Suffrage North, and withhold it from the whites? If the States South have not the sovereign power in this regard, have the States North?" A few days later, editor Wilbur Storey of the Chicago *Times* accused one Anthony O. Hesing of being the leader of a drive, already in progress, to disfranchise northern whites.[18]

Although it is not clear how many southern whites were deprived of the vote, it is clear that a great many of them who could have voted refused to register, or after registering refused to vote. They often refused to vote because, under the first three Reconstruction Acts, the adoption of a new state constitution required a majority of the registered voters, not simply a majority of the votes cast. Thus it was easier to defeat a proposed constitution by registering and not voting than by voting against it. The fourth Reconstruction Act, passed on March 11, 1868, and requiring only a majority of votes cast, remedied this situation. In any case, many whites wallowed in self-pity and complained about the radical grip of Congress when they should have been blaming themselves for it. As arrangements were being made for the various state constitutional conventions under the Reconstruction Acts, the editor of the Charlottesville (Virginia) *Chronicle* bitterly criticized those whites who, "sullen and discontented," had declared that they

recent interpretation is Forrest G. Wood, "On Revising Reconstruction History: Negro Suffrage, White Disfranchisement, and Common Sense," *Journal of Negro History*, LI (Apr. 1966), 98–113.

would refuse to register. Their announcement that they "would prefer military government to negro suffrage" was based on a delusion. To guarantee white control, he insisted, all eligible whites had to register and vote. But such admonitions generally went unheeded. In a typical gesture, almost half the white conservative delegates to the Mississippi Constitutional Convention walked out, to protest an impartial suffrage article.[19]

However, most Southerners lacked even the energy for protest; their general torpor was obvious to many Northerners, including some of the same Copperheads who complained of mass disfranchisements. The editor of the Columbus *Crisis* an avowed opponent of radical recon-struction, denounced those southern whites who, "paralyzed by supine-ness," were just as responsible for the detestable carpetbag governments as the enfranchised blacks. By organizing on Democratic principles, he insisted, the southern whites could easily cast off the radical-Negro yoke—but they refused to do so. In Congress, Senator Aaron H. Cragin, a Republican from New Hampshire, cited the results of the constitu-tional referendums in nine of the ten reconstructed states to show that it was the white voters, not the Negroes, who were responsible for the new state governments. His figures showed that many southern whites apparently supported the radical programs, and that most did nothing. It was within their power to control the elections, but they refused to register, Cragin said; thus, "If a man sleep upon his rights shall he complain if he lose them?"[20] Though it is impossible to know how many southern whites were discouraged from even trying to register because of the threat of being disfranchised, it is clear that many whites were defiant or intimidated, or simply did not care. Whatever the case, they forfeited their right to self-government.

There were numerous reasons for the political abdication of the southern white voter, some so obvious that critics frequently overlooked them. For example, many whites simply could not accept the idea of standing next to a Negro—perhaps one of their own former slaves—at the polls. "God save the people of the South," Representative Andrew Jackson Rogers of New Jersey cried, "from the depradations by which they would be obliged to go to the polls and vote side by side with the negro." In addition, the continuous racist reference to the "savage African" certainly frightened many potential voters. Northern writer J. R. Hayes stated that most whites would "deny themselves the fran-chise, rather than be brought in collision at the polls with a race whose savage fiendishness is well known, and whose weapon of defense is a 'razor.' "[21] Some whites declined to vote in order to avoid an implied recognition of racial equality; others considered their refusal to register an act of protest. To show their contempt for the radicals, they decided to dissociate themselves completely from all things related to reconstruction.

More important, white Southerners shared a feeling of humiliation and disillusionment. Surrounded by the ruins of war, disenchanted over their Lost Cause, stunned by the presence of an army of occupation, and—after putting their faith in men who had led them into a disastrous war—reluctant to become involved in politics and government, many southern whites decided to refrain from participation in political affairs. A defeated, war-weary population, faced with the monumental task of rebuilding a ravaged countryside, had no time for the luxury of partisan politics, and, as Howard K. Beale observed, "remained politically indifferent through the various turns of political fortune."[22]

Since the right to hold public office in America has usually accompanied the right to vote, the racist critics were quick to predict that the ex-slave would elect men of his own race—as ignorant and barbaric as he was—to positions of public trust. And it would not end at the local level, they complained, but would reach up to the highest offices in the land—to the House of Representatives, the Senate, and perhaps even the White House. "Would our Senators allow blacks to sit with them as equals in the Senate?" Montgomery Throop, a New York jurist and legal writer, asked. "Would our Representatives tolerate the presence of black delegations in the House."[23]

Even the most harmless and irrelevant statement provoked angry racist rebukes. After an officer of the Freedmen's Bureau suggested that colonies be established in Florida for all of the ex-slaves, the New York *Daily News* accused the radicals of supporting the idea so that Florida's black senators could sit "cheek by jowl with their *somewhat* colored brethren from Massachusetts!" The New York *World* joked that Frederick Douglass might take John C. Calhoun's old seat in the Senate, "if the race of his mother do not disown in him the part of his white father." The *World* presumed that if Douglass declined, "both the Senatorial seats will be filled by wooly Africans." And "De Intelligent Woter," a cartoon character in the La Crosse *Democrat* said, "I'se gwine to perpose to de gentlum ober dar de ijee ob not havin' none but men ob larnin' in de law in de Leguslater, as I'se hab de ijee ob perposin' for to come to de Leguslater myself."[24]

But there was no laughter from the critics when a Negro actually won an election. After Hiram Revels of Mississippi presented his credentials to the Senate in February 1870, the racist opposition, led by Saulsbury, Garrett Davis, and John Potter Stockton of New Jersey, resurrected scores of old arguments. Stockton insisted that the Senator-elect from Mississippi was not a citizen; and Saulsbury said, "I do not wish to wound the tender sensibilities of the majority. . . . I know how vastly superior in your estimation are the members of this negro race to the members of that race to which you yourselves belong." He later pointed out that the military governor of Mississippi was not the legal and duly-elected chief executive of the state, and hence had no authority to sign Revels's credentials. But the radicals smothered all opposition, and Revels, escorted to the swearing-in ceremony by Senator Wilson of Massachusetts, took his seat.[25]

While poets, songwriters, and cartoonists were making jokes about a Negro president, some critics expressed a genuine fear that the radicals might nominate a Negro vice-presidential candidate, thereby putting a black man only a heartbeat away from the White House. The Detroit *Free Press* noted that the *Anti-Slavery Standard* supported John Mercer Langston, a prominent Ohio Negro, for the 1868 Republican nomination. With the idea catching on among Negroes and "Negro-philists," the *Free Press* continued, "the chances of having a negro Vice-President [are] strong." The Omaha *Weekly Herald* snidely condemned a suggestion by Wendell Phillips that a Negro "should be placed on the radical ticket for the next Vice Presidency," saying that the logical choice was Samuel Wade: "There are no mixed colors in SAMUEL. He is very black and very wooly."[26]

But at the same time, racist critics, in attempts to expose the radical Republicans' hypocrisy, also accused them of discouraging Negro office seekers. Republican leaders, "with professions of Negro suffrage hot in their mouths," a Virginia journalist wrote in 1868, "have been sending advice to southern conventions that Negroes should not run for Congress, or aspire to any conspicuous office; that they should be satisfied to fill the lowest seat in political synagogues." However, if we were to grant universal suffrage, he added, "we must perfect it by universal license to office." Such criticisms were not without their inspirations. In 1869 a bipartisan congressional conference committee, formed to reconcile House-Senate differences on the proposed Fifteenth Amendment, eliminated a section that guaranteed the right to public office. Even the carpetbaggers in South Carolina were beginning to fear the Negro's desire for public office, James S. Pike, a journalist, observed; and the La Crosse *Democrat*'s "Intelligent Woter" was not altogether wrong when he complained, "Dis ijee ob nigro suprimecy is gittin' intirely too much feared an' talked ob and even de Ripublicans was beginning to be scared on it, too."[27]

To most extremists, giving Negroes the right to vote and hold office had only one end—total "Africanization" of the South. The charge of Africanization had many facets, but all of them reflected the fear that the South would become a black man's country, with Negroes in public office, Negroes in places of business and commerce, Negroes in the churches and schools, Negroes controlling every aspect of life. In 1865 and 1866, Democratic organizations in Pennsylvania and Indiana denounced Negro suffrage and the Freedmen's Bureau because they would "Africanize a large portion of the country." At the 1868 Democratic National Convention, the Committee on Resolutions accused the Republican party of trying to Africanize the South by subjecting ten states, "in time of profound peace, to military despotism and negro supremacy." An Alabama delegate underlined the Committee's mood by bringing along an ex-slave in order to show the other delegates the kind of person that the radical Republicans had entrusted with "the political destiny of the South."[28]

Implicit in many of the Africanization charges was the belief that black politicians, once in office, would be beyond the control of white radicals. In its "pursuit of vengeance," Congress dared go only so far, the New York *Herald* argued, "but it delegated its power to the niggers, and they are relied upon to go farther." In a typical racist speech, Ohio's George Pendleton charged that the Republicans had subjugated eight million white people, "flesh of our flesh, blood of our blood," to the "tender mercies of the barbarous African." At the 1868 New York State Democratic Convention in Albany, Tilden added his voice to the growing chorus, speaking of the "untutored negroes" who, "drunk with unusual power and goaded on by bad and designing men," exercized "uncontrolled power" over ten states. Through most of 1867 and 1868, the Detroit *Free Press* regularly published articles on "African domination."[29]

Northern and southern critics, despite their obvious sincerity, based their complaints of Negro political domination on some rather illusory arguments. To begin with, they defined "majority" in a peculiar way. If one used the racists' definition, John R. Lynch, a Negro state legislator in Mississippi, argued, one could credit the Negroes of New York with deciding some presidential elections. As the racists put it, the freedmen did not need a numerical majority in order to enjoy a political majority. Rather, if the total number of eligible Negro voters was greater than the difference between the numbers of white voters registered in each party, the Negroes had a "majority." By voting as a bloc for the candidate who promised them the most, the ex-slaves presumably would have had the balance of power. Though the definition assumed certain preconditions that probably did not exist in any state, North or South, few defenders of the radical program challenged it.

Other types of questionable thinking appeared continuously in the complaints against the government's reconstruction policies. Representative Daniel Voorhees of Indiana claimed that seventy electoral votes from a Negro-dominated South could select a president regardless of how the North voted. "The negroes in Georgia, in their dense barbarity, are to outvote the freemen of Indiana," he claimed. "The negro on the levees of the Mississippi is to drown the voice of the intelligent farmer of the North." The black man would "make the next President." Speaking before the Jackson Central Association in New York City, Horatio Seymour, disregarding the fact that senators represented states rather than populations, declared, "You cannot give three millions of negroes more senators than are allowed to fifteen millions of white men living in New York, Pennsylvania, Ohio, Illinois, Indiana, Wisconsin, Iowa, Kentucky, Missouri, and Michigan."[30] Seymour, of course, did not consider that these same senators would also be representing the white people of the South. Speaking at Leavenworth, Kansas, on July 31, 1868, Francis P. Blair, Jr., with a bewildering display of histrionics, tried to prove that a few million freedmen would have more congressmen than twenty million whites. Subsequently, he attacked the Reconstruction Acts for allegedly making "three millions" of ignorant blacks "supreme over six million of the white race in the South." The congressmen and electoral votes controlled by the ex-slaves would, he said, "overcome the majority against the Radicals in the North, and enable a minority to control a majority in both sections."[31]

Similarly, Democrats in Michigan complained that the radicals, with one-fourth of the electorate, could control the political fortunes of the North; but they declined to explain just how one-fourth could outvote three-fourths. Without proving it with statistics, Thurman and Cox asserted that the freedmen's "balance of power" would lead to black control of all the elections in the South, and, in turn, the nation. The editors of the New York *Herald*, the Detroit *Free Press*, the Philadelphia *Age*, the New York *World*, and the La Crosse *Democrat*, in articles with such titles as "Puritan and the Nigger," "New England Puritan and Southern Negro," and "A Southern Negro Oligarchy over Northern White Free Men," condemned the attempt to commit the welfare of ten states to "a mob of ignorant, brutal, and purchaseable negroes." The South, they said, since it was already decimated, had little to lose; but the North was "fat enough to be worth squeezing and straining." The Reconstruction Acts, James Gordon Bennett insisted, since they gave the Negroes the balance of power, would make a radical president regardless of the votes of northern whites. And Pomeroy charged that the "Rump Star Chamber" hoped to "maintain its reign over the whole Union" by "negroizing" the South.[32]

Another of the racist's favorite tricks was to quote statistics that included very large numbers, perhaps on the theory that the audience would be awed by bigness. Eighteen million northern white voters would be controlled in the Senate, Michigan Democrats insisted, by four million black voters. Although the ratio was correct, there were in the North eighteen million white people, not voters—and in the South four million black people, not voters. Using such patently flimsy arguments, the white supremacists continuously maintained that a "minority" of "millions" would control a "majority" of many more millions.[33]

When it came to numerical escalation, the most popular topic among racist critics was the cost of "Africanization." During the state elections of 1866, Democrats in Pennsylvania published campaign posters that listed the expenses of the Freedmen's Bureau at 25 million dollars for its first two years. The Detroit *Free Press* accused the government of spending 21.5 million dollars of northern taxes to support idle Negroes, plus a hundred million to enforce Negro suffrage and ten million per year to support the Bureau. These figures were modest compared to the estimates of the La Crosse *Democrat*, whose editor apparently included the entire cost of the Civil War when he accused the government of spending seven hundred million per year for the "Africanized government" of the South.[34]

The Negroes of the South, of course, dominated no state or national election, a fact that has been obvious to anyone who has looked beyond the facade of racist rhetoric. Only in South Carolina did Negroes make up a majority of the delegates to a constitutional convention. On the other hand, in Texas only nine out of 90 delegates were black. In South Carolina, where the first reconstruction legislature had 87 Negroes and 40 whites, the whites controlled the state senate from the beginning, and had the leadership in the lower house during most of the period. In all the other southern states, the extent of Negro participation was considerably less. The black men who held responsible positions in state governments were conspicuous by their rarity. Lieutenant-Governors Alonzo J. Ransier and Richard H. Gleaves, State Supreme

Court Justice Jonathan Jasper Wright, and Speaker of the House Samuel J. Lee in South Carolina, Lieutenant-Governor A. K. Davis and Speaker John R. Lynch in Mississippi, Lieutenant-Governors Oscar J. Dunn, P. B. S. Pinchback, and C. C. Antoine in Louisiana, are at the top of a very small list of notable Negro public officials of the period. The racist's "balance of power" complaint only made sense in a state where the parties were evenly divided and the Negroes could be counted on to vote together—which was nowhere. In 1914 Lynch pointed out that the freedmen often had been unpredictable as a political bloc, despite the efforts of the Republican-controlled Union Leagues to unify them in the radical cause.[35] Bill Arp's caustic observation that "slavery for the white foaks and freedum for the nigger runs mity well together now-a-days," was completely groundless.[36]

Probably no prediction struck more terror in the hearts of fearful whites in both the North and the South than the prediction of racial violence. Although most of the critics probably did not believe their own ominous prophecies, they recognized the topic's propaganda value and hammered away at it so relentlessly that they could very well have been accused of fomenting violence. In 1867 and 1868, delegates to the annual state Democratic conventions in Ohio said that they feared "disastrous conflicts." In January 1868, in Indianapolis, Democratic convention president Joseph E. McDonald told the delegates to the annual convention in his state that America must either surrender to the "barbarism of Africa," or face a race war in the South. In June, delegates to a state convention of the so-called Conservative party in Tennessee forecasted racial violence in their state. Three of New York City's racist newspapers gloomily predicted a "direct conflict between the Anglo-Saxon and African races," "a war of races—the worst of all wars," "a desperate collision between the two races in the South," and a "bloody and exterminating war of races." In a speech in Brooklyn on July 23, 1868, S. S. Cox shouted, " 'Let us have arms,' say the negroes. 'Let us have peace,' says the General [Grant]; and he gives them— arms!"* And in Brunswick, Maine, on September 3, he charged that "already a war of sanguinary proportions is being aroused between the two races South."[37]

To dramatize their predictions, many critics recounted some of the

---

* In 1865, two Ohio abolitionists, contemplating a possible northern-Copperhead– southern-conservative fusion, predicted a race war if the Negroes were *not* granted complete equality. See J. D. Cox, "Reconstruction and the Relations of the Races," (Columbus, O., 1865), p. 4.

unfortunate events and barbaric conditions of life in Africa and Latin America. After a major Negro insurrection in Jamaica in October 1865—the fourth outbreak of the century on that island—Democratic newspaper editors filled their pages with descriptions of the "murder and mutilation" of scores of whites by "infuriated negro savages, bent on destroying the civilization which surrounds and vexes them." One newsman quoted numerous "eyewitness accounts" of the grisly atrocities, and said that what the blacks did in Jamaica they were "pretty likely to do in this country, if trusted in the same manner." The editors of *American Annual Cyclopedia* considered the rebellion momentous enough to merit nine pages of double-column coverage.[38]

In 1866, the British government's official report on the rebellion, the "Jamaica Papers," received a limited circulation in the United States; but these accounts, far less inflammatory than the racist descriptions, were ignored by white supremacy propagandists. The Philadelphia *Age* printed a series of articles on the barbarity of the Caribbean Negroes, charging that the radical Republicans were "more corrupt and reckless" than the men who championed Negro suffrage in Jamaica. When the British government dissolved the elected assembly of Jamaica in 1866 and left the administration of island affairs in the hands of the crown-appointed governor and royal council, Thomas Hartley stated that the whites in Jamaica preferred the abolition of self-government because it prevented the "representatives of hordes of ignorant negroes" from gaining control of the colonial legislature. The action, of course, had been initiated in London, not in Jamaica, and its object was not to deny the democratic process but to prevent the outbreak of another revolt. Nevertheless, by claiming that Jamaican whites preferred this (as most of them did), Hartley was illustrating the similarity of their views to the views of southern whites, who, it was said, preferred radical military rule to Negro suffrage.[39]

As reports of violent incidents in various parts of the South spread, uneasy racists everywhere began to anticipate another Jamaica. Whites saw any public gathering of Negroes as a prelude to violence. In July 1866, the New Orleans *Times* described a meeting of Negroes, carpetbaggers, and scalawags, called to discuss Negro enfranchisement. After the assembly hall had filled to capacity, Dr. Anthony P. Dostie, a local radical white dentist, allegedly urged the restless freedmen milling around outside to prepare for a fierce struggle. "I want the negroes to have the right of suffrage, and we will give them this right to vote," the *Times* quoted him as saying. "There will be another meeting here tomorrow night, and on Monday I want you to come in your power. I want no cowards to come." To dispel fears that militant whites might interfere with the meeting, Dostie claimed that the three hundred thousand Negroes of Louisiana, plus the one hundred thousand loyal whites, could whip the three hundred thousand "hell-hound rebels" of the state. Of course, this was the entire population of Louisiana, thus the radicals were as prone to tossing around big numbers as the racists were. Referring to a recent riot in Memphis, where a quarrel between a Negro and a white man resulted in a raid by poor whites and police in a Negro neighborhood where they killed and burned indiscriminately, Dostie reassured his listeners that they need not fear such a "puerile affair." If his group were interfered with, he threatened, "the streets of New Orleans will run with blood!"[40]

The publicity that the affair received, in addition to the War Department's failure to take preventive action—thereby throwing the problem of policing the meeting into the lap of the city's mayor, who opposed Negro suffrage—was bound to draw a crowd. The result was the bloody New Orleans riot of July 30, 1866. When, on Monday, Negroes walked in procession to the assembly hall, someone fired a shot. In the ensuing melee, forty Negroes and three of their white supporters were killed; and more than a hundred Negroes and seventeen white sympathizers were wounded. Of the angry white bystanders and hecklers who had opposed the march, one was killed and ten were wounded. To the racist, of course, it was the barbaric Negro or the white agitator, such as Dr. Dostie,* who had incited the outburst. Anyone who suggested that the local whites might have been responsible was immediately labeled a radical. Unless he was an "instigator," a white man who committed an act of violence was only protecting himself, his home, and his family.[41]

But the rolls of the dead and wounded in New Orleans, and the circumstances of that riot as well as the circumstances of most other incidents, flatly belied the charge that Negroes and radical agitators precipitated most of the trouble. Clemenceau noted how odd it was that in the telegraphic reports, "there was always a band of heavily armed negroes attacking a handful of of harmless whites," yet when it came to counting the casualties, "a few negroes are always down, but

---

* Dr. Dostie had arrived in Louisiana from New York in 1852 and had established a flourishing practice, but he moved to Chicago in 1861 when his ardent unionist views made him unpopular among his neighbors. He returned with the Union army in 1862, and until his death in 1866 he was active in reestablishing a loyal local government. For a highly partisan biography, see Emily Hazen Reed, *Life of A. P. Dostie; or, The Conflict in New Orleans* (New York, 1868).

of white men, not a trace." It was both ironic and amusing to Whitelaw Reid that some of the same Southerners who were complaining of African barbarism had formerly defended slavery because of its civilizing influence. It now appeared, and they admitted, that they had been mistaken. Reid concluded that if they had been wrong then about the Negro's progress, they could also be wrong now about his alleged lack of it.[42]

However, the South was not without its dispassionate realists. In February 1866, a delegate to the white conservative Texas Reconstruction Convention reminded his colleagues that all "the bloody feuds between the white and black races" could be traced to "injustice and oppression" perpetrated by whites. In addition, federal authorities in the South were not sympathetic to whites, conservative or radical, who encouraged violence. In November 1867, Brevet-Major General Edward O. C. Ord, commander of the Fourth Military District (Mississippi and Arkansas), instructed a subordinate to report any person who made "inflammatory speeches to freedmen" or excited "one class or color against another." Such offenders would receive "prompt arrests and trial."[43] While there surely were instances of Negroes committing violence, the whole idea of race war was largely a product of the demagogue's fertile imagination. It was the white man who talked about race war; and if it were to come, the white man would have to start it.

Like the election of 1864, the presidential election of 1868 was a decisive event, a test of whether or not the race issue was as critical as the racist had hoped. During the Civil War, many opponents of the Union government saw the Lincoln-McClellan election as a national referendum on the Emancipation Proclamation. Similarly, white supremacists now saw radical reconstruction as the major issue of the Ulysses S. Grant–Horatio Seymour election. Grant could not be identified with Negro suffrage as easily as Lincoln had been identified with emancipation. However, in 1864, the racist had been speculating about future dangers, or dreaming up imaginary threats, like miscegenation; whereas in 1868 the critic had, or thought he had, substantial and convincing evidence of actual damage. The South, reconstructed with Negro voters, Negro office holders, Negro "violence," martial law, and carpetbag politicians, was both monumental and real. All the political propagandist had to do was make it "wicked" as well.

But the Democrats themselves disagreed on the significance of the race question as a campaign issue. Party members were not as consistent or unified on this point as the extremist would have liked. Two months before the Democratic National Convention, the Detroit *Free Press* cited government corruption, scandal, usurpation of authority, and congressional dictatorship—with no reference whatever to the Negro—as the primary issues of the coming election. Yet four months later, the same newspaper called the race problem the leading issue of the year and condemned those who belittled its significance. Edward A. Pollard, one of the South's most vociferous racists, was just as equivocal; though he insisted that it was one of America's "great duties" to "let the negro severely alone as a subject of political controversy," he himself consistently ignored that "duty."[44]

The Democratic party platform was less equivocal; it condemned the radicals for subjecting ten states to "military despotism and negro supremacy." A short time later, David G. Croly observed in a biography of Seymour that the campaign had "opened very bitterly." A question of "race superiority" was involved, he said, "while the passions and prejudices generated during the war have been stimulated into a new life, so as to affect the result." Much of the campaign oratory and writing reflected these "passions and prejudices." In urging his listeners to vote for candidates who would overthrow the congressional reconstruction program, Tilden told an audience in Washington, D. C.: "In this great contest we shall wage no war of defense. We carry our arms into Africa." And a few days before the election, Voorhees asked what the reaction of northern soldiers would have been if they had been told that "they were to fight for negro suffrage and negro supremacy in any state of this fair land?" According to some Democrats, Anna Dickinson's novel *What Answer?* (1868), a story of a love affair between an octoroon woman and a socially prominent white man, was a major campaign document of the radical Republicans.[45] Since Miss Dickinson was a leading abolitionist, the racists, of course, leaped at the opportunity to make the association.

A more accurate reflection of the real impact of the race issue could be seen in the manuevering of the prospective Democratic nominees. In 1868, as in 1864, there was no "logical" choice. The New York *Herald*'s James Gordon Bennett had recommended, almost facetiously, an "experimental sectional reconciliation ticket of General Grant and General Lee."[46] In the weeks before the Convention, the list of potential candidates narrowed down to half a dozen men including Chief Justice Salmon P. Chase, a former radical Republican who had a sizable Democratic following, and George Pendleton, who had been McClellan's running mate in 1864. On the race issue the two were poles apart. Pendleton, with Washington McLean's vituperative Cincinnati *Enquirer* as his mouthpiece, was one of the nation's most outspoken white supremacy demagogues and had succeeded Vallandigham as leader of the midwestern extremists; Chase, on the other hand, was committed to Negro suffrage and civil equality. But while Chase alienated midwestern Democrats because of his racial views, he endeared himself to eastern Democrats by favoring specie payment of the national debt, in opposition to Pendleton's well publicized pro-greenback position. Moreover, Chase seemed to be a sound compromise candidate in the North; he was popular with conservatives of both parties—partly because he annoyed the radicals with his impartial handling of the President's impeachment trial. As a Democratic candidate with the support of many Republicans, his chances seemed excellent. "The only question remaining," Clemenceau observed, "is whether the Democratic party is really ready to renounce its former errors and to admit the negro on a footing of perfect equality with the white man."[47]

Thus, the possibility of Chase's winning the Democratic nomination was much more remote than the possibility of his winning the election. From the earliest days of radical reconstruction, the Democratic party was moving toward a stronger anti-Negro stand, not a weaker one. Nowhere was this clearer than in the speeches of Horatio Seymour, the eventual candidate. Basically, Seymour was not a racist demagogue. In October 1866, when presidential politics had not been a factor, he had insisted that the "question of tariffs and taxation, and not the negro question, keeps our country divided." The race issue, he said, had been used "to lead the people . . . by their prejudices," a comment that would have been more appropriate coming from a Republican. But the growing militancy of party leaders gradually changed Seymour's views, and *he* soon began leading the people by their prejudices. It was the Republican "negro military policy" that was the cause of all the country's financial troubles, he proclaimed early in 1868. And in his view the crucial campaign issue was Negro suffrage: in order to stay in power the Republicans had to maintain Negro suffrage, and Negro suffrage meant that the "government of the South [was] to go into the hands of the negroes."[48]

As it happened, Seymour himself was a compromise candidate. The eastern Democrats, unwilling to support Pendleton and the greenback, forced a deadlock. To break it, the delegates agreed on Seymour, who satisfied both the hard-money Democrats from the East, and, as a result of his recent decision to kowtow to them, the militant racists throughout the country. In assessing the convention of 1868, one delegate said that Seymour was a man "whom the presidency has sought and who has not sought the presidency," and historian Charles H. Coleman has argued that Seymour "was not a party to his nomination."[49]

But the evidence is not conclusive. Seymour, the former governor of New York, was serving as the president of the convention, and was not even nominated until the fourth ballot. After he insisted that he could not accept, his name was dropped until the twenty-first ballot. This would suggest that his candidacy was a spontaneous thing and came as something of a surprise. However, his speeches both before and after the convention raise some doubt. Although he probably believed that he had no more than an outside chance of winning the nomination, it is naïve to suggest that he never considered himself a potential candidate. "On the negro suffrage issue, and on all the points involved in the so-called radical reconstruction," the *Enquirer* wrote a short time after his nomination, "Mr. Seymour occupies the most advanced Democratic ground, as is well known to everyone who has read his many magnificent addresses denunciatory to the whole radical Congressional scheme." In fact, the *Enquirer* continued, Seymour's views on reconstruction "render him particularly acceptable to the Democracy of the Great West."[50] Perhaps Horatio Seymour personified the ideological conflict within the Democratic party only reluctantly. But if he was reluctant, he nevertheless accepted white supremacy as a political expedient; and had he asserted his original views immediately before the convention and not made his "many magnificent addresses," he probably would never have won the nomination.

Seymour's behavior after his nomination reaffirmed his reluctance to exploit the race question. Even before the delegates had adjourned, he reverted to his earlier position. In his letter of acceptance he assailed the Republicans but failed to mention the Negro. All of his speeches, except for those of the first six months of 1868, generally ignored the race issue. After the convention, campaign strategy called for Seymour to remain in the East and emphasize financial issues, while vice-presidential candidate Blair stumped the West highlighting radical reconstruction and the race issue. Though Tilden received credit for suggesting it, the idea was probably Seymour's.[51] As a demagogue, Seymour was out of character. For him to have continued carrying on as he had just before the convention would have meant maintaining a charade that he certainly found distasteful. His ambivalence also showed that the race issue was not the most vital problem to a large number of voters in both parties—and Seymour probably recognized this as an obstacle which the Democrats had been unable to overcome in 1864. Seymour apparently realized that a lot of Americans simply could not get excited over the threatened "Africanization" of the South.

Nevertheless, while Seymour was devoting his attention to questions other than race, Blair earned the reputation of being the most outspoken political Negrophobe of the campaign. In the 1850's, Blair, an ardent Free Soiler, had joined the Republican party. In 1859 he helped organize a committee to raise sixteen thousand dollars to finance the printing of a hundred thousand copies of Helper's *Impending Crisis of the South*, a blistering criticism of slavery, and one that many Americans erroneously associated with the abolitionists. Blair served in the Union army during the war, and was still thought to be a staunch Republican until he bolted the party over what he called radical excesses. Trying to minimize Blair's Republican past, the *Enquirer* pointed out that he had never supported "the atrocious doctrine of negro equality, but always favored the supremacy of the white race, and insisted that to it alone should be intrusted the destinies of the country." From the convention to the election, Blair did everything he could to justify the *Enquirer*'s description and to destroy whatever image of abolitionism his former Republican affiliation might have conveyed.* White supremacy was, in his mind, the "main issue" of the campaign.[52]

In retrospect, it appears that Blair had deliberately paved the way for his own nomination, by emphasizing purely racist themes before the convention. In the spring of 1868 he had made several speeches, all stressing white supremacy.[53] Then, on June 30, he wrote Colonel James O. Brodhead a letter that received a great deal of publicity. In his letter, Blair advocated martial law enforced by federal troops under direct orders from the President. Otherwise, he insisted, any Democratic chief executive would be powerless to "stop the supplies by which idle negroes are organized into political clubs—by which an army is maintained to protect these vagabonds in their outrages upon the ballot." Under martial law, Blair noted, the President could "nullify and abolish" all the reconstruction laws, and force back to work "all the lazy negroes, who are nothing but a band of organized vagabonds, and who are bringing dishonor on the franchise."[54] Since Blair had been mentioned as a possible presidential candidate, he obviously thought it necessary to express his views on how to resolve the reconstruction crisis; and the letter to Brodhead detailing his ideas on the subject, while it was not sufficient to win away many of the delegates committed to the other presidential hopefuls, made him the ideal choice for balancing the ticket.

* Though remaining a Democrat, Blair cooperated with the Liberal Republicans in Missouri, was appointed by the state legislature to the United States Senate in 1871, and supported Horace Greeley for the presidency on the Liberal Republican ticket in 1872, but was defeated for reelection to the Senate in 1873.

Although the letter to Brodhead did more than anything else to advertise Blair's extremism, it was not his most virulent statement; on July 13, in a less publicized letter to George W. Morgan, who was serving as one of the convention's committee chairmen, he repeated these views in even stronger language: "The same usurping authority [Congress] has substituted [as] electors in place of men of our own race . . . , a host of ignorant negroes, who are supported in idleness with the public money, and combined together to strip the white race of [its] birthright. . . . And to complete the oppression, the military power of the nation has been placed at their disposal, in order to make this barbarism supreme." Moreover, militant racism was virtually the only topic of his acceptance speech: as he saw it, the impending struggle not only was one for "the restoration of our government," but also was one for "the restoration of our race." During the campaign, in a series of frenzied speeches in the Midwest—at Omaha, Leavenworth, St. Joseph, Cincinnati, and Matoon—before wildly cheering audiences, Blair resurrected scores of old anti-Negro arguments.[55] Before he was finished, he had become the personification of the racist faction of the Democratic party, and was the object of Republican joking:

> Blair, Blair, Black sheep,
> Have you any wool?
> Yes, my master, seven bags full—
> Nigger scalps from Georgia,
> Ku-Klux got them all,
> So many less nigger votes
> Against us in the Fall.[56]

Toward the end of the campaign, Blair's extremism became so violent that some Democrats began to wonder about his mental stability; and the New York *World*, convinced that his strident audacity antagonized the uncommitted voter and solidified the opposition, suggested that he be replaced on the ticket. Since several party leaders apparently agreed and put pressure on him, Blair, in the final weeks of the campaign, began emphasizing economic issues.[57] Thus the sword of white supremacy was double-edged; although it was often effective when used carefully in appropriate situations, its indiscriminate application could injure the racist cause.

As far as the racists were concerned, the results of the election of 1868 were essentially the same as the results in 1864. The Democrats were no more successful in their attempts to exploit the race issue than they had been four years earlier; nor did the race issue appear to be more effective than any other issue. The long struggle to secure a

Democratic candidate had indicated clearly that party leaders and nominees did not agree. That Chase, a Republican Chief Justice of the Supreme Court, could have been considered at all is highly revealing. Since the Democratic party had never made a united and rational commitment to white supremacy, how did it expect the electorate to do so? The racist's failure, of course, lay largely in the northern voter's refusal to become deeply concerned about the alleged iniquities of carpetbag corruption and Negro domination in distant states. To win a national election on a campaign against racial equality in the South was far more difficult than to win a state or local election over Negro suffrage close to home. Whatever the evils of radical reconstruction, fabricated or genuine, most Northerners simply could not get excited over remote issues. Moreover, the appeal of a military hero when compared to that of an honest but colorless former governor was more than the Democratic party could overcome. The radicals, of course, saw the results of the election as a public vindication of their program.

Chapter Seven

THE SPECTER
OF SOCIAL EQUALITY

In 1874 the Alabama conservatives issued a ringing denunciation of all laws that prohibited following "the rules and maxims of our social intercourse," and all attempts to punish the South for refusing "to admit an ignorant and barbarous race to equal participation with our families in our social institutions."[1] Thus did they sum up a fear of social equality that white Southerners, and probably most white Americans, had shared for generations. Emancipation had only meant that a man could no longer barter in human beings and that he had to pay his black laborers. Impartial suffrage, distasteful as it was, simply defined the Negro's political rights; he had only one vote and it was equal to a white man's. Emancipation and Negro suffrage did not mean that the white man had to associate with the Negro; standing together at the polls was the closest the two would ever come together. Even economic equality had a saving grace—at day's end each worker would go his own way. In the privacy of a man's home and during his leisure hours, complete segregation would prevail.

Though the racists did not always explain just what they meant by "social equality," it was obvious that it involved the most personal aspects of human relationships. It meant, most of all, that a black man could court a white woman. It also meant that the Negro could send his children to the white man's schools, use the same recreational facilities, ride on the same streetcars and trains, attend the same theaters and galleries, join the same clubs, and eat in the same restaurants. It did not matter whether a racist said he had intellectual objections to sharing these privileges with an "inferior" person or whether he admitted that he was emotionally unable to associate with Negroes on a personal level; the suggestion that Negroes "should be received on an equality in white families" was totally unacceptable to most whites.[2]

Yet racist opinions on this point were far from uniform. During the debates over the Reconstruction Acts, Maryland's Reverdy Johnson, a Senator who had been Attorney-General under Zachary Taylor, advised his fellow Democrats in the Senate to stop worrying about social equality. During the Civil War, rumors had circulated that Johnson— who during his flourishing and lucrative private practice in the 1850's had been counsel for the defense in the case of *Dred Scott* v. *Sandford* (1857)—had been the real author of that controversial Supreme Court decision. No proof of this ever appeared, but the language and tone of the opinion handed down by Chief Justice Roger Taney (who was also from Maryland) were characteristic of Johnson. Johnson's main interest was constitutional law, and he believed that the question of "social enjoyment" for Negroes was beyond the reach of legislation and was not subject to precise constitutional clarification. "I should have no objection to [riding] in a car with Negroes, provided they are clean," he said, "and I have just as much objection to sitting alongside a dirty white man as to sitting alongside a dirty black man." Though the senator conceded that prejudice must be considered in discussions of political and social rights and that he disapproved of the election to the Senate of even those Negroes who "have as much intellect as white men," he was nevertheless one of the more moderate members of the Democratic party when it came to the race issue. The extreme racists, of course, considered him a renegade.[3]

One of the extremists was Hinton R. Helper, whose hatred of Negroes was so intense that in his rambling and occasionally incomprehensible *Nojoque* (1867) he recommended forced emigration, "speedily and prudently effected," or else quick and complete extermination—what he called "fossilization." Helper believed that members of "dingy-hued" races should be "no longer required nor tolerated north of the northern boundary of Mexico," and considered them "drones, sluggards, and vagabonds" who should have been rendered extinct like "toxodons, glyptodons, and mastodons." He said the Copperheads who had insisted, ten years earlier, that he had written *The Impending Crisis of the South* in the slaves' interest were "shallow-brained and babbling blockheads," who "ought to have their necks rung."* Two years after

---

* Misunderstood and misinterpreted in his own time, Helper remains somewhat enigmatic. In one of his postwar books, *Noonday Exigencies in America* (1871), he urged unionist Democrats and conservative Republicans to join in the formation of

Nojoque's publication, Helper became involved in a scheme to sell a hundred thousand acres of undeveloped land in North Carolina to northern and European immigrants—specifically Germans, Swedes, Swiss, Danes, and Norwegians. "Great numbers of such elements of population as these are much needed all over the South," he wrote to a friend, "and it is a work of deep and far-reaching patriotism to facilitate their introduction among us."[4]

Although they were not virulent, as the extremists were, moderates in both parties had mixed feelings about social equality. As early as July 1862, a northern clergyman expressed doubt that "the two races can ever on this continent abide on terms of social equality." Shortly after the war, the editor of the Nebraska *Republican* chided Democratic newsmen who, he said, had a "mortal fear of the negroes' and Indians' becoming their social equals," and added that "ghosts of niggers and Indians are forever floating through their social dreams. They are trembling with fear of actual social equality." Since they apparently did not trust their own prejudices to keep the races apart, he said, nothing short of "legislative inter-position can save them." Three years later, two North Carolina Republicans urged their neighbors to approve the new state constitution, drawn up under the Reconstruction Acts, because it did *not* mean social equality. "With the social intercourse of life, government has nothing to do; that must be left to the taste and choice of each individual." The conservatives, they stated, made their hysterical predictions of social equality in order to "excite a false prejudice" for political purposes, and only created "ill-will between races that are destined to live on the same soil, and ought to live together in peace."[5]

Attitudes toward social equality were, of course, also influenced by local and regional mores and by economic conditions. In the South, generations of slavery had shaped the outlooks both of slaveowners

---

a white-supremacy third party. After reviewing *Nojoque* on July 3, 1867, the Columbus *Crisis* called Helper a confirmed radical Republican; three months later editor Albert Taylor Bledsoe of the *Southern Review* (October) claimed that Helper was not the sole author of the book. Among subsequent treatments of Helper's writings, David Rankin Barbee's two articles in *Tyler's Quarterly Historical and Genealogical Magazine* (January and April 1934), which say *The Impending Crisis of the South* and *Nojoque* were written by others, are monuments to historical inaccuracy and undocumented opinion. Hugh T. Lefler's pamphlet, "Hinton Rowan Helper" (1935), and William Polk's article in *South Atlantic Quarterly* (April 1931) are scholarly capsule treatments but leave a great deal unsaid. The most accurate and best balanced summary of Helper's postwar writings is Chapter Six in Hugh C. Bailey's *Hinton Rowan Helper: Abolitionist-Racist* (University, Ala., 1965).

and of poor whites—and of the slaves themselves. As Postmaster-General Montgomery Blair said in March 1863, southern racism was not just the "fruit of mere ignorance," nor was it "confined to the white people of the South."[6] Although Blair was incorrect when he implied that northern attitudes had the same origins as southern attitudes, there were similarities in the reasons for these attitudes. The prewar migration of non-slaveholding southern whites into the Ohio Valley made that section a stronghold of resistance to suggestions of social equality, as was evidenced by the hostile and sometimes violent reactions that midwestern abolitionists frequently provoked.

In the eastern cities, the counterparts of the southern poor whites were the many immigrants, especially poor Irish peasants who had come to the United States in the decade and a half before the Civil War. (Over a million arrived between 1847 to 1854.) During the economic boom of the 1850's, rapid expansion in manufacturing, food processing, trades, and railroad building had brought relative affluence to many of these new Americans. But since most of them were wage earners, the inflation and dislocation brought about by the war created among them a great and growing sense of economic insecurity. Though the Negro was in no way responsible for this insecurity, he was a convenient scapegoat because the war had made the immigrants extremely sensitive to anything they thought, rightly or wrongly, might jeopardize their status—a situation that unscrupulous political demagogues readily exploited. And complicating the matter was the renewal of heavy immigration after Appomattox; an average of over three hundred thousand immigrants a year came in the last half of the 1860's.

Because legislators and other state officials in the North and the South shared both racism and an economic fear of Negroes, most state governments decided to wait and see what course the federal government would pursue and therefore declined to take the initiative in ensuring social equality. Since Congress had enacted a major civil rights bill in 1866, those states that might have had an inclination to do likewise saw no reason for it. In the decade following the war, less than half a dozen states passed supplementary civil rights legislation.[7] But except for these isolated examples that in actuality accorded only a modicum of social equality, the state legislatures were reluctant to go beyond the federal minimums.

The most common expression of the white man's aversion to social equality was found in the term "Jim Crow." The name presumably originated in the 1830's, when one Thomas D. Rice, a Negro minstrel, staged a song-and-dance show called "Jim Crow," in Washington, D. C. In 1841, railroad officials in Massachusetts used the term to designate a passenger car set aside for blacks. Subsequently, northern and southern Negroes encountered Jim Crow practices everywhere, though in its most precise application the term referred to segregation in public conveyances.

It has been argued by historian C. Vann Woodward that "the era of genuine segregation" did not begin until the 1880's, when conservative southern state governments began the mass disfranchisement of Negroes, and passed sweeping Jim Crow laws. More recently, one of Professor Woodward's students has asserted that "in the areas of transportation and public accommodations the South groped its way only gradually toward Jim Crow."[8] But in spite of these arguments, it was in 1865 that S. S. Cox observed, "In the school-house, the church, or the hospital, the black man must not seat himself beside the white; even in death and at the cemetery the line of distinction is drawn." And it was in the following year that the New York *Daily News* justified Jim Crow practices by calling them a defense of the "social rights of the white race." Negroes must be excluded from all "theaters and other places of public resort," the editor declared. "Pseudo-philanthropists may preach till doomsday about the perfections of the negro, but they will never succeed in blanching or deodorizing him." New York's Representative James Brooks predicted that social equality would lead to "mongrel schools and school-houses, to mongrel cars, to mongrel taverns, to a complete mongrel social existence from the cradle to the grave."[9]

Thus, although the Woodward thesis is essentially correct as far as the statutory codification of Jim Crow practices was concerned, to suggest that "genuine segregation" did not become "institutionalized" until some time after reconstruction is to misrepresent the reality of racial discrimination, as well as the racist attitudes behind that discrimination.* One of the most obvious facts about race relations in the 1860's and 1870's was that the vast majority of Americans, white and black, took racial separation for granted. The draconic black codes (the first mass codification of Jim Crow practices) were only the most conspicuous examples of this assumption. The Thirteenth Amendment did not send ex-slaves rushing into the white man's streetcars, hotels,

---

*Though he claims to agree with the Woodward thesis, George B. Tindall points out that many of the arguments used to defend the "new" Jim Crow practices originated in antebellum defenses of slavery and were popular during the reconstruction. See "The Central Theme Revisited," in Charles Grier Sellers, Jr. (ed.), *The Southerner as American* (Chapel Hill, N. C., 1960), pp. 108–114.

and restaurants. Most of the freedmen segregated themselves through choice and habit. It is common knowledge that segregation came about almost immediately in the schools and the churches, places to which southern Negroes had virtually no access before the war. Hence it is both naïve and unrealistic to suppose that the races were separated in schools and churches but mixed in other places.

The federal government itself had a hand in perpetuating Jim Crow practices. During the war, for example, white and Negro troops had been segregated in the army. Before debating certain civil-rights proposals early in 1866—proposals that, ironically, were to become part of the Fourteenth Amendment—the Senate without controversy had segregated its own galleries. The practice of segregation by the federal government was, as Joseph B. James has pointed out, "obviously accepted as a matter of course by most people."[10] That the backers of the Civil Rights Act of 1875 found it necessary to include explicit provisions pertaining to public accommodations was a testimony to the extent of the institutionalization of segregation. References to time-honored customs of social separation were frequent during the later era of Jim Crow codification, and were even used to justify the new laws. Indeed, in the landmark decision in the case of *Plessy* v. *Ferguson* (1896), which upheld a Louisiana law requiring "separate but equal" accommodations on railroads, the Supreme Court majority based its opinion in part on "established usages, customs, and traditions."[11] The new laws, in reality, merely formalized common practices.

Travel accounts from the period carry many testimonies of de facto segregation. While visiting the North in 1862, British journalist Edward Dicey took special note of the absolute separation of the races in transportation and public accommodations. Describing the South after the war, David Macrae mentioned that on all trains there were "nigger cars to which all coloured passengers [had] to confine themselves." Though the Civil Rights Act of 1866 had presumably made such restrictions illegal, Macrae emphasized that wherever he went "the old rule was still practically enforced." The reasons for the Negro's habitual compliance were not hard to discover. William H. Dixon, shocked at the filthy conditions on a Negro passenger car in Ohio, asked a conductor why the black people did not use the "common cars," since the law was on their side. " 'Well,' said he, with a sudden lightening in his eyes, 'they have the right; but damn them, I should like to see them do it. . . . Sam likes his free condition . . . but he also loves his skin.' "[12]

Nor was the well-to-do Negro's financial status a passport to equal treatment. In September 1868, en route to Washington, D. C., on a river steamer, a middle-class Negro named Robert G. Fitzgerald and a traveling companion were ordered to "a dark place under the forecastle" and were later subjected to other indignities. The previous year, in a suit brought by a Negro woman, the Pennsylvania State Supreme Court had ruled in favor of the West Chester and Philadelphia Railroad Company. The line had lost a lower court decision, but the justices reversed it on two counts: (1) the attempt to force the plaintiff into the Jim Crow car had occurred before the passage of a state law prohibiting discrimination, thus the original action had been an ex post facto judgment, and (2) the carrier had the right to make regulations for the comfort of its passengers.* The second reason was especially far-reaching because, in addition to upholding a specific Jim Crow regulation, it was a precedent that provided the racist with the cloak of judicial dignity.[13] The first such case to reach the United States Supreme Court was *Washington, Alexandria, and Georgetown Railroad Company* v. *Brown* (1873)—and in this instance the plaintiff, another Negro woman, won. But the decision set no precedent. Between 1868 and 1937 the Supreme Court heard fourteen cases, in which Negroes claimed the right to use the *same* facilities in common carriers, public accommodations, and schools, yet only one other was decided in the Negro's favor. Indeed, it was not until 1946, in *Morgan* v. *Virginia*, that the Court specifically invalidated a state law *requiring* segregated carriers, a decision based not on the Fourteenth Amendment† but on the commerce clause of the Constitution.[14]

Black citizens also suffered in cases involving city transportation companies. In a letter to the Philadelphia *Press*, three Negro men, Miles R. Robinson, James Wallace, and R. C. Marshall, complained of the treatment they had received from both the conductor and the male

* It is possible that the United States Supreme Court had this decision in mind almost thirty years later when it established the "separate but equal" principle in *Plessy* v. *Ferguson* (1896). Speaking for the majority in *West Chester and Philadelphia Railroad Company* v. *Mills*, Judge Agnew argued that separation in public conveyances was justified "so long as accommodations were not denied to either party, of as good a quality as were offered to the other."

† It is one of the ironies of the history of civil liberties that the Fourteenth Amendment, created to guarantee the civil rights of minorities, became the guardian of captains of industry seeking to escape state regulation. From 1868 to 1911, the Supreme Court handed down decisions in 604 cases involving the Fourteenth Amendment, but Negroes were parties to only 28 of them—and of the 28, 22 were decided against the Negro. For an extensive discussion of the Court's activities in the seventy years following the ratification of the Fourteenth Amendment, see Morroe Berger's *Equality by Statute: Legal Controls over Group Discrimination* (New York, 1950), pp. 37–71.

passengers on a local trolley. When some white men objected to their presence, the conductor decided—to avoid a fight, he said—not to allow the Negroes to board. Someone called a policeman, a scuffle ensued, and the Negroes were arrested for disorderly conduct. Though the charges were dropped, the three men questioned Philadelphia's claim to the title the "City of Brotherly Love."[15] There was no city ordinance prohibiting integrated streetcars, but the incident was an illustration of the public feeling on the issue of Negroes on trains and streetcars.

In its broader application, the term Jim Crow involved almost every aspect of social intercourse, including churchgoing. Before the war, Negro house servants had occasionally attended church with their masters, but had sat in separate sections. However, the few attempts by the Union army to have Negroes, especially soldiers, freely admitted to churches in occupied Confederate territory met with little success. In February 1864, after Brigadier General Edward A. Wild had replaced secessionist ministers in Norfolk, Virginia, with loyal clergymen, and had ordered all of the city's churches to admit northern soldiers "white or colored," John Bell Robinson, a northern racist cleric, predicted angrily that the time was approaching when everyone "shall be forced to sit in church promiscuously with black African heathens and barbarians."[16]

But during the first few years of the reconstruction era, just the opposite occurred; segregation on Sunday morning became universal. Seven months after Appomattox, the General Assembly of Southern Presbyterians, meeting in Macon, Georgia, defeated a motion that it reunite with the northern branch, because it opposed the northern branch's position on the race issue. Although the institution of slavery may have been evil, the delegates resolved, the master-servant relationship was the proper one for whites and Negroes. On questions of "social morality and Scriptural truth," the relationship remained unchanged. Northern Methodists, working for the peaceful integration of their southern congregations, met identical resistance. In the meantime, Negroes organized their own churches and joined existing all-black bodies—such as the African Methodist Episcopal Church and the African Methodist Episcopal Zion Church. By 1870, whites and blacks together had thoroughly segregated southern Methodism.[17]

Jim Crow practices also reached far into the education systems in both North and South. White supremacists everywhere opposed school integration, on the grounds that children were too young to exercise mature judgment and might unwittingly embrace the idea of social equality. Most northern schools had been segregated for decades, but the antislavery movement had brought proposals for reform in the North. In 1864, an unsuccessful attempt to integrate public schools in Troy, New York, met a caustic attack from the editor of the Albany *Atlas and Argus*. Three years later the Detroit *Free Press* lashed out angrily at a new Michigan law enforcing school integration; and as late as 1878, various whites in Baltimore told traveling English M.P. Sir George Campbell that the threat of white students walking out of the public colleges was what led to the establishment of separate colleges for blacks. At a special convention of Negroes in Indianapolis in November 1866, called to dramatize a drive to win equal rights in Indiana, the delegates conceded that complete social equality was an impossibility because it did not exist "in any country or community"; but they pleaded for educational opportunities, which would give Negroes a chance to overcome their illiteracy and would disprove charges that they were ignorant. In the South, of course, school integration was inconceivable. Before the Civil War, education had been a luxury that many white children had not had access to. After the war, the Freedmen's Bureau established schools for ex-slaves and their children; but these were not integrated schools, since the ignorant poor whites who could have used them refused to do so.[18]

It was the northern influence in schools for Negroes that many southern whites considered almost as intolerable as integration itself. Thirty years after the end of radical reconstruction, Myrta Lockett Avary complained that white men had been forced out of the Freedmen's Bureau technical training schools because Northerners in the Bureau had set them up primarily for the freedmen. "To limit the negro to these and these to the negro," she said, "is to put a stigma on manual labor in the eyes of white youth and to continue the negro's monopoly of a field which he does not appreciate."[19] It is true that the educational program of the Bureau, both academic and vocational, aimed to meet the needs of the former slaves, but whites were not specifically excluded, and they could have used many of the services if they had been able to overcome their prejudices. In effect, Mrs. Avary was saying that asking a white man to attend the same trade schools as a Negro was asking too much, and that therefore failing to provide separate schools amounted to denying deserving whites opportunities open to Negroes. Since the Fourteenth Amendment was silent on this point, segregation in the public schools of the South became virtually universal, in spite of the sincere efforts of many people north and south. In fact, according to Campbell, it was a Negro in the radical legislature of Georgia, arguing that the freedmen would rather remain separate than associate with whites as inferiors, who introduced the motion that segregated schools be maintained in that state.[20]

A few ostensibly well-meaning northern educators opposed school integration in the South on the grounds that white parents would refuse to send their children to school and the children would thus receive no education at all. For example, the Peabody Education Fund, established in 1867 by philanthropist George Peabody to promote public education in the more destitute areas of the South, consistently supported segregated schools for this reason, and, in fact, gave most of its support to schools for whites. When, in 1870, the Louisiana Superintendent of Education, a radical, asked for money from the Fund for schools for Negroes, Dr. Barnas Sears, the Fund's principal agent, pointed out that the money was supposed to benefit underprivileged children of both races. Since the Negroes were served by the Freedmen's Bureau, and since the white children refused to go to school with Negroes, Dr. Sears said, "we must give preference to those whose education is neglected. It is well known that we are helping the white children of Louisiana, as being the most destitute, from the fact of their unwillingness to attend mixed schools." With an endowment of almost two-and-one-half million dollars, the influence of the Peabody trustees reached all the way to Washington, where spokesmen for the Fund persuaded the members of Congress to delete from the Civil Rights Act of 1875 a provision calling for desegregation of public schools.[21] Thus did an organization committed to humanitarian objectives become a party to the perpetuation of racial discrimination.

Racists especially feared that the promise of social equality would make the ex-slaves brash and impulsive. "We ought to know the negro nature well enough to understand that it becomes unendurably saucy under concession," the Richmond *Southern Opinion* pointed out, "and that it is daring in exact proportion to our timidity." The slightest action by a Negro that did not conform to the white's conception of his "place"—such as his failure to address a white man as "sir"—was certain to provoke accusations that he was arrogant and insolent. After a Negro spectator in the Senate galleries had hissed some remarks by Senator Hendricks—remarks belittling the role of the black soldier during the war—the Philadelphia *Age* condemned the so-called social equality laws of the District of Columbia for encouraging that sort of conduct. To many racists, the northern Negro, not used to subservience, was the

most irritating of all. The radical drive for social equality, they complained, would make the southern Negroes behave the same way; they
would become absolutely insufferable. The rudeness with which two
former slave women had treated a white salesgirl, Mrs. Avary complained, was typical; and the worst part of it all was that the white girl
quietly tolerated it.[22]

Magnifying the southern white man's complaint was the fact that
the sudden prominence of many Negroes in state and local government
led to some bizarre but understandable conduct. After all, the slave had
been at the center of a controversy that had raged for decades. Suddenly
he found himself not only free to behave like a white man, but in a
position of some authority as well. Since he modeled his actions on the
most conspicuous example he had—the supercilious planter-politician
of the prewar era—it should have been no surprise that he did not
always act with prudence and discretion. During his travels through
South Carolina in 1872, reporter James S. Pike of the New York *Tribune*
made a particular note of the outlandish buffoonery of the black members of the state legislature. "It is the slave rioting in the halls of his
master," he wrote, "and putting that master under his feet." But even
Pike was forced to concede that underneath all the "shocking burlesque" there was something very real. "They have an earnest purpose,
born of a conviction that their position and condition are not fully
assured, which lends a sort of dignity to their proceedings. The barbarous, animated jargon in which they so often indulge is on occasion
seen to be so transparently sincere and weighty in their own minds
that a sympathy supplants disgust."[23] As a newspaper correspondent,
Pike was perceptive enough to make this observation; it was not likely
that the average southern white was able to do the same.

A far more widespread racial affront to the white Southerner's vanity
was the presence of the Negro militias, organized by radical state governments to keep the peace, but occasionally becoming aggressive political weapons. Nurtured for decades on a slave code that had had as
its prime factor the fear of insurrections, many southern whites saw
the armed Negro as a potential assassin. In addition, less fearful
Southerners, conditioned for generations by the military mystique,
resented Negro soldiery for the same reasons that they objected to
Negro office holders: there was an unwritten law that positions of
rank, authority, and prestige were the exclusive prerogatives of the
"superior race." Hence the southern white man was repelled by
what he considered the degrading sight of ex-slaves in uniform who
seemed, as the *Southern Opinion* had described them, "unendurably

saucy." In truth, the Negro militia was never all Negro. The militia in each state was commanded by whites, and there were varying numbers of whites in every unit. But, as historian Otis Singletary has pointed out, "the longstanding Southern indifference to logic" led to the labeling of every state militia force as "Negro militia." "As in heredity, so in the militia, a touch of Negro was sufficient to brand it as all Negro in the eyes of most Southern whites."[24]

Complaints of insolence were usually forthcoming when Negroes insisted on rights that white people took for granted but denied blacks. For example, Negro men were legally and ontologically entitled to be addressed as "sir" no less than white men, but to the white Southerner such an idea would have been the height of impertinence. "When Southern people speak of the insolence of the negro," Senator Carl Schurz of Missouri pointed out, "they generally mean something which persons who never lived under the system of slavery are not apt to appreciate." It was not the same thing as insolence among whites. "A negro is called insolent," Schurz continued, "whenever his conduct varies in any manner from what a southern man was accustomed to when slavery existed." For this reason, he added, occurrences of real antisocial behavior were comparatively rare. "On the whole, the conduct of the colored people is far more submissive than anybody had a right to expect."[25]

Since insolence injured only the white man's vanity, predictions and reports of disrespect and temerity were less disturbing than those of overt violence. Inflammatory descriptions of Negro crime were almost daily features of the racist press. Many of them were essentially reverse-color doubles of what the New York *World* called "bogus stories" about crimes against Negroes, which had been written to "create prejudice against the South." Under such circumstances, they were almost admittedly distorted for the sake of overall balance. The *Southern Opinion*, complaining of the "frequent discriminations made on all hands against us and in favor of the black man," criticized the lack of speedy police action following the attack in Richmond of a "black mob" on a drunken white man. After publishing a story describing how four hundred Negroes had robbed and beaten a white family in New Orleans, the Columbus *Crisis* observed that its "exchanges and telegraphic accounts" were filled with reports of the "most atrocious crimes" perpetrated by Negroes and "renegade whites, and committed in the name of loyalty."[26] (It neglected to specify the object of this loyalty.) The political motivation behind many of these complaints can be seen in the fact that they were most numerous in major Democratic newspapers

like the *World*, the Philadelphia *Age*, and the Chicago *Times* during
the months immediately preceding the presidential election of 1868.

Tales of horror also echoed through the halls of Congress. A white
witness in South Carolina told a congressional investigating committee
about two Negro domestics who had been well treated all of their
lives, and who had nonetheless conspired to burn their mistress's
home. According to the same witness, another Negro girl, "a bright
mulatto still living with her old owner," had said "she would delight to
be in hell, to have a churn-paddle, and churn the whites to all eternity."
In January 1868, Thomas A. Hendricks told the Indiana State Democratic Convention of "burning houses," and "pillaging bands of negroes." The white Northerner would withdraw in horror from the
sight of a "mother and children escaping from the burning home that
has sheltered and protected them," he declared. "If ever he venerated a
mother, or loved a sister or wife, his heart and hand will be for the
pale-faced woman and child of his own race." Like most racists, Hendricks did not mention the whereabouts of the white father or husband.
The emotional impact was greatest if it seemed that all isolated rural
homes in the South were occupied by widows, their children, and the
elderly, and that the war had claimed all the able-bodied men. According to Mrs. Avary, Negro criminal tendencies were aggravated by
unscrupulous white radicals, who deliberately provoked atrocities.
During the trial of Jefferson Davis, she said, a carpetbagger was heard
cautioning a group of local Negroes against doing anything reckless
while the trial judge was still in Richmond; but after he left, said the
carpetbagger, the Negroes could have a "high carnival" if they wished.
"It is not for me to advise you what to do," racists quoted the alleged
rabble-rouser as saying, "for great masses do generally what they have
a mind to."27

In truth, complaints and predictions of Negro crime were just as
exaggerated as other racist criticisms. The ex-slaves violated the law
"less often than we would be led to expect," Philip Alexander Bruce
admitted, and Carl Schurz pointed out that "acts of violence by freedmen against whites were relatively few compared to those committed
by whites against Negroes." Crimes actually attributed to Negro militiamen were surprisingly infrequent, in spite of almost continuous
white discussions of them. Similarly distorted were the crimes Negroes
reportedly committed among themselves. In March 1870, in order to
enlighten the public on the "present state of society amongst the Freedmen," Major-General O. O. Howard printed a collection of nineteen
letters he had received in January and February from John W. Alvord,

the Freedmen's Bureau's General Superintendent of Education. Howard said he hoped the letters, which described Negro progress, would "correct the false impressions which have gone abroad with regard to the colored people of the South," since they refuted racist charges of infanticide and inebriation, and similar accusations.[28]

If there was one thing that was behind the white man's resistance to social equality, it was his obsession with the issue of sexuality, especially as it related to the white woman. In the South, virtually every racist action could be justified, in the long view, on the grounds that it perpetuated, exalted, and, indeed, sanctified the myth of white womanhood. Although the attitude had its origins in the antebellum cavalier heritage of the planter class, poor and middle-class whites quickly embraced it during the postwar era and made it a fetish. The opportunity to adopt the code of the masters was in itself appealing; but far more fundamental, now that the protective barrier of slavery had been swept away, were the white man's feelings of sexual insecurity and his fears that Negro men possessed super sexual powers. Accordingly, specific references to sexual matters and white women became part of the litany of organized racism. The Ku Klux Klan glorified the honor and purity of white womanhood; and in a general condemnation of social equality, initiates to the Knights of the White Camellia, to avoid "degenerate and bastard offspring," swore to oppose intermarriage and miscegenation. Though the white woman herself was not the principal architect of the myth of white womanhood, she did, of course, subscribe to its rules. Sir George Campbell observed that the white woman encouraged the attitude of patronizing deference on the part of white men by her refusal even to "sit in the same room with a colored man," regardless of his social position.[29]

Negroes who actually showed an interest in white women were particular objects of racist contempt—and sometimes of racist violence. According to some critics, the Negro considered the right to marry a white woman the ultimate reward of social equality. A prosperous Negro in Leavenworth, Kansas, allegedly admitted that social equality made the black man too proud to marry a woman of his own race: "Lord, sar!" he said, "you not think I marry a black nigger wench?" Describing a debate over the elimination of Jim Crow laws at the radical state convention in Alabama in 1867, the Detroit *Free Press* identified several "buck negroes" who insisted on the right *"to ride in the sleeping cars with the white women!"* Some of the white delegates, the editor sneered, "seem actually to have opposed the sleeping together of their wives, sisters, mothers, and daughters with gentlemen of African descent." But there were others, "more true to their professions," who thought it was a good idea.[30]

Many of the complaints, however, were not so much expressions of concern for white women as they were manifestations of the white man's fear that the Negro's sexual powers would prove irrestible. Through all of his rantings and ravings against intermarriage, the racist showed so little faith in the white woman's judgment and her ability to resist a Negro's advances that one wonders if many white women did not consider all this reverence downright insulting.* As Herman H. Heath, editor of the Nebraska *Republican*, satirically put it, "They will marry niggers if someone don't stop them!" A suggestion of "love and wedlock among white women and black men excites the wildest rage," William Hepworth Dixon remarked in 1867. White men "will clench their hands and gnaw their lips at any allusion to the subject," he wrote revealingly. "Americans are not squeamish as to jokes; but you must not jest in their society about the loves of black men for white women." The day may come when the two could marry, he concluded, but the day when they could solemnize their vows in church without "exciting the wrath, provoking the revenge, of these masculine protectors of white women, is evidently a long way off."[31]

Most contemptible and threatening of all, in the eyes of the racist, was the willing white woman. In an article entitled " 'Dote' and His Lady Love; A Miscegenation Romance," the Peoria *Democrat* dramatized this contempt with a fictional story of a Negro brakeman and a white schoolteacher from New England who carried on a romance as his train passed the schoolhouse each day.[32] Similarly, the Detroit *Free Press* identified as Cassa Boynton and Nellie Woodward two young women who, at a party in Green Lake, Wisconsin, allegedly had kissed a Negro servant on a dare. Since each was the daughter of a well-known radical miscegenationist, the editor noted, it was no surprise that they were "depraved in taste and vulgar in habits." He went on to say that "as the old cock crows the young one learns," and that it was certain the girls had "heard their fathers boast of the delicious nectar they had, in their younger days, sipped from colored lips." Fathers who

---

* The obsession appears to be as strong today as ever. "These nigger civil rights, they're gonna end in the white man's bedroom," journalist Stewart Alsop quoted Raymond Cranford, Exalted Cyclops of the Ku Klux Klan in North Carolina, as saying. "I love my daughter, but I find her with a nigger, I'll take my gun and I'll blow her brains right out of her head." See "Portrait of a Klansman," *Saturday Evening Post* (April 9, 1966), pp. 23–27.

favored social equality could expect their daughters to end up like the daughter of a radical in Jefferson County, Missouri, the La Crosse *Democrat* surmised. After eloping, the girl returned home to present her father with a grandchild of "pumpkin hue." Nor were willing white women confined to the North. Whites in Port Gibson, Mississippi, were outraged when a local girl named Ellen Smith married a black state legislator. To Hinton R. Helper, such women were "sexless creatures in petticoats—human hermaphrodites in female garb."[33]

Thus the racist not only feared the Negro's sexual powers, but feared the white woman's sexuality and what it might lead to. The southern white woman who was spirited enough—"brazen," a racist would say— to make up her own mind exposed the hypocrisy of a corrupt way of life. For generations, southern white men had successfully dehumanized their women in order to perpetuate their own privileged position and rationalize their own sexual excesses. If white women took it upon themselves to express their sexuality fully, the presence of high-powered animalistic Negroes would allow them to destroy completely the socio-sexual culture that had evolved over the decades. The Civil War abolished slavery, it did not abolish the southern way of life.

In the mind of the fearful white supremacist, the sexual threat could manifest itself in two ways: rape and intermarriage. To Mrs. Avary, rape was the "most frightful crime which negroes commit against the white people," and the Negro rapist was essentially a product of the reconstruction period. Sir George Campbell observed, "The blacks are popularly said to be prone to that kind of crime, with what justice I cannot say." Indeed, the racist argument that emphasized Negro crime but failed to mention or at least suggest the iniquity of rape—the "scream of beauty and innocence in the flight from pursuing lust," as Hendricks put it—was hardly half an effort.[34] No words were too strong to describe such a violation, and few were withheld because they might have offended delicate ears. The Detroit *Free Press* luridly reported that two Negro men had raped a young German immigrant woman while she was convalescing after the birth of her fourth child. Similar stories appeared in many other racist newspapers: a Negro in New Haven, Connecticut, assaulted a thirteen-year-old girl; in Brookfield, Connecticut, a Negro struck one woman with a rock and raped another who was pregnant and who subsequently died with her unborn child; in South Orange, New Jersey, a black man was caught trying to seduce a five-year-old white girl; near Chambersburg, Pennsylvania, a Negro named Cam Morris raped two white women and a thirteen-year-old white girl; and in Washington, D. C., a six-year-old white girl contracted syphillis after an unsuccessful rape attempt by a Negro.[35] These were the stories as the racist press reported them; in most cases, the public never learned what really happened.

To the white Southerner, rape by a Negro was catastrophic; and the shock displayed by the victim only intensified the rage of everyone else. Mrs. Avary described a friend who had been raped as "a beautiful, gentle, high-born creature," who could not enjoy a moment's sleep as a result of her ordeal. "She would start from a slumber with a shriek, look at us with dilated eyes, then clutch us and beg for help," she reported. "But the most unspeakable pity of it all was her loathing for her own body, her prayers that she might die and her body be burned to ashes." When the sheriff came to investigate, the doctor refused to let her repeat the "horrible story." Some angry white men brought a group of Negroes for identification, but her brothers and her fiancé said, "Only over our dead bodies." Southern newspapers seemed just as anxious to catalogue lurid details as northern ones. In the summer of 1868, the Georgia *Clarion* told how ten Negroes in Swain's Mill, North Carolina, led by a black candidate for the state legislature, raped a white widow and her eight-year-old daughter. Allegedly, after accomplishing their purpose on the child with a knife, they finally killed her and her brother and left their mother insensible in a burning house.[36]

When Negroes were accused of rape, retribution was always quick. Between 1868 and 1874, Professor Singletary has pointed out, several Arkansas militiamen accused of rape received speedy trials and sentencing, and almost immediate execution. As Dixon observed, it was "generally the case when there [was] an alleged assault of any kind by a black on a white woman" that a lynching followed. Naturally, many who were innocent lost their lives. An uncertain or spiteful white woman held life in her hands; and before she had a chance to change her mind or realize the magnitude of her accusation, an innocent person often died. In 1869, police in Missouri arrested a sixteen-year-old Negro boy on suspicion of attempted rape. The "victim," the young wife of a blacksmith, had escaped unharmed; in fact, the accused had not even touched her, and everyone knew it. Nevertheless, a gang of angry whites intercepted the jail wagon and shot and killed the prisoner. Some years later, an "experienced judge" told Sir George Campbell of "many accused and many hanged," but none convicted after due process. "The mere suggestion that a black man would *like* to do something of the kind if he could seems enough to hang him," Campbell noted.[37]

While it seems preposterous to an enlightened generation in the twentieth century that any intelligent person could justify lynching, respectable people in the nineteenth century often considered it necessary. A scholarly Virginian, Philip Alexander Bruce, suggested that Negroes committed rapes in proportion to the decline in their respect for whites; therefore to eliminate the crime the certainty and severity of the punishment had to be increased. Mrs. Avary defended lynch mobs by pointing to the degree of hysteria that the act of rape created. "Only people on the spot, writhing under the agony of provocation, comprehended the fury of response to the crime of crimes," she reasoned. In her opinion, rape by a black man was so "outside of civilization" that it was not worthy of "dispassionate discussion" or "civil trial and legal penalty." Besides, she remarked almost as an afterthought, most of those lynched were probably guilty anyway. As an example she cited the case of a young Negro who had raped a ten-year-old white girl and confessed immediately, blaming a "white man f'om de Norf" for encouraging him. A rope was quickly slipped around his neck and "he dropped into eternity," Mrs. Avary said, thus saving the state and the courts a great deal of time, effort, and expense. Of course it did not occur to her that Negro rape cases which got to court were probably handled with more dispatch and less expense than any other kind of legal proceedings.[38]

Lynching was indirectly defended on the grounds that most Northerners, especially the Republicans, cared little what happened to the white women of the South. The Negro rapist "commanded observation North less by reason of what he did than by reason of what was done to him." According to Southerners, the radical press, excited over the punishment, accused the South of trying to reenslave its blacks, all the while overlooking the act that provoked the punishment. Said Mrs. Avary, "It was a minor fact that a woman was violated, that her skull was crushed or that she sustained other injuries from which she died or which made her a wreck for life—particulars too trivial to be noted by molders of public opinion writing eloquent essays on 'Crime in the South.' " She complained that there were many outraged editorials against lynching but there was "not one word of sympathy or pity for the white victim of negro lust!" From such articles, she said, the black man could draw only one conclusion—lynching was a "monstrous crime" and rape "an affair of little moment."[39]

The racists commonly accused those advocating due process of encouraging rape. According to the Columbus *Crisis*, three Negroes convicted of attacking a white woman were astonished—because they had been taught to believe that rape was trivial—at the intensity of the public outcry and at the pronouncement of the death sentence. The Ottumwa (Iowa) *Copperhead* featured a story about a Negro servant who raped a white servant girl in the same household. After the rapist had fled to a different city and had taken another job as a domestic, he was caught in the act of sexually assaulting his new employer's daughter. "We understand that the darkey seems to think rather lightly over the affair and considers that he did no more than any white man," the *Copperhead* sneered; he feels that "there is nothing to make a fuss over."⁴⁰

To the perceptive observer, all these racist reactions to rape by Negroes revealed a basic dilemma in American, and especially southern, attitudes toward interracial sexual relations. There were, undoubtedly, cases of white women who invited black men into their beds—perhaps to get even with husbands who kept Negro mistresses—but troubled by feelings of guilt, cried "rape." Accordingly, the white man's eagerness to lynch was partly the result of a subconscious suspicion that his woman might find a black man sexually desirable. In such a situation, the Negro was the victim of the "rape," as well as the victim of a false accusation and a murder.

It was also very likely that the Negro, though uneducated, was familiar enough with the system to know the risk he was taking. Yet, in a sense, he was doing nothing more than imitating his "betters." Southern slaveowners, enduring no punishment and little criticism, had been seducing Negro women for generations. Although it might have been technically impossible to call this rape, the hardships of a system that drove a black woman to acquiesce in the master's demands, if for no other reason than to survive, made it, in effect, rape. The institution of slavery had taught the Negro to look up to the white man as the "standard of perfection," David Macrae asserted, "and therefore the pattern for imitation."⁴¹ With such an example, it is easy to see how a Negro might have minimized the seriousness of rape, thinking, as the *Copperhead* suggested, "that he did no more than any white man."

Less dramatic and emotional than the fear of rape but in reality more fundamental to the contradiction in white beliefs about interracial sexual relations was the belief that social equality would lead to intermarriage. "If a negro may stand by a white man and vote, sit by him in a jury box, testify against him in court, and hold office *over* him," a delegate to the Indiana State Democratic Convention asked in 1866, "why may not the races marry and be given in marriage?" According to the Detroit *Free Press*, a Negro (nameless, of course), had said, "I want the privilege of going to see any white man, of eating with him, of sleeping with him—and, if I choose to, why shouldn't I marry his daughter?"[42] Aware of the prevalence of Negro concubinage in the antebellum era, and of the common complaint of whites that moral laxity was an inherent characteristic of the black race, many Negroes doubtless saw the glaring hypocrisy in the racist argument against intermarriage.

In its appeal to the white man's sexual insecurities, this aspect of the postwar white-supremacy crusade was similar to the rape scares and to the miscegenation controversy of 1864. But in other ways it was quite different. In the first place, there was no promotion involved— there were no publications to match Croly's "Miscegenation" or Van Evrie's "Subjenation." In the second place, postwar feelings did not erupt in one brief climacteric of hysteria, like the 1864 presidential campaign. Third, the miscegenation controversy had been confined largely to the eastern cities; but intermarriage—although if it had become widespread it would have had its most profound consequences in the South—concerned many people in all sections of the country. Finally, during the war, racist issues were easily overwhelmed in the public mind by military matters. But now, with the war over and four million ex-slaves involved, the public had time to think about the potential effects of emancipation.

With intermarriage as with many aspects of their cause, racists sought sympathy for the unfortunate "poor whites." They asked who the victims of the radical drive toward social equality through inter-marriage would be, and answered that it was the lower-class whites who would be forced into unnatural unions with blacks. After Governor Richard Oglesby of Illinois innocently suggested at a meeting of the Irish Republican Brotherhood (the Fenians) that Negroes were the equals of white men, the Chicago *Times* accused him of encouraging black men to court Irish women. In 1873 an obscure religious writer named A. C. Harness published a pamphlet (expanded in the same year into a 372-page book) condemning radical reconstruction in which he asked, "For whom is miscegenation intended?" In answering his own question, he asked, "Why, who is it that bears all the wrongs of society? Who has to dress plainer, eat less, and work harder to pay taxes?" If human mules were to be made in America, he said, Ireland and Germany would supply "fresh horses (poor white trash), and the supply of asses (negroes) on hand is pretty large."[43]

Although racists accused the Republicans of fostering mulattoism, there were numerous indications that most Republicans were just as opposed to intermarriage as the racists were. The Republican party controlled most of the northern state legislatures during the reconstruction

era, but they did nothing to repeal existing state laws prohibiting intermarriage. Indeed, racists frequently pointed to these anti-miscegenation
laws to prove that white people everywhere, and in both parties, opposed race mixing. Speaking in the Senate in 1870, Garrett Davis of
Kentucky named four New England states, supposedly the heartland
of abolitionism, that had had, at one time or another since the eigh-
teenth century, laws prohibiting marriage between races. "Will the
pretty daughter of the bondaucrat marry a buck negro?" Harness
asked (referring to the new group of conservative Republican financiers,
like Jay Cooke, who had made fortunes marketing government bond
issues during the war). "Will his rich son kiss the thick, husky lips of
a negro wench? Hardly, I think."[44]

Nevertheless, most racists were convinced that intermarriage was
part and parcel of Republican reconstruction policies. The Richmond
Southern Opinion called a gathering of local scalawags and Negroes the
"Mongrel Convention." And the Chicago *Times* reprinted a story from
the Nashville *Banner* about a despicable affair in which two black men
had fought for the attentions of a married white woman. According to
the *Times*, after the woman had divorced her white husband and had
married one of the Negroes, her white teenage son inadvertently discovered her and her new spouse engaging in marital intimacies. The
Negro husband, mistaking the white boy for his old rival, shot and
killed the innocent youth. Charging that Republican race policies led
to this sort of thing, the *Times* concluded that "miscegenation and
murder" were essential ingredients of social equality.[45] In the spring
of 1868, the New York *World* accused the congressmen and senators
from the five New England states of conspiring at that very moment to
"force negro equality and miscegenation upon the people of ten American states." According to the *World*, Senator Sumner endorsed the
"bounty of the flesh," calling for the impressment of white women
into unnatural relations with black men. A few months later, the
Indianapolis *State Sentinel* charged that David M. Long, an Indiana
Republican, forced his sixteen-year-old-daughter to marry a Negro
after the girl had refused to accept as her stepmother her father's Negro
bride. Reprinting the story, the Columbus *Crisis* insisted that this situation was typical among the radicals. The most dastardly crime a man
could commit, Buckner H. Payne's notorious "Ariel"* reflected, was
to "give his daughter in marriage to a negro—a beast—or to take one
of their females for his wife."[46] Long had done both.

* "Ariel" is discussed in Chapter 1, pp. 6–7.

To hear the critics tell it, the carpetbaggers were intermarrying on a grand scale. A Negro woman in Florida was reported to have said, "Rich Yankees in de wintertime; crap uh white nigger babies in de fall." Such affairs were doubly evil, racists complained, because they set bad examples for simple-minded ex-slaves. One carpetbagger whose marriage received much publicity was A. T. Morgan, a former Ohio farmer who had moved south and became sheriff of Yazoo County, Mississippi. He married a young, part-Negro schoolteacher from New York, and was quoted as telling his brother, "She is a wonderful creature, that girl of mine. Her breath is as pure and sweet as if it came off a bed of spring violets." Though the new Mrs. Morgan was only one-eighth Negro, racists north and south made the marriage one of their favorite propaganda topics, and even some of Morgan's radical friends frowned on it. In 1871, while attending a session of the Louisiana State Senate—a session presided over by a Negro—Scotsman Robert Somers said that a white senator who had married a black woman was just one of many "negro-marrying legislators in Louisiana and South Carolina."[47]

Extremists cried that the government was falling into the hands of amalgamationists, the leaders of the "new era of miscegenation, amalgamation, and promiscuous intercourse between the races"; these leaders agreed that "the pretty Caucasian women of America were fit only to be used as bait to catch Sambo and Cuffee." According to the Columbus *Crisis*, the staunchly Republican *Harper's Weekly* was the major organ of pro-miscegenation propaganda. But to most Republicans, and probably to most Americans, the charge of forced intermarriage was too absurd to deserve a reply. The satirists, of course, could not let the issue pass without an answer. "Let the shuddrin' uv Democratic damsels over the horrors uv bein forst to contract matermonyel alliances with niggers be got up immejitly," David Locke wrote, "and let their shudders be strong."[48] What Locke so clearly perceived, of course, was the implicit racist admission that the white woman could not be trusted to resist, and indeed might even welcome, an opportunity to marry a Negro.

There was another side to the masculine glorification of womanhood, but one that the white supremacist would certainly not admit existed. Negro men, after generations of watching slaveowners gratify their lust at the expense of Negro women, were just as sensitive about their womenfolk as white men, and, in truth, had far greater cause for alarm than whites. Considering the state of dependency of the female slave and the total absence of legal protection for the southern black woman, slave or free, the element of coercion was almost always present in her sexual liaisons with white men. In 1868, a black delegate to the Mississippi State Constitutional Convention agreed to support a proposed law against intermarriage if it included a section prohibiting white men from keeping Negro mistresses. Negro delegates to other conventions supported similar resolutions for largely the same reason.* As late as 1883, Negroes in Texas were still pleading for a stronger law against concubinage—a law with a punishment at least equal to that for intermarriage. Like the statutes in most other southern states and a few northern states, the original Texas law encouraged promiscuity because the punishment for concubinage was slight and the penalty for intermarriage was severe. Furthermore, as a Negro carpenter from Montgomery, Alabama, pointed out to a Senate investigating committee, the black woman did not have the same opportunity for legal redress of grievances that the white woman enjoyed. "This is what I want," he argued, "to protect the virtue of our girls."[49]

Despite racist outcries against miscegenation, and despite pleas from several quarters for stricter laws against concubinage, southern white men were reluctant to acknowledge any wrongdoing. An old man in Mississippi told Morgan that concubinage, since it provided a valuable "training ground" for young unmarried white men, should be legalized and protected. As a "safety valve" for the white man's supposedly superabundant sexual energies, it played a vital role in glorifying white womanhood. Prohibiting sexual relations between white men and Negro women, he concluded, would eliminate a valuable "stabilizing" social element. To satisfy the "demand" for an outlet, white women would be forced into prostitution. Other Southerners, for less outlandish reasons, opposed such a ban because they simply resented any meddling in their personal lives. A report made by the Grand Jury of Madison, Georgia, condemning the open interracial philandering of certain local white citizens aroused the anger of the men implicated—they insisted that the "private affairs of the people should not be intruded upon." And, some years later, even Mrs. Avary claimed that most black women preferred white men to Negroes. According to her, a mulatto woman was supposed to have said, "Nigger gal ain' nuvver gwi have a black chile ef she kin git a white one."[50]

* Beginning around 1830 and continuing through reconstruction, these were numerous conventions of Negroes, most of them unrelated to any special organizations. They were generally ad hoc meetings, called to air some particular grievance. See J. H. Franklin, *From Slavery to Freedom* (second edition, New York, 1956), pp. 233–234.

The racist's fears and predictions notwithstanding, intermarriage was the exception rather than the rule. It was easy to cite examples because they were conspicuous, not because they were numerous. There were sweeping changes in most southern state constitutions under the Reconstruction Acts, but no radical state government repealed existing laws against intermarriage. Even in the courts, racism, however absurdly rationalized, held sway. In *Charlotte Scott, defendant in error,* v. *The State of Georgia* (1869), State Supreme Court Justice C. J. Brown, ruling that no legislature can regulate social status, *upheld* an anti-intermarriage law on the grounds that its repeal would "force" people into unnatural relations. To abolish the statute, he said, would be to use legislation to interfere with social status. As it stood, the law left "social rights and status where it finds them" and prohibited "the legislature from repealing any laws in existence which protect persons in the free regulation among themselves of matters properly termed social."[51] In short, Justice Brown was saying that the law prohibiting intermarriage was merely a legal acknowledgment of an existing natural condition, but that its repeal would be "interference" with "social rights and status."*

To many racists, the radicals to fear were those who actually practiced social equality. For example, after a carpetbagger in Richmond had apologized to a gathering of Negroes for some unkind remarks in the northern press and concluded by expressing mock shame for being a white man, a member of the audience was heard to shout, "Ne'm min', boss! Yo' heart's black! Dat's good enough." Although most of those present may have seen this as a compliment, the racist press saw it as

---

* Despite a century of civil rights agitation, state legislatures have been notoriously slow in repealing anti-miscegenation statutes. Oregon rescinded its law in 1951, followed by Montana in 1953, North Dakota in 1955, Colorado and South Dakota in 1957, California, Idaho, and Nevada in 1959, Arizona in 1962, Nebraska and Utah in 1963, and Wyoming and Indiana in 1965. Thus, by the centennial anniversary of Appomattox, only the seventeen southern and border states still had laws against racial intermarriage. These laws usually involved only white-Negro marriages. In most cases, Negroes and other non-whites were still permitted to marry. One exception was in North Carolina where the "Croatoan" Indians, whose ancestors had presumably absorbed Virginia Dare's "lost colony" of Roanoke Island between 1587 and 1591, were likewise prohibited from marrying Negroes on the grounds that some of them *might* be part white. Finally, on June 12, 1967, almost a century after the ratification of the Fourteenth Amendment, the United States Supreme Court in the case of *Loving* v. *Virginia* invalidated all remaining anti-miscegenation laws on the grounds that no state had the right to deny a person his choice of spouse because of race.

a statement of disgusing fact. Testifying before a congressional committee investigating the Ku Klux Klan, a white Southerner asserted that carpetbaggers gave the freedmen hard liquor, brought them home to meet their wives and families, and attended their picnics.[52]

But the evidence did not support these accusations. In most of the South, carpetbaggers and other radicals who preached social equality seldom practiced it. In the summer of 1867, more than two thousand Negroes and carpetbag and scalawag whites met at a Republican Convention in Morgantown, North Carolina. They resolved that "no sensible person of any complexion desires or expects social equality," and said that anyone who suggested it was one of the objects of the Republican party was a "base slanderer." Over twenty years later, a Negro in Montgomery, Alabama, told a touring Senate committee, "I don't want no social equality with the white people, and I don't want them to have none with me." Yet the racists continued to search out those who were most alarmed by the thought of social equality. For example, the scalawags, many of whom had been non-slaveholding Southerners before the war, abhorred the thought. Charles Nordhoff, a Northerner who traveled in the South in 1875, remarked that racist Democrats critical of radical reconstruction had "naturally worked upon [the scalawags'] fears on this point, and thus found their best argument put into their hands by these Republican leaders in the North," who were insisting on civil rights for the freedmen.[53]

But most white supremacists agreed that the radicals rarely concerned themselves seriously with the ex-slave's social condition, and believed that the Republican party actually opposed social equality. Even in Washington, D. C., where the freedmen had been the beneficiaries of considerable federal aid, they remained wretchedly destitute. Edward A. Pollard charged that as a result of Republican neglect, ex-slaves, instead of winning social equality, were living on the brink of starvation. In a similar vein, Robert L. Dabney, a southern clergyman and former Confederate officer, said that starvation was the only thing the African in America had to thank the selfish radical for. Senator John B. Henderson of Missouri remarked that while Republicans cried for social equality, they increased discrimination. Except for a few fools and fanatics who would prove their sincerity by intermarriage and social mixing, the Chicago *Times* argued, most Republicans only pretended to endorse social equality. President Grant "won't shampoo in a nigger barber shop, but we must," Bill Arp commented. "He wouldn't set by em in a car, or a hotel, or a meetin house, but we've got to."[54]

At no time during the reconstruction era, of course, did Negroes north or south secure anything even resembling social equality. Most white Americans simply did not consider such a situation possible; and many Republicans discouraged or at least evaded the issue. Thus, there were very few sincere efforts to see that Negroes achieved social equality, and there was no chance at all that what efforts there were would succeed.

Chapter Eight

THE ELECTION
OF 1872 AND THE DECLINE
OF THE RACE ISSUE

With Liberal Republican campaign posters blaring "Turn the Rascals Out!" in 1872, racist demagoguery, as a major force in national politics, began to fade. The Democratic party, naming no presidential candidate of its own, did not even acknowledge the race issue in its platform, a move that James Gordon Bennett considered a "radical change of base." The party had abandoned the old war issues, he observed, and had accepted the constitutional amendments as "fixed facts."[1]

Signs that the race issue was losing political importance appeared as early as March 1867, barely two weeks after the passage of the first Reconstruction Act. "It is certain that the next Presidential election cannot be carried on the negro question," the New York *World* forecasted. It stated that with the passage of the supplementary Reconstruction Bill, which was then pending, race would "be taken out of national politics," and that affairs could no longer revolve around the Negro. A few weeks later, the Philadelphia *Age*, less optimistic than the *World*, cautiously predicted that the country would "not always be deluded with the negro question." The black man would probably get the ballot, the editor said, and "find his level"; then the nation could get on to other matters. The race issue was "rapidly solving itself," George Lunt, a contemporary historian, noted, "cruelly for the black man, prejudicially for the white."[2]

Although the decline of the race issue was not as early or as rapid as these observers suggested, it was nonetheless obvious on several fronts. As an object of both radical sympathy and racist scorn, the Negro grew progressively less popular in books, pamphlets, newspapers, periodicals, and speeches. In 1869, complaining of the "diminished product" of serious books and pamphlets, the literary editor of the *American Annual Cyclopedia* pointed to the drain on the "mental energies" of the American people that had been imposed by the crucial issues of the war and reconstruction. As a result of this exhaustion on the part of both writers and reading public, he wrote, our most productive and important authors have grown "apathetic to our most pressing public interests." After the ratification of the Fifteenth Amendment in March 1870, most of the conservatives (and not a few of the radicals) in the Republican party, believing that their work on the ex-slave's behalf had been accomplished, did indeed begin to grow "apathetic to our most pressing public interests." The three great amendments were, to many, the finished products of a humanitarian reform movement that had begun half a century earlier. From now on, many people thought, the Negro had to advance his own cause.[3]

An example of Republican ambivalence about one aspect of the race question can be seen in the change in policy of Senator Carl Schurz of Missouri. As a radical journalist, Schurz had toured the South shortly after the war and had recommended unqualified Negro suffrage. However, realizing by 1870 that the uneducated freedmen had been too easily manipulated by political opportunists who were concerned only with their own fortunes, Schurz asserted that his original recommendation had been wrong, or at least premature.[4] Although there were certainly other important questions involved, this reaction was influential in the formation of the Liberal Republican faction of 1872 and the later Mugwump movement. The race issue had some political effects on the national level after 1872, but the Republicans themselves were frequently divided over its significance and political utility.

Such inertia was bound to lead to a corresponding weakening of racist zeal (although it is possible to argue that it was the other way around). In fact, it appears that racist demagoguery faded faster than the equalitarianism it was supposed to be counteracting. From the early 1870's on, talk about the race issue became more and more monologue; Republicans who continued to argue for the rights of the freedmen and wave the "bloody shirt" were increasingly talking to themselves. Most of the Democratic state party platforms of 1870 ignored the race issue; and only a few state conventions passed resolutions concerning the Negro's status. Nebraska's Democratic newspapers had furiously and frequently denounced both Republicans and Negroes

between 1865 and 1870. By 1872 such denunciations were coming in a
trickle, and in 1873 they were almost nonexistent. In 1876, making a
belated reply to his critics, Buckner H. Payne, the author of the notorious book *The Negro: What Is His Ethnological Status?* (1867),
could only offer a picayune theological cavil over the writings of Moses.
As Dixon observed in the same year, the bloody shirt fervor of the
early postwar years was rapidly disappearing. Feeling sympathy for
their "oppressed" white brethren in the South, he wrote, "Americans
begin to cry—'close ranks!' "[5]

But the most startling change of all was in the writings and speeches
of some opponents of radical Republicanism who had been (and presumably still were) white supremacy fanatics. Five years after his unsuccessful bid, on a racist platform, for the governorship of Ohio,
George W. Morgan denounced the policies of the Republican party
but completely ignored the Negro. In March 1871, the Columbus *Crisis*
praised a speech by Charles Sumner, calling it sober and statesmanlike.
Such a reaction would have been inconceivable a few years earlier, but
the Massachusetts senator, because of his disaffection from the Grant
administration, apparently had won some favor among the racists.
Two months later, at a Democratic rally in Ohio, none other than
Clement L. Vallandigham pleaded for a "new departure" in party principles. It was time to stop attacking accomplished facts like the Fifteenth
Amendment, the old Copperhead said; secession, slavery, and inequality
before the law were dead. His concessions shocked even the *Crisis*. In
Congress, similar arguments were heard from many who had been
ardent Negrophobes. There were, of course, exceptions. Van Evrie continued to advertise and distribute some of his own pamphlets, most of
them written a decade or more earlier, under the label "The White
Man's Political Library."[6]

The emerging apathy of the Republicans and the changing views
of the Democrats had two fundamental causes. The first was a growing
realization among most Americans that the threat of "Africanization"
was groundless, that the racists' ominous predictions were not material-
izing. The most important political offices in the South were filled by
white men, not Negroes; and the hated carpetbaggers and scalawags
lost their power very quickly in most states. Georgia was under radical
control for less than a year and a half—from the summer of 1870 to the
fall of 1871—and North Carolina and Texas "endured" for only two
years. Tennessee, never subjected to the terms of the Reconstruction
Acts, became, in October 1869, the first former Confederate state to
return to the control of the white conservatives. With the ascendancy

of similar interests assured at about the same time, Virginia returned to the Union in the following January. Ten months later, conservatives in North Carolina regained control of their state, and conservatives soon took power in the other southern states: Texas in 1873, Arkansas and Alabama in 1874, Mississippi in 1875, South Carolina in 1876, and Louisiana and Florida in 1877. Thus, the immediate aim of most southern racists was, in reality, accomplished fairly quickly.[7]

As southern whites regained control of their region, most Northerners, never especially eager to interfere on the Negro's behalf in the first place, grew more and more willing to accept the idea that the South was indeed "different." Thus although the "peculiar institution" ceased to exist, a peculiar "way of life" survived. The rejection of radical control and the resistance to racial equality did not, of course, come about easily. Racist demagogues in the postwar South worked long and hard to guarantee white supremacy. But there were some basic differences between northern and southern racism, differences that partially account for many of the unique developments in southern politics in the years since reconstruction. Although the South produced its share of malignant editorials, outraged pamphlets, and fiery speeches, southern whites did not have to be convinced of the black man's "place" and "inferiority" or asked to hate the radicals or to vote a certain way.[8] From Appomattox on, the white South was staunchly anti-Republican and anti-Negro.

Because of these fundamental differences, racism in the South was physical rather than verbal, overt rather than furtive, obtrusive rather than devious. Southern white supremacists exhibited their hatred of Negroes, carpetbaggers, and federal authorities with threats, intimidation, social and economic pressures, and outright violence. As members of the Ku Klux Klan, the Knights of the White Camellia, the White Leagues, or just an unorganized gang, they soon made life intolerable for many Negroes and for whites working on the Negroes' behalf. Although the original aims of the Ku Klux Klan had been social, leadership soon fell "into the hands of utter scoundrels," and racism became its exclusive mission. Initiates to the Knights of the White Camellia had to swear "to maintain and defend the social and political superiority of the White Race on this Continent"; this implied that violence would be used when necessary, and it was used. Smaller and less well known, but equally menacing, were such groups as the Pale Faces in Tennessee, the Constitutional Guard and the White Brotherhood in North Carolina, the Council of Safety in South Carolina, the Men of Justice in Alabama, the Society of the White Rose in Mississippi, and the Sons of Washington in Texas.[9]

Among the most numerous and militant societies were the so-called White Leagues and the White Line clubs. "Let there be White Leagues formed in every town, village, and hamlet of the South," the Atlanta *News* proclaimed in 1874. "Every Southern State should swarm with White Leagues." The acknowledged object of the leagues was to oppose the "Black Leagues," and to "save the White race." The White Leagues were an army, Dixon noted in 1876, "ready, on two hours' notice, to fall in." To many Republicans, the Leagues were the most dangerous of all southern racist groups. Senator Morton of Indiana denounced the brutal treatment of Negroes in Mississippi at the hands of its members. Representative James A. Garfield of Ohio accused the White League of New Orleans of using force to prevent Negroes from voting. A few days later, George F. Hoar of Massachusetts stood on the same rostrum in the House of Representatives, and stating that the New Orleans White League had twenty-five hundred to three thousand members, repeated many of Morton's and Garfield's accusations.[10]

Though southern racist demagoguery attracted men from all walks of life, the rowdier elements of white society, including idle boys who intimidated Negroes for amusement and hardened fanatics who willingly committed murder to guarantee white supremacy, dominated the secret organizations. Humiliated by defeat, loitering in busy places with no money, jobs, education, or supervision, understanding neither the significance of Negro freedom as advocated by most Northerners nor the cavalier traditions of upper-class southern whites, they resorted to violence almost spontaneously. Nevertheless, respectable whites could not escape some responsibility for inciting or encouraging acts of violence against the freedmen. Many organizers and officers of the Knights of the White Camellia and the White Leagues were also recognized community leaders. In South Carolina, Ku Klux Klan activity was closely linked with the state Democratic machine. Angered over the cruel treatment of ex-slaves, a northern writer named James Brewster insisted that prominent white Southerners had caused most of the organized violence. There was no doubt that white leaders often tacitly encouraged violence; and on most occasions they at least refused to speak out against such actions, thus by their silence endorsing the racist excesses of their more impulsive neighbors.[11]

Scores of incidents apparently unrelated to specific organizations made life miserable for Negroes and southern radicals. A Negro postal agent, whose appearance on a railroad mail car in Kentucky had offended local whites, endured a savage beating—for which Democrats and Republicans blamed each other. Southern racists persistently intimidated and harrassed northern "do-gooders" and the "nigger-loving" agents of the Freedmen's Bureau and Union Leagues. In a letter to the white schoolmaster of a Negro school in Pike County, Alabama, quoted in the Alabama *State Journal*, an anonymous racist urged the "outsider," in order to avoid "one of the worst scourings that a man ever got," to dismiss his "nigger school" and "leave this settlement with [his] negro children." In 1876, after listening to extensive testimony, a special committee of the United States Senate reported similar threats and actions against both Negroes and whites in Mississippi.[12]

Yet despite the overwhelming evidence to the contrary, many observers—and not all of them Southerners—claimed that race relations in the South were improving; that there was no violence, no discrimination, and no prejudice—in short, that there was no racism. Writing from Meridian, Mississippi, in January 1871, Robert Somers insisted that the Ku Klux Klan was "dying fast, if not already dead." Consequently, the "distrusts and animosities" of earlier years were "rapidly dying out." The main objective now before the South, he said, was "to secure a more efficient administration of justice, without respect to party or color." Louisiana White League officials, convinced that they should suppress suspected Negro rebellions for the good of both races, paradoxically asked their members to "forget all differences of opinion and race prejudices of the past," and for the "common good of both races," work "to reestablish a white man's government." An officer of the Knights of the White Camellia, Dr. George P. L. Reid, former commander of the Central Circle in Perry County, Alabama, actually declared, "I have no knowledge of a single case of violence by the Camellias, and I was in a position to know if there were any."[13]

Some of the testimony on the so-called harmonious relations between southern whites and blacks bordered on the preposterous. During a congressional investigation into charges of mistreatment of ex-slaves, a Georgia newspaper editor named C. W. Howard flatly denied that there had ever been any racist sentiment among whites in his state. On the contrary, he added, their behavior had been unexpectedly commendable. In view of the Negro's newly won rights and privileges, it would have been "very natural to suppose that the whites, as a mass, would have a feeling of the strongest animosity toward them." But such had not been the case, Howard concluded, and the two races, "in their intercourse with each other, have acted in a manner which no former experience would have led us to anticipate." Even the Negroes, one writer remarked, had great hopes for the future. Race prejudice, a freedman in Florida was quoted as saying, "is passing away." In 1871, at a community meeting of local whites and Negroes in Holly Springs, Mississippi, those in attendance agreed that there had been less racial violence after the war than at any time before. Northern travelers in the South often made less optimistic but similar observations. Charles Nordhoff crossed the deep South in the spring of 1875 and reported to his editor, in a series of controversial letters, that the freedmen enjoyed all the rights of their white neighbors, who, in fact, regarded the black community as an "integral and important part of the population."[14]

The second fundamental element in the decline of racist demagoguery was the emergence of new issues that were largely unrelated to the race question and that encouraged critics to abandon their old, frequently ineffective clichés and take a fresh approach. The problems "bequeathed by the civil war," a literary reviewer noted in 1869, had yielded to questions of taxes, free trade, women's suffrage, and other matters. "The difficulty is not that important matters are neglected," he said, "but that the best thought of the community is brought only so indirectly into relation with its governing forces."[15]

However, although the Democrats were gradually losing interest in the race issue, the topsy-turvy presidential campaign of 1872 indicated that they could not find another issue of equal impact and unanimity of sentiment. The Republican party, divided over questions of government corruption and inefficiency, nominated two candidates. Unable or unwilling to take advantage of the schism (they took advantage of a similar split later, in 1912), Democratic leaders, meekly endorsing Horace Greeley over the protests of the more vociferous dissenters, forfeited their opportunity to offer the voters a party choice and nominated no candidate. Perhaps no single event reflected more clearly the dwindling importance of the race issue and the emergence of other questions. The Liberal Republicans had repudiated the traditional party leadership to defend the same principles that the Democrats had been turning to—namely, ending both corruption and the spoils system. "Turn the Rascals Out!" could have been a Democratic slogan had not the Greeley forces snatched it.

The extent of the Democratic shift can be seen in the identities of some of Greeley's most outspoken supporters. In August 1872, "Sunset" Cox himself asked the staunchly Democratic Hickory Club of New York City's Fifteenth Ward to support the Liberal Republican candidate. A similar plea came from Richmond's Edward A. Pollard. Unlike Cox, Pollard did not ignore the race issue, but invited Negroes to assist in unseating the radicals. "The bringing together of the negro and the 'Conservative' whites of the South on the question of Mr. Greeley's election," he declared, "is its happiest and most peculiar circumstance." Denying the insidious accusations of intractable Democratic "stalwarts" who complained of a sellout, Pollard insisted that Greeley had always opposed integrated schools and endorsed the same kind of equality that all right-thinking Southerners advocated—equality with the races separate. In fact, he said, Greeley had never been a genuine abolitionist. Similarly, Francis P. Blair, Jr., was confident that the German voters of the Midwest, under the prodding of Senator Schurz, would swing the election to Greeley.[16] It is not unreasonable to assume that many voters rubbed their eyes in disbelief.

There was some justification for the racist support of Greeley. One of the ostensible reasons for the decline of racist demagoguery was that the Republican party appeared to have abandoned the Negro cause in a relatively short time—and no one personified this abandonment better than Greeley. During a trip through the South in 1871, he ignored the freedmen; and in April of the following year he accused them of lacking initiative.[17] Thus, even among equalitarians, political or economic expediency occasionally overshadowed humanitarian zeal. The issue of corruption among public officials was new, and therefore superseded the race question in the arena of political debate. Critics of the government began pointing to events like the Crédit Mobilier scandal involving Congress and the Union Pacific Railroad Company. Although this financial manipulation did not involve the President—and it actually occurred in 1868, before Grant began his first term—the episode came to light in the election year of 1872; thus the Democrats tried hard to identify it with the Grant regime. Other questionable developments—such as the President's scheme to annex Santo Domingo, essentially to safeguard American speculative interests there, the Salary Grab Act of 1873, the Indian affairs scandal involving Secretary of War W. W. Belknap, and the so-called whiskey ring affair—further tarnished the government's image. Though it was true that not all of these unsavory events had occurred or come to light during Grant's first term, the growing tendency among public officials to compromise their public trust for personal gain, ranging from carpetbag corruption in the South to the Tweed ring in New York City, was obvious enough to become a major issue in the presidential election of 1872.

There were, of course, dissident Democrats and conservatives who refused both to endorse Greeley and to abandon the race issue. Many Southerners, for example, simply could not support a man who had

stood so strongly for emancipation. To them it would have been tanta-
mount to supporting Garrison, Phillips, or Sumner. The chairman of
Kentucky's Democratic Executive Committee urged all the county
chairmen in his state to oppose Greeley's candidacy because of his
earlier *Tribune* editorials endorsing racial equality. Other Democrats
in both North and South, for essentially the same reasons, made similar
protests.[18] In the end, the voters, probably a little indifferent and certainly somewhat confused by the erratic obfuscation of party loyalties,
gave Grant a majority twice as large as his margin over Seymour and
almost twice the size of Lincoln's over McClellan.

> To be sure there is always a bit of a row,
> When we choose our tycoon, and especially now;
> For things are so mixed, how's a fellow to know,
> What party he's of, and what vote he shall throw[?]
> White's getting so black, and black's getting so white,
> Republic-rat, Dem-ican, can't get'em right![19]

After the election, the Democratic–Liberal Republican coalition sput-
tered into oblivion.

This is not to say that racism was politically insignificant after 1872.
Although it was becoming obvious to the demagogues that they could
not arouse the intense emotions they had aroused in earlier years, the
race issue was far from dead. Debates over the Civil Rights Act of 1875
included many heated exchanges between its Republican supporters
and its Democratic opponents. After reconstruction, southern whites
skillfully exploited white supremacy to ensure their takeover of government and guarantee the demise of southern Republicanism, a move
that even had some Negro cooperation. The race issue played a role in
the various federal and state elections from 1876 to 1892 (and especially
in the congressional and presidential elections of 1880). But the debate
went increasingly one way. It had been the very rise of Liberal Republicanism that signaled the beginning of the end of an era in racist
demagoguery. Although many Republicans continued to champion
the Negro's cause for some years, the party as a whole did not display
the same unity it had shown in the early reconstruction period. Dis-
illusioned and desperate, James G. Blaine resurrected the bloody shirt
in 1884; but the Mugwump element, anxious to drop the Negro question altogether, mustered enough support to split the party.[20]

The decline of the race issue can only be fully understood when
viewed in relation to the decline of radicalism. It must be remembered

that the radicals had come to power in the flush of strong northern feelings against the South. Aggravating the hatreds generated by the war had been the President's assassination by a southern sympathizer, the de facto reenslavement of the Negro through the black codes, the incorrigibility of many southern whites, and Andrew Johnson's unwillingness to even consider moderate Republican proposals. But public enthusiasm was bound to wane, and when it did the militants would lose much of their support. As Northerners grew weary of the bloody shirt, candidates for office who had campaigned with antisouthern slogans turned to other tactics. The division within Republican ranks, which began with the rise of the liberals in Missouri in 1870, portended trouble for the radicals.

When it became obvious that the radicals could not depend on the southern black vote forever, racist demagoguery began to lose its political purpose. The practical impossibility of maintaining the Negro power base must have been increasingly apparent to all parties. The Negro vote had ensured the radical control of Congress, and it had guaranteed Ulysses S. Grant his popular majority in 1868 (though he would have won the electoral vote without it). But the Republican party could expect this support only while it controlled the southern state governments. How long could the equalitarian cause continue to depend on federal bayonets? It was obvious that military rule would have to come to an end sooner or later, and when it did the freedmen would cease to be the unified bloc that guaranteed the "perpetual ascendancy" of the Republican party. Surely the Negro, after generations of learning to accommodate the master in order to safeguard his own welfare, could see the expediency of coming to terms with the white power structure.

It appeared that the radicals, if they expected to ensure their future with a combination of black votes and antisouthern feeling, had based their hopes on a slender reed. Of course, there had been more enduring components of their power base—the firm alliance between the Republican party and business and financial interests, for example. But the entrepreneurs did not control enough votes to keep the radicals in office, and it was largely over the radicals' economic transgressions that the radical and liberal factions had polarized; thus, the business community's identification with the Republican party hurt the cause of radicalism just as much as it helped. Whatever the effect, it was not enough by itself to ensure the continuation of the hard radical line. Though it might be attributing more perception to the liberals than they possessed, it is not unreasonable to assume that they were aware

of the handicap of being too closely identified with the economic elite
but failed to capitalize on the situation because of the intrinsic nega-
tivism of intraparty disputes.

In the last analysis, the radical front must have seemed, at least to
the intellectuals in the liberal camp, an inappropriate base from which
to maintain a humanitarian program. In their view, the idealism of
the war and early reconstruction had broken down under the brutalizing
effects of power and the increasing misuse of public office. It was the
worst sort of hypocrisy for the selfish to appear selfless. How could
congressional endorsements of civil rights for black men be sincere,
some liberals probably asked themselves, when dozens of congressmen
seemed so patently insincere in everything else? Disenchanted by the
intrigues of erstwhile equalitarians, Republican reformers must have
viewed the government's humanitarian overtures with mounting in-
credulity.[21] The Liberal Republican's "liberalism" was, in a very real
sense, a conservative manifestation—a desire to restore the genuine
reform spirit of earlier times. But the term "conservative" was still
associated in the public mind with the southern "incorrigibles" and
the old Copperheads; thus, none of the conventional labels applied
any more. Even the language of politics had been corrupted.

To most Northerners, the status of the Negro was the South's problem, and Southerners had their own way of handling it. Many Americans, though committed to the principle of equality, continued to
believe that certain people were innately superior to others. The Republican party controlled the presidency until 1885, but by then the
race issue, elbowed aside by charges of scandal and economic bungling,
found itself in the shadows. Even the Civil Rights Act of 1875, the
effort of a diminishing congressional majority, was marked by a spirit
of finality. As journalist Alexander K. McClure belatedly observed in
1886, Grover Cleveland's election in 1884 ended "all effort at political
organization on the race line." Though the Republicans had had many
opportunities for "partial success," he said, the Democratic victory had
completely eliminated the Negro issue. "Today there is nothing left of
race organization in politics."[22] McClure was correct, though late; the
attempt to incorporate the Negro electorate in the Republican party
had collapsed with the end of radical reconstruction.

But while Republicans failed at "political organization on the race
line," Democrats likewise failed at political organization on the racist
line. They failed partly because the bumbling Democratic leadership
never agreed on a consistent policy. During the Civil War, Van Evrie

had castigated his fellow Copperheads for evading their responsibilities. If these men had "nothing to offer the people but the dry husks of expediency, they must be swept aside," he raged. "We must get down to the hard pan of principle, or we are lost." After the war, Van Evrie urged the formation of "some such organization as The White Sons of Liberty," an agency that would presumably do for the Democratic party what the Union League was doing for the Republican party. Clemenceau's response to such hopes was an attack on those who, "blinded by long established prejudices, have gone on fighting not the means but the principles." Though he was a strong supporter of the Republicans, Clemenceau, as an ostensibly unbiased foreign observer, conceded that the Democrats would have been more successful in electing candidates and influencing legislation if they had been less dogmatic on the race issue. Accusing the extremists of being unrealistic, James Gordon Bennett of the New York *Herald* similarly criticized "Democratic blunders." After dissenters in the Indiana State Legislature walked out on an attempt to ratify the Fifteenth Amendment, he asked in an editorial why the Democrats persisted "in this folly of fighting the nigger when they have been almost destroyed in their successive disasters on the nigger question since 1854?" Thus, although white supremacy propaganda was rampant throughout the nation during the Civil War and reconstruction era, it never resulted in a clear-cut positive policy like the policies on tariffs, public lands, and other more traditional political issues. The racists, their strength usually dissipated by little or no organization or unity, failed to take full advantage of their opportunities.[23]

Nevertheless, racist demagoguery did draw quick and anxious replies from equalitarians. American political parties "hang upon the applause of the rabble," T. Thomas Fortune, Negro editor of the New York *Globe*, reflected. "Not alone do parties defer to the wishes of the illiterate, the 'great unwashed' majority," he wrote, but it is done by "individuals as well, who prefer to ride upon the wave of success as the champions of great wrongs rather than to go into retirement as the champions of just principles. The voice of the Charmer is all too powerful to be successfully resisted." Speaking in opposition to the New York State Legislature's reversal of its earlier ratification of the Fifteenth Amendment, Senator Roscoe Conkling accused the Democrats of willfully spreading fear throughout the North. After emancipation they had predicted that the Negroes of the South would "sweep like a black wave" across the country, Conkling reminded his colleagues in the Senate, but that had not happened, and peace had prevailed. An anonymous Republican pamphleteer summed up postwar politics in 1876, saying "For the past fifteen years the policy of the Democratic party has been to systematically misrepresent, in every possible way, the men and measures of the Republican party."[24] Except for the fact that the racists had rarely been systematic, this statement was essentially correct.

Emancipation and reconstruction presented white America with its most severe racial tests to that time. Before the Civil War, Americans had concentrated their energies on occupying and consolidating a continent (though not without sharp conflicts over race). At that time, when the Negro segment of the population was so far removed from the mainstream of economic, social, political, and intellectual life, the question of racial equality had been largely academic. The existence endured by the vast majority of Negro slaves had not been comparable to that of even the most oppressed white group. But the antislavery movement, the rise of the Liberty and Free Soil parties, and the spectacular emergence of the Republican party in the 1850's amidst Democratic epithets of "black Republicanism," portended the turmoil to come. When Negro freedom became a war aim, a new strain was placed on political communication. The Civil War and the reconstruction era wrought radical changes in American life in an incredibly short span of years; and no change was more radical or rapid than the freeing of four million black slaves. Not having faced the reality of mass Negro freedom before, Americans were now being asked to embrace a new way of thinking. Though long committed to principles of liberty, equality, democracy, and justice, most white Americans had brushed aside every suggestion that these principles should apply to nonwhite races. Caught between the fact of Negro freedom and the legacy of the Anglo-Saxon self-image, many tormented Americans simply could not adjust; thus, what is best described as a national trauma followed. The shock was more than their collective systems could withstand; and of shocked Americans, the racist demagogues were the most articulate and opportunistic—and little more. The result was a spate of white supremacy propaganda.

That the Civil War and reconstruction period has represented something of a "Golden Age" to subsequent Negro generations there can be little doubt. But despite the absence of a recognizable phalanx of racist demagogues, it also represented a "Golden Age" for subsequent generations of white supremacists—the successors of Van Evrie, Payne, Hayes, Cox, Croly, Helper, Pomeroy, and Pollard. These men, the hard core of nineteenth century white supremacists, popularized such terms as "social equality," "Africanization," "negro domination," "nigger," "kinky-head," "miscegenation," and "mongrelism"—popular terms in the vocabulary of modern, twentieth-century extremists. Furthermore, the racists of the 1860's and 1870's operated in an intellectual climate that was passing from an age of romanticism to an age of realism and naturalism, and the new age posed new problems for the Negro. Social Darwinism, for example, introduced new interpretations of man's place in nature and of his relationship to his fellows.[25] Whatever revisions of human order might result from these interpretations, many years would have to pass before the prophecy in this short poem by Herman Melville, inspired by a painting of a slave woman, would be realized:

> Her children's children they shall know
>   The good withheld from her;
> And so her reverie takes prophetic cheer—
>   In spirit she sees the stir.[26]

Reference Matter

Notes

Full publication data for works cited in the Notes with short titles in quotation marks may be found in the Bibliography under Pamphlets (p. 193). Full data for works with short titles in italics may be found under Other Works cited (p. 203). Magazine articles are cited in the Notes in full. The following abbreviations are used in the Notes:

AC	*The American Annual Cyclopedia and Register of Important Events.* 84 vols. New York, 1870–1903.
CG	The Congressional *Globe.*
JNH	*Journal of Negro History.*
JSH	*Journal of Southern History.*
MVHR	*Mississippi Valley Historical Review.*
OG	The *Old Guard.*

CHAPTER ONE

[1] S. S. Cox, "Speeches," p. 23.

[2] [William Aikman], "Future of the Colored Race in America," *Presbyterian Quarterly Review,* XI (July 1862), 134; also available in two pamphlet editions. See also the Indianapolis *State Sentinel,* June 24, 1865.

[3] Andrews, *South since the War,* p. 22.

[4] Gossett, *Race,* pp. 88–89; Seabury, *American Slavery,* pp. 222–223; Democratic Party, Pennsylvania, "Issues of the Hour," p. 6.

[5] Dawson, "Speech," p. 15; Helper (ed.), *Negroes in Negroland,* p. 186; Hayes, "Negrophobia," p. 29.

[6] Philadelphia *Age*, Aug. 4, 1863; Hartley, "Universal Suffrage," p. 37; Dickinson, *WhatAnswer?*, p. 238.

[7] Grayson, *Hireling*, p. 71; New York *World*, Feb. 15, 1866; Fleming (ed.), *Documentary History*, I, 84; E. McPherson (ed.), *Political History*, p. 385; Richmond *Southern Opinion*, Sept. 7, 1867; W. T. Grant, "The Southern Negro," *Scott's Monthly Magazine*, II (Nov. 1866), 856–862; E. B. Teague, "Relations of the Races," *Scott's Monthly Magazine*, VII (Apr. 1869), 254–256.

[8] Andrews, *South since the War*, pp. 21, 395.

[9] New York *World*, Aug. 22, 1868; Philadelphia *Age*, Aug. 27, 1868; E. McPherson (ed.), *Political History*, p. 53; New York *Daily News*, Oct. 1, 1866; Walter (ed), "Vallandigham Song Book," p. 14; S. S. Cox, *Eight Years*, p. 246; *CG*, 39 Cong., 1 Sess. (Jan. 22, 1866), p. 343; C. H. Smith, *Bill Arp's Peace Papers*, p. 183.

[10] Tarbox, *The Curse*, pp. 9–10; Clemenceau, *American Reconstruction*, pp. 115–116 (letter of Oct. 2, 1867).

[11] Horlacher, "Is Slavery Condemned"; Hopkins, "Bible View of Slavery"; Robinson, "Pictures of Slavery" and "Reply to the Resolutions"; Detroit *Free Press*, Mar. 22, 1863; Crosby and Morse, "Letter of a Republican," pp. 8, 10.

[12] Hopkins, "Bible View of Slavery," p. 2 (italics in the original).

[13] Read, *Negro Problem Solved*, pp. 36–50; Tarbox, *The Curse*, pp. 14–21; Feeks (pub.), "Copperhead Minstrel," pp. 21–24.

[14] Prospero (pseud.), "Caliban"; Sister Sallie (pseud.), "The Color Line"; anon., *The Mystery Finished*.

[15] [W. J. Scott], "Our Tripod: The Ethnological Status of the Negro," *Scott's Monthly Magazine*, V (Mar. 1869), 149–151; Young, "Reply to Ariel"; anon., "Adamic Race"; Berry, "Reply to Ariel."

[16] Stanton, *Leopard's Spots*, p. 174; Wish (ed.), *Ante-Bellum*, pp. 11–12.

[17] Duberman (ed.), *Antislavery Vanguard*, p. 166; Lurie, *Louis Agassiz*, pp. 257–258, 260–262, 305–306.

[18] Lowie, *History of Ethnological Theory*, pp. 16–18.

[19] Stanton, *Leopard's Spots*, p. 192.

[20] *Ibid.*, pp. 192–193.

[21] Van Evrie, "Six Species of Men"; John H. Van Evrie, "Types of Mankind," *OG*, VI (Jan. 1868), 62–72, (Feb.), 139–148, (Mar.), 216–222, (Apr.), 302–308, (May), 362–365, (June), 458–470; [Albert Taylor Bledsoe], "Baker's African Explorations," *Southern Review*, II (Oct., 1867), 330–358.

[22] "Ape-Like Tribes of Men," *OG*, IV (Sept. 1866), 557–562; "Uncivilized Races," p. 24; Spring, *Negro at Home*; Helper (ed.), *Negroes in Negroland*; Hayes, "Negrophobia," pp. 18, 30–35.

[23] Feeks (pub.), "Democratic Songster," pp. 60–61.

[24] Pollard, *Black Diamonds*, illustrates, in collected letters, the empirical southern view.

[25] *CG*, 37 Cong., 2 Sess. (June 3, 1862), p. 245; Black, "Doctrines Contrasted."

[26] Quoted in Columbus *Crisis*, Feb. 27, 1867.

[27] Feeks (pub.), "Copperhead Minstrel," pp. 21–24.

[28] Macrae, *Americans at Home*, p. 311; Helper, *Nojoque*, pp. 99–100.

29 Helper, *Nojoque*, pp. 81–192; C. H. Smith, *Bill Arp's Peace Papers*, p. 183.

30 Locke, *Ekkoes from Kentucky*, pp. 233–237; Columbus *Crisis*, Jan. 6, 1869.

31 Columbus *Crisis*, Nov. 26, 1862.

32 James M. McPherson, "Abolitionists and the Civil Rights Act of 1875," *Journal of American History*, LII (Dec. 1965), 494–495; anon., *Inquiry into the Condition and Prospects of the African Race*, pp. 151–152; W. G. Allen, *American Prejudice*, p. 1; Litwack, *North of Slavery*; G. G. Johnson, "The Ideology of White Supremacy, 1876–1910," in Green (ed.), *Essays*, p. 138; Fleming (ed.), *Documentary History*, I, 189; Woodward, *Strange Career of Jim Crow*, pp. 19–21.

33 Francis B. Simkins, "New Viewpoints of Southern Reconstruction," *JSH*, V (Feb. 1939), 56; Democratic Party, Pennsylvania, "Issues of the Hour," p. 9; Leslie H. Fishel, Jr., "Northern Prejudice and Negro Suffrage, 1865–1870," *JNH*, XXXIX (Jan. 1954), 12, 18–19; Hans L. Trefousse, "Ben Wade and the Negro," *Ohio Historical Quarterly*, LXVIII (Apr. 1959), 170; Beale, *Critical Year*, pp. 179–187; *AC, 1865*, pp. 745–746; *CG, Appendix*, 35 Cong., 2 Sess. (Feb. 21, 1859), p. 193; Columbus *Crisis*, Nov. 19, 1862; New York *World*, Nov. 26, 1862; J. McPherson, *Struggle for Equality*, pp. 143–147; G. S. Henry, *Radical Republican Policy*.

34 Fredrickson, *Inner Civil War*, pp. 47, 115–117, 124, 126–127, 161–162, 171–172.

35 Hans L. Trefousse, "Ben Wade and the Negro," *Ohio Historical Quarterly*, LXVIII (Apr. 1959), pp. 161–176; Tarbox, *The Curse*, p. iv. For a discussion of the accomplishments of equalitarianism in converting public opinion and in securing various civil rights measures at both the state and federal levels, see Cochrane, *Freedom without Equality*.

36 [C. Chauncey Burr], "Is the Democratic Party United?" *OG*, VI (May 1868), 383–388.

CHAPTER TWO

1 Feeks (pub.), "Copperhead Minstrel," pp. 46–47·.

2 New York *Journal of Commerce*, Aug. 3, 1863; New York *Tribune*, Mar. 17, 1863; Wilson, "Copperhead Catechism," p. 16.

3 John Van Evrie, " 'American Slaveholders,' The Founders of American Liberty," *OG*, VI (Nov. 1868), 831–838.

4 Litwack, *North of Slavery*, p. 286.

5 Democratic Party, National Committee, "The Great Issue," pp. 4, 12–15.

6 "War Democrats—Their Crimes," *OG*, I (Aug. 1863), 200–204.

7 Feeks (pub.), "Songs and Ballads," p. 15·

8 S. S. Cox, "Puritanism in Politics," pp. 4–6; Columbus *Crisis*, Jan. 21, 1863, Aug. 3, 1864; Hartford *Times*, quoted in Columbus *Crisis*, Mar. 30, 1864; Black, "Speech," pp. 1–6.

9 Columbus *Crisis*, Oct. 14, 1863; "God Bless Abraham Lincoln," p. 4; "Omnium," *OG*, I (Sept. 1863), 239; New York *Weekly Day Book*, Oct. 10, 1863;

Detroit *Free Press*, July 16, 1864; Cleveland *Plain Dealer*, Jan. 19, 1863; *CG*, 38 Cong., 1 Sess. (Jan. 27, 1864), p. 386; W. J. Allen, "Speech"; Dean, "Emancipation Proclamation," p. 8; New York *World*, Nov. 23, 1863, Feb. 15, 1864; Feeks (pub.), "Copperhead Minstrel," p. 50, and "Songs and Ballads," p. 38.

[10] John D. Barnhart: "Sources of Southern Migration into the Old Northwest," *MVHR*, XXII (June 1935), 49–62, "Southern Contributions to the Social Order of the Old Northwest," *North Carolina Historical Review*, XVII (July 1940), 237–248, and "The Southern Element in the Leadership of the Old Northwest," *JSH*, I (May 1935), 186–197; Beale, *Critical Year*, p. 179; Jacque Voegeli, "The Northwest and the Race Issue, 1861–1862," *MVHR*, L (Sept. 1963), 235–251; Frank L. Klement, "Midwestern Opposition to Lincoln's Emancipation Proclamation," *JNH*, XLIX (July 1964), 169–183.

[11] Vallandigham, *Record*, p. 150; Detroit *Free Press*, Feb. 13, 1864; Columbus *Crisis*, Mar. 23, 1864, quoting the Philadelphia *Presbyterian*, Feb. 20, 1864; Indianapolis *State Sentinel*, Mar. 26, 1864.

[12] Quoted in Hickok, *Negro in Ohio*, p. 47.

[13] S. S. Cox, *Eight Years*, pp. 244–245; Klement, *Copperheads*, p. 13; Gray, *Hidden Civil War*, p. 150; Reed, "Southern Slavery," *passim*; Columbus *Crisis*, Dec. 17, 1862.

[14] Cleveland *Plain Dealer*, Jan. 22, 1863; Columbus *Crisis*, Apr. 6, 1864.

[15] Columbus *Crisis*, Oct. 29, 1862; Democratic Party, Ohio, "Address to the Soldiers," p. 6; Bliss, "Response," p. 6.

[16] S. S. Cox, *Three Decades*, p. 80; Walter (ed.), "Vallandigham Song Book," p. 3; Grinnell, *Men and Events*, p. 142; Columbus *Crisis*, Dec. 31, 1862, Mar. 15, 1865.

[17] Gray, *Hidden Civil War*, pp. 211–212; New York *Weekly Day Book*, Mar. 25, 1865; "Abolition Philanthropy," pp. 1–4.

[18] Williston H. Lofton, "Northern Labor and the Negro during the Civil War," *JNH*, XXXIV (July 1949), 256–262, 267–271; Klement, *Copperheads*, pp. 13–14.

[19] Cleveland *Plain Dealer*, Dec. 17, 1862; Columbus *Crisis*, Dec. 3, 1862; Philadelphia *Age*, Aug. 27, 1863; Albany *Atlas and Argus*, Jan. 29, 1863; New York *Journal of Commerce*, Oct. 10, 1864; Northend, *Speeches and Essays*, pp. 66–67; Van Evrie, "Free Negroism," pp. 13–32.

[20] Dean, "Emancipation Proclamation," p. 8; Albany *Atlas and Argus*, Jan. 17, 1863.

[21] Detroit *Fress Press*, Feb. 16, 1863; Cleveland *Plain Dealer*, Apr. 10, 1863; Columbus *Crisis*, July 15, 1863, Mar. 23, 1864; Philadelphia *Age*, Aug. 11, 12, 15, 17, 21, Sept. 7, 8, 12, 25, 29, Oct. 12, Nov. 3, Dec. 4, 1863, Feb. 12, Apr. 8, 9, May 3, 17, June 1, 8, 15, July 2, Sept. 8, 21, Nov. 10, 1864, Mar. 24, 1865.

[22] Albany *Atlas and Argus*, Mar. 9, 1863; Gray, *Hidden Civil War*, pp. 99–100, 135.

[23] McCabe, *Life of Horatio Seymour*, pp. 89, 95–96; Dickinson, *What Answer?*, pp. 242–259.

[24] Philadelphia *Age*, Oct. 8, 1863; Black, "Speech," p. 4; Democratic Party,

Kentucky, "Address to the People," pp. 4, 13; Nicholas, *Conservative Essays*, pp. 29–30.

[25] Columbus *Crisis*, Nov. 5, 1862.

[26] New York *World*, Oct. 18, 1862; Albany *Atlas and Argus*, Feb. 28, 1863.

[27] Schmidt, "Guide Post," pp. 7–9; Columbus *Crisis*, Dec. 3, 1862; New York *Daily News*, Mar. 19, 1864; Van Evrie, "Free Negroism," pp. 6, 32.

[28] Feeks (pub.), "Copperhead Minstrel," pp. 31–32.

[29] Robbins, "Civil Rights," p. 4; Hartley, "Universal Suffrage," pp. 33–34; Burton, *Mission to Gelele*, II, 200; Helper, *Nojoque*, p. 206.

[30] S. S. Cox, *Eight Years*, p. 246; Vallandigham, "Great Civil War," pp. 189–190; *CG, Appendix*, 37 Cong., 3 Sess. (Feb. 28, 1863), pp. 137–138; Spence, *American Union*, pp. 125–126; Mason, "Election in Iowa," pp. 3–4; Boston *Post*, Nov. 5, 1863; Philadelphia *Age*, Dec. 4, 22, 1863, Feb. 4, 6, 1864, Jan. 23, Mar. 22, 24, 1865; Detroit *Free Press*, Jan. 15, Mar. 1, July 28, 1864; Columbus *Crisis*, Mar. 16, 30, 1864, Nov. 8, 1865; Cleveland *Plain Dealer*, Mar. 26, 1863; Indianapolis *State Sentinel*, Aug. 3, 1865.

[31] Feeks (pub.), "Songs and Ballads," p. 15.

[32] New York *Journal of Commerce*, Apr. 15, June 19, Dec. 3, 1863; Omaha *Weekly Herald*, Jan. 22, 1866, quoted in Workers of the Writers' Program (eds.), *Nebraska and Reconstruction*, pp. 12–13. Eight months later, the *Herald* modified its position by admitting that the free Negro was here to stay and that the white man had the responsibility of caring for him. See *Nebraska and Reconstruction*, p. 32.

[33] Nicholas, *Conservative Essays*, p. 31; "Modern Philanthrophy Illustrated," p. 6.

[34] Brooks, "Two Proclamations," p. 6; New York *World*, Oct. 18, 1862; Albany *Atlas and Argus*, May 9, 1863; Detroit *Free Press*, Jan. 7, Sept. 3, 1863; Philadelphia *Age*, Jan. 16, 1865.

[35] Black, "Speech," pp. 4–6.

[36] *Harper's Weekly* (1862) p. 672; "Catechism of Negro Equality"; "Facts for the People."

[37] Kedar (pseud.), "A Vision" and "Visions"; Mitchell, "Letter," p. 10; Read, *Negro Problem Solved*, pp. v–vi.

[38] Basler (ed.), *Collected Works of Lincoln*, V, 370–375; Charles H. Wesley, "Lincoln's Plan for Colonizing the Emancipated Negroes," *JNH*, IV (Jan. 1919) 7–21.

[39] J. D. Cox, "Reconstruction," p. 8; Columbus *Crisis*, Aug. 9, 1865; "General Cox's Plan," *OG*, III (Nov. 1865), 481–484.

[40] Feeks (pub.), "Democratic Songster," pp. 53–54.

[41] Mott, *American Journalism*, p. 400, contends that the political cartoon did not become a regular feature of the American press until 1867.

[42] Ray H. Abrams, "Copperhead Newspapers and the Negro," *JNH*, XX (Apr. 1935), 131–133. The title of this article is misleading; it deals almost exclusively with the *Age*.

[43] Milton, *Lincoln and the Fifth Column*, pp. 240–245.

[44] Woodward, *Burden of Southern History*, pp. xi, 73, 75; Gray, *Hidden Civil*

War, pp. 174–175; Klement, *Copperheads*, pp. 43–48; Ryan (ed.), *Civil War Literature of Ohio*, p. 9.

45 Despite its continuous financial trouble, Van Evrie's sheet had a fairly long career. There are presently in existence copies of the *Day Book* dating from Jan. 1848 to Feb. 1879. See Gregory (ed.), *American Newspapers*, p. 464.

46 The first seven issues—June to December 1862—were not numbered as part of a volume. Volume I began in January 1863.

47 *OG*, VII (Dec. 1869), 960.

48 Hopkins, "Bible View of Slavery"; Spring, *Negro at Home*, Chapter 3.

49 "Democratic Gospel of Peace," pp. 5, 7–8; Feeks, "Revelations: A Companion to the 'New Gospel of Peace,' According to Abraham," pp. 35–37.

50 "Editor's Table," *OG*, III (Feb. 1865), 93; New York *Weekly Day Book*, Aug. 12, 1865.

CHAPTER THREE

1 Brooks, "Speech at 932 Broadway," p. 13.

2 Quoted in the Columbus *Crisis*, Oct. 22, 1862.

3 Baird, "General Washington," pp. 1–8; "Notes on Colored Troops," p. 11; *Dictionary of American Biography*, XIII, 170–171; Morrison, "Speech," p. 16.

4 Randall and Donald, *Civil War and Reconstruction*, pp. 391–392; Franklin, *Slavery to Freedom*, pp. 273–274.

5 Albany *Atlas and Argus*, Oct. 24, 1864; New York *Daily News*, Oct. 13, 14, Nov. 7, 1864; Detroit *Free Press*, Nov. 2, 1864.

6 Brooks, "Two Proclamations," pp. 5–6; New York *Journal of Commerce*, Mar. 5, 1864; Albany *Atlas and Argus*, Feb. 2, 3, Sept. 1, 1863, Jan. 7, 1864; "Congressional Address," pp. 12–13; Philadelphia *Age*, July 18, 19, 1864; Detroit *Free Press*, Feb. 12, 20, 24, Apr. 12, June 3, Aug. 14, 21, 25, Sept. 6, 1863, Jan. 3, 14, 16, Mar. 29, Apr. 21, June 15, July 26, 28, Nov. 2, 1864; Columbus *Crisis*, Jan. 27, 1864.

7 New York *Journal of Commerce*, Mar. 5, 1864; New York *Daily News*, Mar. 8, 1864; New York *World*, Mar. 7, 1864.

8 Philadelphia *Age*, Mar. 14, May 3, 1864.

9 *CG*, 37 Cong., 3 Sess. (Feb. 2–5, 1863), pp. 680–690, and *Appendix* (Feb. 2, 1863), p. 93; White, "Speech."

10 Halpine, *Private Miles O'Reilly*, p. 55; Feeks (pub.), "Songs and Ballads," pp. 35–36.

11 Philadelphia *Age*, Sept. 26, Nov. 23, 1863; Cleveland *Plain Dealer*, Jan 28, 31, Feb. 27, 1863; New York *Weekly Day Book*, Oct. 10, 1863; New York *World*, Dec. 18, 1863, Feb. 12, June 4, 1864; *CG*, *Appendix*, 37 Cong., 3 Sess. (Feb. 2, 1863), pp. 83–86; "Beecher Blasphemy and Negro Patriotism," *OG*, II (Feb. 1863), 38–39; Albany *Atlas and Argus*, Jan. 19, 1863.

12 Philadelphia *Age*, July 29, 1863; New York *World*, Feb. 20, 1864; Indianapolis *State Sentinel*, June 21, 1864; Albany *Atlas and Argus*, June 20, 22, 1864; "Editor's Table," *OG*, II (Apr. 1864), 94.

13 Albany *Atlas and Argus*, July 19, 1864. All italics in the original.

14 New York *World*, July 20, Aug. 4, 12, 1864; Philadelphia *Age*, July 2, Aug. 11, 1864; Democratic Party, National Committee, "Miscegenation," p. 3.

15 Brooks, "Two Proclamations," p. 6; Feeks (pub.), "Songs and Ballads," pp. 5–6; Morrison, "Speech," p. 17.

16 Halpine, *Private Miles O'Reilly*, p. 55; Feeks (pub.), "Songs and Ballads," pp. 35–36.

17 "Alarming Evidences of Demoralization in the Army," *OG*, II (Feb. 1863), 36–37; Democratic Party, National Committee, "Address," pp. 4–5; Indianapolis *State Sentinel*, May 6, 1864; New York *Daily News*, Aug. 2, 1864; Philadelphia *Age*, May 24, 1865.

18 Herbert Aptheker, "Negro Casualties in the Civil War," *JNH*, XXXII (Jan. 1947), 15–17; Franklin, *Slavery to Freedom*, pp. 286–290.

19 Albany *Atlas and Argus*, Aug. 17, 1864, italics in the original; Democratic Party, National Committee, "Address," p. 4.

20 New York *World*, Mar. 30, 1864; Indianapolis *State Sentinel*, Apr. 21, 1864.

21 "Beecher Blasphemy and Negro Patriotism," *OG*, II (Feb. 1863), 38–39; Philadelphia *Age*, Aug. 10, 1863; Croly and Wakeman, "Miscegenation," p. 56.

22 "For Peace and Peaceable Separation," p. 19; Nicholas, *Conservative Essays*, pp. 148–149; Philip Ripley to Marble, New Orleans, Aug. 7, 1863, Barlow manuscript, Huntington Library, italics in the original; *AC, 1864*, pp. 447–449.

23 Gray, *Hidden Civil War*, pp. 121–122; Columbus *Crisis*, Aug. 17, 1864; Abrams, "Copperhead Newspapers and the Negro," *JNH*, XX (Apr. 1935), 136–139; Philadelphia *Age*, June 8, Nov. 19, 1864, Feb. 16, 1865, Jan. 12, 13, Feb. 21, 1866, Feb. 18, 1867.

24 Columbus *Crisis*, Aug. 19, 1863; Mar. 16, 1864; New York *World*, Sept. 29, 1864; New York *Daily News*, Aug. 2, 3, 7, 13, 28, 1866.

25 Albany *Atlas and Argus*, Feb. 2, 1863; "Congressional Address," pp. 12–13; Philadelphia *Age*, July 18, 19, 1864; Cleveland *Plain Dealer*, Jan. 29, 1863; Walter (ed.), "Vallandigham Song Book," pp. 23–24; Feeks (pub.), "Copperhead Minstrel," pp. 14–15; *CG, Appendix*, 37 Cong., 3 Sess. (Feb. 2, 1863), pp. 91–94.

26 Philadelphia *Age*, July 2, 1864.

27 Blair, Sr., "Shall the Usurpation Be Perpetuated?" p. 8; Philadelphia *Age*, Jan. 1, 13, Feb. 21, Mar. 29, 1866.

28 Quoted in *Public Opinion* (London), Apr. 14, 1866.

CHAPTER FOUR

1 Columbus *Crisis*, Nov. 19, 1862.

2 *Dictionary of American Biography*, IV, 560.

3 Sidney Kaplan, "The Miscegenation Issue in the Election of 1864," *JNH*, XXXIV (July 1949), 284–285; Julius Bloch, "'Miscegenation' in the American Language: Story of an Emotion-Laden Word," *Gregg Press Newsletter*, II (Dec. 1964), 1–2.

[4] Croly and Wakeman, "Miscegenation," pp. 8, 11, 16.

[5] *Ibid.*, pp. 19–25.

[6] *Ibid.*, pp. 29–32.

[7] *Ibid.*, pp. 42–45, 57.

[8] *Ibid.*, pp. 26, 53, 65. On p. 66 they quote Phillips at Framingham, Mass., July 4, 1863. For similar statements by Phillips and the New York *Independent*, see the Detroit *Free Press*, Feb. 26, 1864.

[9] *CG*, 38 Cong., 1 Sess. (Feb 17, 1864), pp. 708–713. "Miscegenation and Amalgamation" is a pamphlet reprint of Cox's speech.

[10] S. S. Cox, *Eight Years*, p. 352.

[11] Indianapolis *State Sentinel*, July 7, 1865; Pollard, *Lost Cause Regained*, pp. 130–131n.

[12] Van Evrie, "Subjenation," pp. iii–iv, 51, 65.

[13] *Ibid.*, pp. 5ff, 30.

[14] Philadelphia *Age*, Mar. 14, 17, 26, Apr. 9, May 4, June 25, 1864; New York *Daily News*, Mar. 17, Apr. 4, 1864.

[15] New York *World*, Feb. 27, 1864; Detriot *Free Press*, Mar. 2, 1864; Albany *Atlas and Argus*, Mar. 7, 1864; Columbus *Crisis*, Mar. 30, 1864; "Editor's Table," *OG*, II (Apr. 1864), 94.

[16] New York *World*, Mar. 30, Apr. 9, 1864; Louisville (Ky.) *Courier*, Mar. 30, 1865, quoted in Avary, *Dixie*, pp. 395–396.

[17] Van Evrie, "Subjenation," p. 45; New York *Daily News*, Apr. 4, 1864.

[18] Feeks (pub.), "Democratic Songster," pp. 60–61; New York *Daily News*, Apr. 9, 1864; Van Evrie "Subjenation," p. 51.

[19] New York *World*, Apr. 4, 1864; Philadelphia *Age*, Nov. 1, 1864.

[20] Feeks (pub.), "Copperhead Minstrel," pp. 54–55.

[21] Massey, *Bonnet Brigades*, p. 272; Dixon, *New America*, II, 324–326.

[22] "God Bless Abraham Lincoln!" p. 14.

[23] *Ibid.*, p. 16; Democratic Party, National Committee, "Miscegenation," p. 3.

[24] *Ohio Statesman*, July 8, 1864, quoted in the Philadelphia *Age*, July 12, 1864; Ray H. Abrams, "Copperhead Newspapers and the Negro," *JNH*, XX (Apr. 1935), 135–136.

[25] Van Evrie, "Subjenation," p. 51.

[26] Macrae, *Americans at Home*, pp. 296–298.

[27] New York *Daily News*, Apr. 6, 1864; New York *World*, Jan. 1, 1864; "Congressional Address," pp. 19–20; S. S. Cox, *Eight Years*, pp. 249, 358; Nicholas, *Conservative Essays*, pp. 30–31.

[28] "The Crimes of Modern Philanthropy," *OG*, III (Nov. 1865), 499–500; Van Evrie: "Subjenation," pp. 21–24, and *Negroes and Negro "Slavery,"* p 160.

[29] Van Evrie, "Subjenation," pp. 20–21, 25–26; Burton, *Mission to Gelele*, II, 189n; Van Evrie, *Negroes and Negro "Slavery,"* p. 163.

[30] U.S. Bureau of the Census, *Negro Population, 1790–1915*, p. 218.

[31] *Ibid.*; Van Evrie, "Subjenation," pp. 45–46.

[32] Dickinson, *What Answer?*, p. 153.

33 Beecher, "Universal Suffrage," p. 18; "Greeley's Amnesty Record"; Macrae, *Americans at Home*, p,. 297.

34 Avary, *Dixie*, p. 395; Macrae, *Americans at Home*, pp. 319–320.

35 Nicholas, *Conservative Essays*, pp. 148–149; Harness, "Genius of Democracy," *passim*; "Democratic Gospel of Peace," p. 8; Van Evrie, "Subjenation," pp. 45–46; New York *Daily News*, June 20, 1866.

36 "Real Chicago Platform"; "Cincinnati Convention"; Potts (ed.), *Freemen's Guide to the Polls*, pp. 24–25; Black, "Doctrines Contrasted," p. 3; Philadelphia *Age*, Oct. 26, 1864.

37 Philadelphia *Age*, June 25, Nov. 1–8, 1864; New York *World*, Sept. 22, 1864; New York *Daily News*, Sept. 20, 1864; Columbus *Crisis*, Oct. 5, 1864; Democratic Party, National Committee, "Miscegenation," p. 3.

38 New York *World*, Sept. 23, 26, 27, 28, 1864.

39 New York *Weekly Day Book*, Oct. 1, 8, 1864.

40 Albany *Atlas and Argus*, Oct. 1, 1864.

41 S. S. Cox, *Eight Years*, pp. 354–361; Democratic Party, National Committee, "Miscegenation," pp. 2–7.

42 Quoted in S. S. Cox, *Eight Years*, pp. 360–361.

43 "Omnium," *OG*, I (Sept. 1863), 239; Indianapolis *State Sentinel*, Mar. 30, 1864; New York *World*, Sept. 22, 1864; Philadelphia *Age*, Sept. 27, 1864.

44 Democratic Party, National Committee, "Miscegenation," pp. 7–8; New York *Weekly Day Book*, Apr. 16, 1864; Philadelphia *Age*, Nov. 1, 1864.

45 Hesseltine, *Lincoln's Plan*, p. 121; James, *Fourteenth Amendment*, p. 28; McKitrick, *Andrew Johnson*, p. 30; Philadelphia *Age*, Apr. 17–26, 1865; "Death of a President," *OG*, III (May 1865), 240.

46 Reid, *After the War*, p. 53; Andrews, *South since the War*, p. 28.

47 McKitrick, *Andrew Johnson*, p. 67; Albert V. House, Jr., "Northern Congressional Democrats as Defenders of the South during Reconstruction," *JSH*, VI (Feb. 1940), pp. 48–50; Kendrick (ed.), *Journal*, p. 195; "How the Democratic Party Fell to Pieces," *OG*, IV (Aug. 1866), 449; [C. Chauncey Burr]: "Is the Democratic Party United?" *OG*, VI (May 1868), 383–388, and "The Positive Democracy," *OG*, VI (June 1868), 408–410; Union League Club of New York, "Report of the Special Committee," p. 22.

48 Democratic Party, Pennsylvania, "Issues of the Hour"; McKitrick, *Andrew Johnson*, pp. 73–74; Columbus *Crisis*, Sept. 13, Oct. 4, 11, 18, 1865.

49 Columbus *Crisis*, Jan. 10, 17, 1866.

50 Democratic Party, Pennsylvania, "Issues of the Hour," pp. 8, 10, 12.

51 New York *Herald*, Sept. 1, 6, 1866.

CHAPTER FIVE

1 Clemenceau, *American Reconstruction*, pp. 35–36 (letter of Sept. 28, 1865), and p. 131 (letter of Nov. 1, 1867); [Chauncey Burr], "Is the Democratic Party United?" *OG*, VI (May 1868), 383–388.

[2] Clemenceau, *American Reconstruction*, pp. 35–36 (letter of Sept. 28,1865).

[3] *AC, 1864*, pp. 237–241.

[4] Detroit *Free Press*, Apr. 7, 27, 1864; Democratic Party, Pennsylvania, "Issues of the Hour," p. 5.

[5] "White Supremacy and Negro Subordination," *OG*, III (May 1865), 193–199; Steiner, *Life of Reverdy Johnson*, pp. 119–120; Hager, "Fifteenth Amendment," p. 11; Democratic Party, Pennsylvania, "Issues of the Hour," pp. 6, 14–15; Cincinnati *Enquirer*, Aug. 25, 1865; Nicholas, *Conservative Essays*, pp. 28–29; *CG*, 39 Cong., 1 Sess. (Jan. 11, 29, 1866), pp. 196, 200, 476–481; Rogers, "White Man's Government."

[6] J. M. McPherson, *Struggle for Equality*, pp. 245–246; New York *World*, June 14, 1867; Welles, *Diary*, III, 524; Haight, "Message."

[7] James, *Fourteenth Amendment*, pp. 12–13; Stephenson, *Race Distinctions*, p. 285; *AC, 1868*, p. 544; John G. Gregory, "Negro Suffrage in Wisconsin," *Transactions of the Wisconsin Academy of Science, Arts, and Letters*, XI (1898), 96–100; Govan and Livingood, *Chattanooga Country*, pp. 282–283.

[8] Columbus *Crisis*, Apr. 3, 1867; E. McPherson (ed.), *Political History*, pp. 353–354; *AC, 1865*, pp. 529–530, *1867*, p. 475, *1868*, p. 542.

[9] *AC, 1866*, p. 508, *1868*, p. 602.

[10] Democratic Party, Pennsylvania, *Nob Mountain Meeting*, pp. 70–72, and "Issues of the Hour," pp. 5–6; *AC, 1865*, p. 812, *1866*, pp. 613–614, *1867*, p. 620, *1869*, p. 563; E. McPherson (ed.), *Political History*, p. 123; Tioga Democratic Club, "Huzza for Seymour and Blair!!!" pp. 11–12.

[11] *AC, 1865*, pp. 441, 610–611, 614, 685, 823, *1866*, pp. 252, 405, *1867*, pp. 407, 529–540, *1868*, pp. 203, 212, 330, 377, 385, 505, 509, 521, 533, 543, 603, *1869*, p. 550, *1870*, p. 752; E. McPherson (ed.), *Political History*, pp. 248, 479; Omaha *Daily Herald*, Oct. 9, 1865, quoted in Workers of the Writers' Program (eds.), *Nebraska and Reconstruction*, p. 1; Democratic Party, Indiana, "Facts for the People," p. 2; Denison, *Iowa Democracy*, I, 221–222.

[12] Chicago *Times*, Nov. 12, 13, 1866.

[13] Columbus *Crisis*, Nov. 21, 1866.

[14] *AC, 1865*, pp. 512–513.

[15] Clemenceau, *American Reconstruction*, p. 231 (letter of Aug. 20, 1868).

[16] Stephenson, *Race Distinctions*, p. 288; Leslie H. Fishel, Jr., "Northern Prejudice and Negro Suffrage, 1865–1870," *JNH*, XXXIX (Jan. 1954), 8–26.

[17] Detroit *Free Press*, Dec. 6, 1867; Croly, *Seymour and Blair*, p. 221; *AC, 1867*, pp. 420, 513, *1868*, pp. 494, 505; New York *World*, Apr. 8, 1868.

[18] E. McPherson (ed.), *Political History*, p. 372; *AC, 1867*, p. 605, *1868*, pp. 386, 494; Columbus *Crisis*, Sept. 4, 11, 1867; Democratic Party, New York, "The Path to Conservative Triumph," pp. 22–23.

[19] Quoted in Oberholtzer, *United States since the Civil War*, I, 170.

[20] *Public Opinion*, Nov. 2, 1867; Dunning, *Essays*, pp. 189–190; New York *Herald*, July 9, 1868.

[21] J. D. Cox, "Reconstruction," p. 4; *AC, 1865*, pp. 589, 605, 610–611, 686, *1868*, pp. 378, 533; Leslie H. Fishel, Jr., "Northern Prejudice and Negro Suf-

frage," *JNH, XXXIX* (Jan. 1954), 12–13; E. McPherson (ed.), *Political History*, p. 124.

22 Woodward, *Burden of Southern History*, pp. 89–94; Daniels, *Freedom's Birthplace*, p. 90n; Louis Ruchames, "William Lloyd Garrison and the Negro Franchise," *JNH, L* (Jan. 1965), 41–46.

23 James, *Fourteenth Amendment*, pp. 12–13; Andrew "Valedictory Address," p. 35; Brodie, *Thaddeus Stevens*, pp. 230–231; Woodward, *Burden of Southern History*, pp. 89–94.

24 *AC, 1865*, p. 458.

25 Democratic Party, Pennsylvania, "Issues of the Hour," p. 6; Helper (ed.), *Negroes in Negroland*, p. 187; Pollard, *Lost Cause Regained*, pp. 133–134.

26 *CG*, 39 Cong., 1 Sess. (Feb. 16, 1866), pp. 879–880; Hendricks, "Speech"; James, *Fourteenth Amendment*, pp. 12–13.

27 *CG*, 39 Cong., 2 Sess. (Jan. 7, 1867), p. 311.

28 New York *Herald*, Dec. 9, 1868; *CG*, 41 Cong., 2 Sess. (Feb. 23, 1870), pp. 1508–1509.

29 Pomeroy, "Condensed History of the War," p. 11; Boston *Post*, Jan. 3, 1864.

30 Northend, *Speeches and Essays*, pp. 127–132.

31 Pomeroy, *Democratic Campaign Song Book*, pp. 21–22; *CG*, 39 Cong., 1 Sess. (Jan. 11, 1866), p. 203; Rogers, "White Man's Government," *passim*; Seymour and Tilden, "Speeches," pp. 12–13; Philadelphia *Age*, Oct. 15, 1868.

32 Hans L. Trefousse, "Ben Wade and the Negro," *Ohio Historical Quarterly*, LXVIII (Apr. 1959), 161–176, and *Benjamin Franklin Wade, passim*.

33 New York *World*, Dec. 14, 1865; *CG*, 39 Cong., 1 Sess. (Jan. 11, 1866), pp. 196, 198; Rogers, "White Man's Government."

34 E. McPherson (ed.), *Political History*, pp. 154–159; *AC, 1868*, p. 127; New York *World*, Jan. 8, 1867; Philadelphia *Age*, Jan. 8, 1867; Democratic Party, Indiana, "Proceedings of State Convention," p. 14.

35 Detroit *Free Press*, Jan. 24, 1867; CG, 39 Cong., 2 Sess. (Dec. 12, 1866), p. 79.

36 Massey, *Bonnet Brigades*, p. 357; Indianapolis *State Sentinel*, July 6, 1865; Philadelphia *Age*, Feb. 5, 1866; Chicago *Times*, Feb. 16, July 25, 1868.

37 New York *World*, Feb. 14, 1866; Columbus *Crisis*, Dec. 19, 1866; *AC, 1867*, p. 439.

38 Detroit *Free Press*, Apr. 28, 1867; Helper, *Nojoque*, p. 85.

39 James, *Fourteenth Amendment*, pp. 7–8; *AC, 1867*, p. 420; Bowers, *The Tragic Era*, p. 145; Detroit *Free Press*, June 11, 1867.

40 Quoted in Dixon, *White Conquest*, II, 270.

41 Hager, "Fifteenth Amendment," p. 7.

42 *AC, 1868*, p. 86; Dixon, *White Conquest*, II, 237–238.

43 *AC, 1868*, p. 533, *1869*, p. 79, *1870*, p. 606; *CG*, 39 Cong., 2 Sess. (Jan. 7, 1867), p. 313; E. McPherson (ed.), *Political History*, pp. 478–488; Omaha *Weekly Herald*, Feb. 9, 1866, quoted in Workers of the Writers' Program (eds.), *Nebraska and Reconstruction*, p. 18.

[44] *AC, 1871*, p. 92.

[45] Field, "Power of the State to Exclude," *passim.*

[46] Field, "The Chinese Question."

[47] E. McPherson (ed.), *Political History*, p. 479; *AC, 1869*, p. 79; Hager, "Fifteenth Amendment," p. 10; Dixon, *New America*, II, 18–19. Nine years later, Dixon was less certain. In *White Conquest*, II, Chapters 19 through 26, he praised the Chinese for their individual thrift, industry, and patience, but still considered them collectively a threat to American democracy.

[48] Black, "Doctrines Contrasted," pp. 2–3; New York *World*, Apr. 4, 1867; Philadephia *Age*, Sept. 14, 24, Oct. 6, 1869; Seymour and Tilden, "Speeches," p. 13; Columbus *Crisis*, Feb. 3, Mar. 24, 31, May 26, June 30, Aug. 11, Sept. 22, Nov. 3, 1869.

[49] Detroit *Free Press*, Aug. 8, 24, 1867; Hager, "Fifteenth Amendment," p. 10; Hayes, "Negrophobia," p. 28; *CG*, 40 Cong., 3 Sess. (Feb. 8, 1869), pp. 989–990.

[50] Hager, "Fifteenth Amendment," pp. 11–12; Columbus *Crisis*, Feb. 3, 1869, June 22, 1870; *AC, 1870*, pp. 211, 217–218, 463, 541, 546, *1871*, pp. 90, 91, 543, 621, 752; Coulter, *South during Reconstruction*, pp. 106–107; Fortune, *Black and White*, p. 18.

[51] Columbus *Crisis*, Feb. 3, 10, Mar. 3, Apr. 21, June 16, Aug. 11, 18, Oct. 6, 13, 20, Dec. 1, 1869, Jan. 26, Feb. 2, 16, May 25, 1870; Saulsbury, "Suffrage Constitution Amendment"; Hager, "Fifteenth Amendment"; E. McPherson (ed.), *Political History*, pp. 488–498, 557–562; *AC, 1870*, p. 543, *1871*, pp. 406–407.

[52] Clemenceau, *American Reconstruction*, pp. 201–202 (letter of June 19, 1868), and pp. 299–300 (letter of Apr. 12, 1780).

[53] Columbus *Crisis*, May 25, 1870; *CG*, 41 Cong., 2 Sess. (May 20, 1870), p. 1870; James G. Blaine *et al.*, "Ought the Negro to Be Disenfranchised? Ought He to Have Been Enfranchised?" *North American Review*, CXXVIII (Mar. 1879), pp. 225–283.

[54] Sinclair, *Aftermath of Slavery*, p. 104.

CHAPTER SIX

[1] Carrollton (La.) *Times*, Nov. 9, 1867, quoted in Coulter, *South during Reconstruction*, p. 59.

[2] *CG, Appendix*, 37 Cong., 3 Sess. (Feb. 2, 1863), p. 105; George Sykes to Fitz-John Porter, July 22, 1863, Barlow manuscript, Huntington Library.

[3] Bliss, "Response," p. 6; Dickson, "Absolute Equality," pp. 14–15.

[4] Holden, *Memoirs*, p. 52.

[5] Fleming (ed.), *Laws Relating to Freedmen*, p. 4 (summarized in Fleming [ed.], *Documentary History*, I, 243).

[6] Prentiss, "Political Situation," p. 33; *AC, 1866*, p. 253; Macrae, *Americans at Home*, p. 293; Harris, *Quest for Equality*, p. 26. See also L. and J. H. Cox, *Politics, Principle, and Prejudice.*

7 *CG,* 39 Cong., 2 Sess. (Jan. 3, 1867), p. 252; Clemenceau, *American Reconstruction,* p. 135 (letter of Nov. 8, 1867); Macrae, *Americans at Home,* p. 337.

8 Hartley, "Universal Suffrage," p. 51; U. S. Bureau of the Census, *Negro Population,* pp. 25–27.

9 New York *World,* Apr. 3, 1868; *AC, 1865,* p. 694; Hartley, "Universal Suffrage," pp. 26–28; S. S. Cox, "Speeches," p. 7.

10 Pollard, *Lost Cause Regained,* p. 137; Democratic Party, Indiana, "Proceedings of State Convention," p. 12; Seymour and Tilden, "Speeches," p. 9; Northend, *Speeches and Essays,* pp. 155–177; Nicholas, *Conservative Essays,* p. 30; Steiner, *Life of Reverdy Johnson,* pp. 119–120; Hartley, "Universal Suffrage," pp. 20–21; New York *World,* Mar. 28, 1868; New York *Herald,* Aug. 17, 1872; U. S. Congress, *Ku Klux Report,* II, North Carolina Testimony (1871), pp. 246–251; Oberholtzer, *U. S. since the Civil War,* II, 17; Reid, *After the War,* p. 371; Kendrick (ed.), *Journal,* p. 211, quoting the New York *Sun; AC, 1865,* p. 781.

11 Dunning, *Essays,* pp. 189–190; Hartley, "Universal Suffrage," p. 32; New York *Herald,* Nov. 6, 9, 1867; *AC, 1867,* p. 55, *1868,* p. 432.

12 R. S. Henry, *Story of Reconstruction,* p. 235; Degener, "Minority Report"; Woodward, *Strange Career of Jim Crow,* p. 34.

13 Hartley, "Universal Suffrage," p. 35; *AC, 1865,* p. 781; Woodward, *Burden of Southern History,* pp. 89–94; New York *World,* Apr. 3, 1867, quoting Jackson (Miss.) *Clarion,* and Apr. 20, 1867; Brodie, *Thaddeus Stevens,* pp. 227–228.

14 *AC, 1867,* p. 763, *1868,* pp. 696, 731, *1870,* p. 457.

15 *AC, 1865,* p. 694.

16 Martin and Gelber (eds.), *Dictionary of American History,* p. 518.

17 William A. Russ, Jr., in "Registration and Disfranchisement under Radical Reconstruction," *MVHR,* XXI (Sept. 1934), 178–179, cites *Letter Book,* First [Military] District, II, 261–262, for the figures on Virginia, and *Senate Executive Document,* 40 Cong., 2 Sess., No. 53, for the statistics on Florida, North Carolina, South Carolina, and Georgia. These are the standard sources, and are quoted in several works, e.g. Croly, *Seymour and Blair,* p. 277, and E. McPherson (ed.), *Political History,* p. 374.

18 New York *Weekly Day Book,* Apr. 15, 1865; La Crosse (Wis.) *Democrat,* Feb. 25, 1868; S. S. Cox, "Speeches," p. 7; Chicago *Times,* July 15, 29, 1868; Pollard, *Lost Cause Regained,* pp. 37–39.

19 Charlottesville (Va.) *Chronicle,* June 18, 1867, quoted in *Public Opinion,* July 6, 1867; *AC, 1868,* p. 509.

20 Columbus *Crisis,* Apr. 1, 1868; *CG,* 40 Cong., 2 Sess. (Jan. 30, 1868), pp. 849–850.

21 Miller (ed.), *Great Debates,* VII, 440; Hayes, "Negrophobia," pp. 6–7.

22 Howard K. Beale, "On Rewriting Reconstruction History," *American Historical Review,* XLV (July 1940), 814.

23 Friese, "Letter," pp. 29–30; "Modern Philanthropy Illustrated," p. 8; Throop, *The Future,* p. 166.

24 New York *Daily News,* Jan. 22, 1866; New York *World,* July 7, 8, 9, 11, 1867; La Crosse (Wis.) *Democrat,* Mar. 24, 1868.

25 *CG, Appendix*, 41 Cong., 2 Sess. (Feb. 24, 1870), p. 121, and (Feb. 23, 24, 25, 1870), pp. 1503–1568; *CG, Appendix*, 41 Cong., 2 Sess. (Feb. 25, 1870), pp. 1557–1560; Oberholtzer, *U. S. since the Civil War*, II, 326.

26 Detroit *Free Press*, July 14, 1867; Omaha *Weekly Herald*, June 7, 1867, quoted in Workers of the Writers' Program (eds.), *Nebraska and Reconstruction*, pp. 39–40.

27 [Edward A. Pollard], "Universal Suffrage in a New Disguise," *The Political Pamphlet*, I (Sept. 12, 1868), 40; Pollard, *Lost Cause Regained*, p. 100; Clemenceau, *American Reconstruction*, pp. 278–280 (letter of Mar. 3, 1869); Pike, *Prostrate State*, p. 45; La Crosse (Wis.) *Democrat*, Mar. 24, 1868.

28 Holcombe, "The Alternative"; Democratic Party, Pennsylvania, *Nob Mountain Meeting*, pp. 13, 28, 66–67; Democratic Party, Indiana, "Facts for the People," p. 4; *AC, 1865*, p. 684, *1867*, p. 424; E. McPherson (ed.), *Political History*, p. 367; Cincinnati *Enquirer*, July 13, 1868.

29 New York *Herald*, Nov. 4, 6, 1867; Columbus *Crisis*, July 24, Oct. 9, 1867; New York *World*, Aug. 26, 1868; Seymour and Tilden, "Speeches," p. 9; McCabe, *Life of Horatio Seymour*, pp. 222–230; S S. Cox, "Speeches," pp. 5, 12, 23–27; Hager, "Fifteenth Amendment," pp. 4–5; Detroit *Free Press*, Mar. 21, Aug. 30, Sept. 12, 28, Oct. 4, 19, 31, Dec. 27, 1867, Mar. 21, July 2, 28, Sept. 11, 1868.

30 Lynch, *Facts of Reconstruction*, pp. 94–99; Columbus *Crisis*, Oct. 29, 1867; Democratic Party, Indiana, "Proceedings of State Convention," pp. 25–26; McCabe, *Life of Horatio Seymour*, p. 222.

31 Chicago *Times*, Aug. 8, 1868; McCabe, *Life of Horatio Seymour*, pp. 460–461, 487–497.

32 *AC, 1868*, p. 495; Columbus *Crisis*, Oct. 23, 1867; S. S. Cox, "Speeches," p. 11; Philadelphia *Age*, Apr. 2, May 17, 19, 25, June 13, 20, 1866, Mar. 8, 1867, Sept. 23, 1868; New York *Herald*, Sept. 9, 1867, Feb. 7, 1868; Detroit *Free Press*, Aug. 30, 1867; New York *World*, July 12, 1868; La Crosse (Wis.) *Democrat*, Feb. 26, 1868.

33 *AC, 1868*, p. 495; Seymour, *Record*, p. 300; McCabe, *Life of Horatio Seymour*, pp. 460–461; Columbus *Crisis*, Oct. 23, 1867; Detroit *Free Press*, Aug. 11, 1868.

34 "The Freedman's Bureau!"; "Only Seven Millions!"; Detroit *Free Press*, Apr. 6, 7, July 19, 1868; La Crosse (Wis.) *Democrat*, Mar. 24, 1868.

35 Macrae, *Americans at Home*, pp. 294–296, 327–338; Franklin, *Slavery to Freedom*, pp. 312–315; Lynch, *Facts of Reconstruction*, pp. 94–99.

36 C. H. Smith, *Bill Arp's Peace Papers*, p. 184.

37 Gilmer, "War of Races," *passim; AC, 1867*, p. 603, *1868*, pp. 603, 721; Democratic Party, Indiana, "Proceedings of State Convention," p. 5; Detroit *Free Press*, Sept. 28, Oct. 29, Dec. 24, 1867; July 25, 26, 1868; New York *Herald*, Jan. 26, 1866; New York *Daily News*, Mar. 21, 1866; New York *World*, Aug. 15, 1867; S. S. Cox, "Speeches," p. 2, 23.

38 "Results of Emancipation in Peru," *OG*, IV (Aug. 1866), 505–507; "The Negro in America," *OG*, IV (Dec. 1866), 732; John H. Van Evrie, "The Mongrel

Republics of America," *OG*, V (Sept. 1867), 695–702; "Negro in Africa," *OG*, V (Sept. 1867), 721–728; "Mongrel Rule or Ruin," *OG*, VI (Apr. 1868), 249–255; New York *Weekly Day Book*, Oct. 7, 1865; Columbus *Crisis*, Nov. 2, 1865; New York *World*, Nov. 15, 17, 18, 29, 1865; *AC, 1865*, pp. 446–454.

[39] Jamaica Committee, London, *Facts and Documents*, and *The Blue Books*; *AC, 1865*, p. 450; Philadelphia *Age*, Mar. 24, 1866; Apr. 16, 22, May 17, June 1, 1867; Hartley, "Universal Suffrage," p. 19n; Charlottesville (Va.) *Chronicle*, June 18, 1867, quoted in *Public Opinion*, July 6, 1867. For an analysis of the underlying causes of racial antagonisms in Jamaica, see Knox, *Race Relations in Jamaica*.

[40] New Orleans *Times*, July 27, 1866, quoted in *AC, 1866*, p. 454.

[41] Randall and Donald, *Civil War and Reconstruction*, pp. 587–588; Richmond *Southern Opinion*, Sept. 28, 1867; Detroit *Free Press*, Dec. 24, 1867.

[42] Clemenceau, *American Reconstruction*, p. 299 (letter of Aug. 13, 1868); Reid, *After the War*, p. 264.

[43] Degener, "Minority Report," p. 15; *AC, 1867*, pp. 54–55.

[44] Detroit *Free Press*, May 8, Sept. 20, 1868; Pollard, *Lost Cause Regained*, p. 185.

[45] Porter and Johnson (eds.), *National Party Platforms*, pp. 37–39; Croly, *Seymour and Blair*, p. 4; W. E. Smith, *Blair Family in Politics*, II, 416; Chicago *Times*, Oct. 25, 1868; Bowers, *Tragic Era*, p. 231.

[46] New York *Herald*, May 13, 1867.

[47] Coleman, *Election of 1868*, pp. 24, 143–44; Clemenceau, *American Reconstruction*, pp. 196–199 (letter of June 12, 1868). For an insight into the Democratic drive to draft Chase, see the correspondence between Chase and his Democratic supporters in *AC, 1868*, pp 749–751.

[48] Seymour and Tilden, "Speeches," p. 1; New York *World*, Mar. 12, 14, 1868; Seymour, *Record*, pp. 295, 333–334.

[49] Coleman, *Election of 1868*, p. 244.

[50] Cincinnati *Enquirer*, July 10, 1868.

[51] McCabe, *Life of Horatio Seymour*, pp. 283–292; Croly, *Seymour and Blair*, *passim*; Seymour, *Record*, *passim*; Chicago *Times*, Oct. 25, 1868; W. E. Smith, *Blair Family in Politics*, II, 414.

[52] Coleman, *Election of 1868*, p. 155; Croly, *Seymour and Blair*, p. 259; Lefler, "Hinton Rowan Helper," p. 22; Cincinnati *Enquirer*, July 10, 1868; McCabe, *Life of Horatio Seymour*, p. 499.

[53] McCabe, *Life of Horatio Seymour*, pp. 439–440.

[54] The Brodhead letter can be found in many places: New York *World*, July 13, 1868; W. E. Smith, *Blair Family in Politics*, II, 406–407; McCabe, *Life of Horatio Seymour*, pp. 462–465; E. McPherson (ed.), *Political History*, pp. 380–381; *AC, 1868*, pp. 746–747; Clemenceau, *American Reconstruction*, p. 212.

[55] E. McPherson (ed.), *Political History*, pp. 369, 381–382; McCabe, *Life of Horatio Seymour*, pp. 477–478, 480–484, 485–497; W. E. Smith, *Blair Family in Politics*, II, 416–417; New York *World*, July 11, 1868; Chicago *Times*, July 28, 1868; Oberholtzer, *United States since the Civil War*, II, 188.

⁵⁶ New York *Tribune*, Oct. 7, 1868, quoted in W. E. Smith, *Blair Family in Politics*, II, 428.

⁵⁷ W. E. Smith, *Blair Family in Politics*, II, 415–417, 428; Oberholtzer, *United States since the Civil War*, II, 192.

CHAPTER SEVEN

¹ *AC, 1874*, p. 15.

² New York *World*, Oct. 18, 1862; Helper (ed.), *Negroes in Negroland*, pp. 185–186; Dawson, "Speech," p. 14.

³ Steiner, *Life of Reverdy Johnson*, pp. 94–95; Kendrick (ed.), *Journal*, p. 196; Chicago *Times*, Oct. 27, 1868.

⁴ Helper to Dr. Bloede, Asheville, N. C., Dec. 8, 1869, Brock manuscript, Huntington library.

⁵ William Aikman, "The Future of the Colored Race in America," *Presbyterian Quarterly Review*, XI (July 1862), 148; Nebraska *Republican*, Oct. 13, 1865, quoted in Workers of the Writers' Program (eds.), *Nebraska and Reconstruction*, pp. 6–7; Rodman and Gahagan, "To the People of North Carolina," p. 3.

⁶. Helper (ed.), *Negroes in Negroland*, pp. 183–184.

⁷ Franklin, *From Slavery to Freedom*, p. 295; Stephenson, *Race Distinctions*, pp. 112–114.

⁸ Stephenson, *Race Distinctions*, p. 208; Woodward, *Strange Career of Jim Crow, passim;* James M. McPherson, "Abolitionists and the Civil Rights Act of 1875," *Journal of American History*, LII (Dec. 1965), 494–495.

⁹ S. S. Cox, *Eight Years*, pp. 249–250; Helper (ed.), *Negroes in Negroland*, p. 189; New York *Daily News*, May 25, 1866; *CG, Appendix*, 40 Cong., 2 Sess. (Dec. 18, 1867), p. 70; Brooks, "Reconstruction."

¹⁰ James, *Fourteenth Amendment*, pp. 200–201. Similar conclusions can be found in Mangum, *Legal Status of the Negro*, pp. 26–30, 163–164, 200, 274, 311, 350–353; Konvitz, *Century of Civil Rights*, pp. 63–64; Harris, *Quest for Equality*, pp. 50–52, 55–56; Myrdal, *American Dilemma*, pp. 579, 580, 580n; and G. G. Johnson, "The Ideology of White Supremacy, 1876–1910," in Green (ed.), *Essays*, pp. 125, 135.

¹¹ Harris, *Quest for Equality*, pp. 99–100; Konvitz, *Century of Civil Rights*, pp. 128–129. People who lived during this so-called disfranchisement era and made similar observations include Blair, *Southern Prophecy*, pp. 89–92; Cable, *Negro Question*, pp. 51–108; Baker, *Following the Color Line*, p. 235; and Stephenson, *Race Distinctions*, pp. 207–236.

¹² G. W. Smith and Judah (eds.), *Life in the North*, pp. 130–131; Macrae, *Americans at Home*, p. 459; Dixon, *New America*, II, 331.

¹³ Murray, *Proud Shoes*, pp. 205–297; *AC, 1867*, p. 621.

¹⁴ Stephenson, *Race Distinctions*, pp. 212–213; Berger, *Equality by Statute*, pp. 65, 92.

[15] Aptheker (ed.), *Documentary Negro History*, pp. 505–506.

[16] Robinson, "Address to the 'People,' " p. 9.

[17] Woodward, *Strange Career of Jim Crow*, p. 15; *AC, 1865*, p. 706; Morrow, *Northern Methodism*, pp. 187–188; Franklin, *Reconstruction*, pp. 190–191; Green (ed.), *Essays*, pp. 144–145.

[18] Alfred H. Kelly, "The Congressional Controversy over School Segregation, 1867–1875," *American Historical Review*, LXIV (1959), 538, 549; Albany *Atlas and Argus*, Mar. 21, Apr 1, 1864; Detroit *Free Press*, Apr. 10, 17, 1867; G. Campbell, *White and Black*, p. 264; *AC, 1866*, p. 405; Reid, *After the War*, p. 249.

[19] Avary, *Dixie*, pp. 389–402.

[20] Woodward, *Strange Career of Jim Crow*, p. 15; G. Campbell, *White and Black*, p. 384.

[21] *AC, 1870*, p. 457; Kelly, "The Congressional Controversy over School Segregation, 1867–1875," *American Historical Review*, LXIV (1959), 553–554; Franklin, *Reconstruction*, pp. 201–202.

[22] Richmond *Southern Opinion*, Oct. 19, 1867; Philadelphia *Age*, Feb. 20, 1866; Avary, *Dixie*, p. 400.

[23] Shenton (ed.), *The Reconstruction*, p. 24, quoting *Pamphlets on Reconstruction*, "Report of Carl Schurz on the States of South Carolina, Georgia, Alabama, Mississippi, and Louisiana"; Pike, *Prostrate State*, pp. 12, 17–21.

[24] La Crosse (Wis.) *Democrat*, May 12, 1868; Singletary, *Negro Militia*, pp. 15–16, 151–152.

[25] Shenton (ed.), *The Reconstruction*, p. 24.

[26] New York *World*, Feb. 24, 1866; Richmond *Southern Opinion*, Aug. 3, 1867; Columbus *Crisis*, Jan. 13, 20, 1869.

[27] United States Congress, *Ku Klux Report*, V, South Carolina Testimony (1871), p. 1430; Democratic Party, Indiana, "Proceedings of State Convention," p. 13; Helper (ed.), *Negroes in Negroland*, pp. 187–188; Avary, *Dixie*, p. 233.

[28] Fleming (ed.), *Documentary History*, II, 443–444; Shenton (ed.), *The Reconstruction*, p. 24; Singletary, *Negro Militia*, p. 49; Alvord, "Letters from the South," p. 3.

[29] Macrae, *Americans at Home*, p. 273; Franklin, *Reconstruction*, p. 155; Fleming (ed.), *Constitution and Ritual*, pp. 27–28; G. Campbell, *White and Black*, p. 309.

[30] Dixon, *New America*, II, 328; Detroit *Free Press*, Nov. 26, 1867.

[31] Nebraska *Republican*, Oct. 13, 1865, quoted in Workers of the Writers' Program (eds.), *Nebraska and Reconstruction*, pp. 6–7; Dixon, *New America*, II, 332–337.

[32] Quoted in Chicago *Times*, Sept. 27, 1866.

[33] Detroit *Free Press*, Feb. 16, 1868; La Crosse (Wis.) *Democrat*, June 2, 1868; Fleming (ed.), *Documentary History*, II, 291–292; Helper, *Nojoque*, p. 84.

[34] Fleming (ed.), *Documentary History*, II, 443–444; Avary, *Dixie*, p. 377; G. Campbell, *White and Black*, pp 171–172; Helper (ed.), *Negroes in Negro-*

land, pp. 187–188; Democratic Party, Indiana, "Proceedings of State Convention," p. 13.

[35] Detroit *Free Press,* Sept. 4, 1867, quoting the Cleveland *Plain Dealer;* Helper, *Noonday Exigencies,* pp. 37–66.

[36] Avary, *Dixie,* p. 382; Georgia *Clarion,* quoted in Columbus *Crisis,* Aug. 19, 1868.

[37] Singletary, *Negro Militia,* p. 44; Dixon, *New America,* II, 337–338; St. Louis *Times,* Sept. 14, 1869; G. Campbell, *White and Black,* pp. 171–172 (italics mine).

[38] Fleming (ed.), *Documentary History,* II, 443–444; Avary, *Dixie,* pp. 381–382.

[39] Avary, *Dixie,* pp. 377, 383–384.

[40] Columbus *Crisis,* Mar. 16, 1864, and Sept. 9, 1869, quoting the Ottumwa *Copperhead.*

[41] Macrae, *Americans at Home,* pp. 310–311.

[42] Democratic Party, Indiana, "Facts for the People," p. 2; Detroit *Free Press,* Dec. 11, 1867.

[43] Chicago *Times,* Oct. 4, 1868; Harness, "Genius of Democracy," pp. 25–26.

[44] G. Campbell, *White and Black,* p. 197; Stephenson, *Race Distinctions,* pp. 89–90; *CG, Appendix,* 41 Cong., 2 Sess. (Feb. 23, 1870), pp. 1511–1512; Harness, "Genius of Democracy," p. 54.

[45] Macrae, *Americans at Home,* pp. 296–298; Richmond *Southern Opinion,* Aug. 3, 1867; Chicago *Times,* Oct. 11, 1868, quoting the Nashville *Banner.*

[46] "Abolition Conspiracy to Destroy the Union," p. 31; New York *World,* Apr. 3, 1868; Pollard, *Lost Cause Regained,* p. 131n; Indianapolis *State Sentinel,* Oct. 3, 1868; Columbus *Crisis,* Nov. 4, 1868; Payne, *The Negro,* p. 48.

[47] Avary, *Dixie,* pp. 397–398; Fleming (ed.), *Documentary History,* II, 289–290; Morgan, *Yazoo, passim;* Wharton, *Negro in Mississippi,* p. 228; Somers, *Southern States since the War,* pp. 226–227.

[48] "The Crimes of Modern Philanthropy," *OG,* III (Nov. 1865), 499–500; "The Results of the War," *OG,* IV (Feb. 1866), 109; "Mongrel Rule or Ruin," *OG,* VI (Apr. 1868), 249–255; Harness, *The Great Trial,* p. 16; Columbus *Crisis,* Oct. 31, 1866; Locke, *Ekkoes from Kentucky,* p. 11.

[49] Thorpe, *Mind of the Negro,* p. 240; Wharton, *Negro in Mississippi,* p. 150; Aptheker (ed.), *Documentary Negro History,* pp. 687–688, quoting *Proceedings of the State Convention of Colored Men of Texas, Held at the City of Austin, July 10–12, 1883;* Fleming (ed), *Documentary History,* II, 445–446, quoting *Senate Report on Labor and Capital,* Testimony, IV, 454.

[50] Morgan, *Yazoo,* pp. 211–212; Fortune, *Black and White,* pp. 108–109n; Avary, *Dixie,* pp. 397–398.

[51] Stephenson, *Race Distinctions,* pp. 78–79, 90–91; E. McPherson (ed.), *Political History,* pp. 474–475.

[52] Avary, *Dixie,* p. 232; Franklin, *Reconstruction,* p. 153; U. S. Congress, *Ku Klux Report,* III, Alabama Testimony (1871), pp. 227–233.

[53] Woodward, *Strange Career of Jim Crow,* p. 15; Raleigh (N. C.) *Tri-*

Weekly Standard, Aug. 31, 1867, quoted in Coulter, *South during Reconstruction*, p. 66; Fleming (ed.), *Documentary History*, II, 445–446, quoting *Senate Report on Labor and Capital*, Testimony, IV, 454; Nordhoff, *Cotton States*, p.111.

[54] Hager, "Fifteenth Amendment," p. 6; Fortune, *Black and White*, p. 18; Philadelphia *Age*, Apr. 13, May 1, 16, June 15, 1866, Jan. 2, 21, 1870; New York *Daily News*, Feb. 5, 14, Mar. 8, May 2, 14, 17, June 5, 15, 1866; *CG*, 39 Cong., 1 Sess. (Mar. 20, 1866), p. 1508; Columbus *Crisis*, June 23, 1869; Edward A. Pollard (ed.), "The Negro Reconstructed," *The Political Pamphlet*, I (Sept. 12, 1868), 44–46; Dabney, *Defence of Virginia*, pp. 293–294; Miller (ed.), *Great Debates*, VII, 176–177; Chicago *Times*, Oct. 4, 1866; C. H. Smith, *Bill Arp's Peace Papers*, p. 180.

CHAPTER EIGHT

[1] Porter and Johnson (eds.), *National Party Platforms*, pp. 41–43; New York *Herald*, Oct. 7, 1872.

[2] New York *World*, Mar. 19, 1867; Philadelphia *Age*, Apr. 13, 1867; Lunt, *Origin of the Late War*, pp. 457–458.

[3] *AC, 1869*, p. 385; Henry, *Story of Reconstruction*, p. 468; Oberholtzer, *U. S. since the Civil War*, II, 269–271; Lewinson, *Race, Class, & Party*, p. 53; Woodward, *Burden of Southern History*, pp. 105–106; Patrick W. Riddleberger, "The Radicals' Abandonment of the Negro during Reconstruction," *JNH*, XLV (Apr. 1960), 93; Leslie H. Fishel, Jr., "The Negro in Northern Politics, 1870–1900," *MVHR*, XLII (Dec. 1955), 468; Hirshson, *Farewell to the Bloody Shirt, passim*.

[4] Hirshson, *Farewell to the Bloody Shirt*, pp. 126–127; Woodward, *Burden of Southern History*, pp. 105–106.

[5] E. McPherson (ed.), *Political History*, pp. 623–624; Workers of the Writers' Program (eds.), *Nebraska and Reconstruction*, editorials compiled from Oct. 9, 1865, through Aug. 13, 1873; Payne, "Ariel's Reply"; Dixon, *White Conquest*, II, 367–368.

[6] Morgan, "Reform"; Columbus *Crisis*, Mar. 29, May 24, 1871; *AC, 1871*, pp. 609, 750; *CG*, 42 Cong., 2 Sess. (Mar. 23, 1872), pp. 1922–1928; New York *Weekly Day Book*, Nov. 30, 1872.

[7] Lewinson, *Race, Class, & Party*, pp. 51–52; Franklin, *Reconstruction*, pp. 200–201.

[8] Duke, *Reminiscences*, Chapter 10; Hesseltine (ed.), *Tragic Conflict*, Chapter 44.

[9] Somers, *Southern States since the War*, p. 155; Franklin, *Reconstruction*, p. 154; Stampp, *Era of Reconstruction*, pp. 199–203; Fleming (ed.), *Constitution and Ritual*, pp. 23–24; Brewster, *Sketches of Southern Mystery*, p. 140; Ezell, *South since 1865*, pp. 95–96.

[10] Atlanta *News*, Sept. 10, 1874, quoted in Hofstadter (ed.), *Great Issues*,

II, 43–44; Dixon, *White Conquest*, II, 24–25; Morton, "Speech"; Garfield, "Can the Democratic Party Be Intrusted?"; Hoar, "Political Condition of the South."

11 *Dictionary of American Biography*, XV, 47–48; Wharton, *Negro in Mississippi*, pp. 218–220; Franklin, Reconstruction, p. 164; Herbert Shapiro, "The Ku Klux Klan during Reconstruction: The South Carolina Episode," *JNH*, XLIX (Jan. 1964), 36; Brewster, *Sketches of Southern Mystery*, *passim*.

12 *AC, 1871*, p. 435; Alabama *State Journal*, quoted in Fleming (ed.), *Documentary History*, II, 206; U.S. Senate, *Outrages in Mississippi*; Aptheker (ed.), *Documentary Negro History*, *passim*.

13 Somers, *Southern States since the War*, p. 155; Fleming (ed.), *Documentary History*, II, 359, quoting U.S. Congress, *House Report No. 101*, 43 Cong., 2 Sess., Part ii, p. 213; Fleming (ed), *Constitution and Ritual*, pp. 6–7.

14 U.S. Congress, *Ku Klux Report*, VII, Georgia Testimony (1871), p. 833; Fleming (ed.), *Documentary History*, II, 448; *AC, 1871*, p. 524; Nordhoff, *Cotton States*, pp. 39–53.

15 *AC, 1869*, p. 385.

16 S. S. Cox, "Grant or Greeley?" p. 9; Pollard, "Appeal for Horace Greeley," pp. 4, 12–32; W. E. Smith, *Blair Family*, II, 432–433.

17 New York *Tribune*, Apr. 12, 1872, quoted in Patrick W. Riddleberger, "The Radicals' Abandonment of the Negro during Reconstruction," *JNH*, XLV (Apr. 1960), 95–96.

18 Democratic Party, Kentucky, "Letter"; Stinchfield, "Principle, Policy, and Practice!"; anon., *Political Oats*; *AC, 1872*, p. 784.

19 S. S. Cox, "Grant or Greeley?" p. 9.

20 Brown, *Southern Attitudes*, *passim*; Woodward, *Origins of the New South*, pp. 103–105; Hirshson, *Farewell to the Bloody Shirt*, pp. 126, 251–255.

21 Fredrickson, *Inner Civil War*, p. 194. For discussions of various aspects of postwar reforms, see Sproat, *Party of the Center*; and Downey, *Rebirth of Reform*.

22 Woodward, *Burden of Southern History*, pp. 78–79; McClure, *The South*, p. 219.

23 Van Evrie, "Subjenation," pp. 51–53; Clemenceau, *American Reconstruction*, p. 231 (letter of Aug. 20, 1868); New York *Herald*, Mar. 10, 1869; "How the Democratic Party Fell to Pieces," *OG*, IV (Aug. 1866), 449–456; "Congress, Not a Congress," *OG*, V (Feb. 1867), 81–89; [Chauncey Burr], "Is the Democratic Party United?" *OG*, VI (May 1868), 383–388; [Chauncey Burr], "The Positive Democracy," *OG*, VI (June 1868), 408–410.

24 Fortune, *Black and White*, pp. 17–18; *CG*, 41 Cong., 2 Sess. (Feb. 22, 1870), p. 1479; "The Contrast," p. 1.

25 Sinclair, *Aftermath of Slavery*, p. 109; Carter, *Angry Scar*, p. 403; Patrick W. Riddleberger, "The Radicals' Abandonment of the Negro during Reconstruction," *JNH*, XLV (Apr. 1960), 98–99; Gossett, *Race*, pp. 144–175; Fredrickson, *Inner Civil War*, p. 192.

26 Melville, *Battle-Pieces*, p. 153.

Bibliography

This Bibliography combines an exhaustive list of racist pamphlets from the Civil War and reconstruction era with a selected list of other works—namely, those actually cited in this book, with the exception of periodicals. The list of Other Works begins on p. 203.

PAMPHLETS

"Abolition and Secession; or, Cause and Effect, Together with the Remedy for our Sectional Troubles." Anti-Abolition Tract No. 1. New York, 1862.

"The Abolition Conspiracy to Destroy the Union; or, A Ten Years Record of the 'Republican' Party." Anti-Abolition Tract No. 3. New York, 1866.

"Abolition Is National Death; or, The Attempt to Equalize Races, the Destruction of Society." New York, 1866.

"Abolition Philanthropy! The Fugitive Slave Law: Too Bad for Southern Negroes, but Good Enough for Free Citizens of Foreign Birth! Handcuffs for White Men! Shoulder Straps for Negroes! Voters Read!" [Philadelphia, 1863.]

"The Adamic Race: Reply to 'Ariel,' Drs. Young and Blackie, on the Negro." New York, 1868.

Adderup, Andrew (pseud.?). "Lincolniana; or the Humors of Uncle Abe: Second Joe Miller." New York, 1864.

Aikman, William. "The Future of the Colored Race in America: Being an Article in the Presbyterian Quarterly Review, of July, 1862." Philadelphia, 1862.

Allen, William. "Speech of Hon. William Allen, of Ohio, on the Enlistment of Negro Soldiers, Delivered in the House of Representatives, February 2, 1863." Washington, D. C., 1863.

Allen, William Joshua. "Speech of Hon. William J. Allen, of Illinois, upon the President's Message, Delivered in the House of Representatives, January 27, 1864." Washington, D C., 1864.

Alvord, J. W. "Letters from the South, Relating to the Condition of the Freedmen, Addressed to Major General O. O. Howard." Washington, D. C., 1870.

Andrew, John A. "Valedictory Address of His Excellency John A. Andrew, to the Two Branches of the Legislature of Massachusetts, January 4, 1866." Massachusetts State Senate Doc. No. 2. Boston, 1866.

Baird, Henry Carey. "General Washington and General Jackson on Negro Soldiers." Philadelphia, 1863.

Beecher, Henry Ward. "Universal Suffrage; An Argument, Including Report of conference between Sec. Stanton, Gen. Sherman, and Freedmen in Savannah." New York, 1865.

Berry, Harrison. "A Reply to Ariel." Macon, Ga., 1869.

Black, Jeremiah S. "The Doctrines of the Democratic and Abolition Parties Contrasted—Negro Equality—The Conflict between 'Higher Law' and the Law of the Land: Speech of Hon. Jeremiah S. Black, at the Hall of the Keystone Club, in Philadelphia, October 24, 1864." [Philadelphia, 1864.]

———. "Speech of Hon. Jeremiah S. Black, at the Democratic Mass Convention, in Lancaster City, September 17, 1863." Harrisburg, Pa., 1863.

Blair, Frank P., Sr. "Shall the Usurpation of the Government, by a Fragment of Congress, Be Perpetuated by Negro Suffrage?: Speech of Gen. Frank P. Blair, Delivered at Memphis, Tennessee, at Odd-Fellow's Hall, on Thursday, September 20, 1866." Washington, D. C., 1867.

Blair, Frank P., Jr. "The Destiny of the Races of the Continent: An Address Delivered before the Mercantile Library Association of Boston, Massachusetts, on the 26th day of January, 1859." Washington, D. C., 1859.

———. "Speech of Hon. Francis P. Blair, Jr., of Missouri, on the Acquisition of Central America; Delivered in the House of Representatives, January 14, 1858." Washington, D. C., 1858.

Bliss, George. "Response of Hon. George Bliss, Representative of the Fourteenth Congressional District of Ohio, to Resolutions of the Legislature of Ohio, Requesting the Senators and Representatives of that State in Congress to Vote for a Proposed Amendment to the Constitution of the United States to Abolish Slavery." Washington, D. C., January 28, 1865.

Brooks, James. "Reconstruction: Speech of Hon. James Brooks, of New York, in the House of Representatives, December 18, 1867." Washington, D. C., 1867.

———. "Speech of Hon. James Brooks, of New York, on the President's Message, in the House of Representatives, December, 1864." N.p., 1864.

——. "Speech of the Hon. James Brooks, at 932 Broadway, Tuesday Evening, December 30, 1862." No. 3 of Papers from the Society for the Diffusion of Political Knowledge. New York, 1863.

——. "The Two Proclamations: Speech of Hon. James Brooks, before the Democratic Union Association, Sept 29th, 1862." New York, 1862.

Carlyle, Thomas. "Occasional Discourse on the Nigger Question." London, 1853.

"Catechism of Negro Equality." Leaflet. N.p. [1863?].

"Cincinnati Convention, October 18, 1864, for the Organization of: A Peace Party, upon State-Rights, Jeffersonian, Democratic Principles and for the Promotion of Peace and Independent Nominations for President and Vice-President of the United States." N.p. [1864].

Clayton, Phillip. "Greeley vs. Grant: The Duty of True Democrats. An Open-Letter by Hon. Phillip Clayton, of Georgia. What a Life Long Democrat Thinks—Letter of Gen. John A. Dix, of New York." Leaflet. [New York, 1872.]

"Congressional Address: An Address to the People of the United States, and Particularly to the People of the States which Adhere to the Federal Government." Washington, D. C., 1864.

"The Contrast: Republican and Democratic Administration, Reviewed and Contrasted." N.p., 1876.

Cooper, Peter. "The Death of Slavery: A Letter from Peter Cooper to Governor Seymour." No. 28 of the Loyal Publication Society. New York, 1863.

"The Copperhead's Prayer" (or, "A Degenerate Yankee"). Chicago, 1864.

Cox, Jacob Dolson. "Reconstruction and the Relations of the Races: Letter from a Committee at Oberlin to Gen. J. D. Cox, the Union Candidate for Governor. Gen. Cox's Response." Columbus, 1865.

Cox, Samuel Sullivan. "Emancipation and Its Results—Is Ohio to Be Africanized?: Speech of Hon. S. S. Cox, of Ohio, Delivered in the House of Representatives, June 6, 1862." Washington, D. C., 1862.

——. "Grant or Greeley?: Speech of S. S. Cox, of New York City, on the Issues of the Presidential Campaign of 1872." New York, 1872.

——. "Miscegenation or Amalgamation: Fate of the Freedman. Speech of Hon. Samuel S. Cox, of Ohio, Delivered in the House of Representatives, February 17, 1864." Washington, D. C., 1864.

——. "Puritanism in Politics: Speech of Hon. S. S. Cox, of Ohio, before the Democratic Union Association, January 13, 1863." New York, 1863.

——. "Speeches of Hon. S. S. Cox, in Maine, Pennsylvania and New York, during the Campaign of 1868." New York, 1868.

[Croly, David Goodman, and George Wakeman.] "Miscegenation: The Theory of the Blending of the Races, Applied to the American White Man and Negro." New York, 1864.

Crosby, Edward N., and Samuel F. B. Morse. "The Letter of a Republican, Edward N. Crosby, Esq., of Poughkeepsie, to Prof. S. F. B. Morse, Feb. 25, 1863, and Prof. Morse's Reply, March 2nd, 1863." No. 4 of Papers from the Society for the Diffusion of Political Knowledge. New York, 1863.

Davis, Jefferson (pseud.[?]). "An Address to the People of the Free States by the President of the Southern Confederacy." Leaflet. Richmond, Va., 1863.

Dawson, John L. "Speech of John L. Dawson, of Pennsylvania, on the State of the Union, Delivered in the House of Representatives, January 31, 1866." Washington, D. C., 1866.

Dean, Gilbert. "The Emancipation Proclamation and Arbitrary Arrests!!: Speech of Hon. Gilbert Dean, of New York, on the Governor's Annual Message, Delivered in the Assembly of the State of New York, February 12, 1863." Albany, 1863.

Degener, E. "The Minority Report in Favor of Extending the Right of Suffrage, with Certain Limitations, to All Men without Distinction of Race or Color Made in the Texas Reconstruction Convention." Austin, 1866.

"The Democratic Gospel of Peace, According to St. Tammany." New York, 1863.

Democratic Party, Indiana. "Facts for the People: The Address Adopted by the Democratic State Convention, Held in Indianapolis, Ind., on March 15, 1866." N.p. [1866].

——. "Proceedings of the Indiana Democratic State Convention, Held in Indianapolis, Wednesday, January 8th, 1868." Indianapolis, 1868.

Democratic Party, Kentucky. "An Address to the People and Congress of the United States." Louisville, 1863.

——. ["Letter from the State Executive Committee to All County Democratic Chairmen."] Louisville, 1872.

Democratic Party, National Committee. "Address of the National Democratic Committee: The Perils of the Nation; Usurpations of the Administration in Maryland and Tennessee; the Remedy to Be Used." Campaign Document No. 13 [and 26]. [New York, 1864.]

——. "Campaign Songs." Campaign Document No. 19. New York [1864].

——. "Corruptions and Frauds of Lincoln's Administration." Campaign Document No. 14. [New York, 1864.]

——. "The Great Issue to Be Decided in November Next! Shall the Constitution and the Union Stand or Fall, Shall Sectionalism Triumph? Lincoln and His Supporters. Behold the Record." Washington, D. C. [1860].

——. "Miscegenation: Indorsed by the Republican Party." Campaign Document No. 11. New York [1864].

——. "Republican Opinions about Lincoln." [New York, 1864.]

Democratic Party, New York City. "The Path to Conservative Triumph. The Successful Policy. The Necessity for New Measures and New Men. The Strength and Claims of Candidates: a New One Recommended; His Antecedents, Ability, Services, Character and Availability Considered." New York, 1868.

Democratic Party, Ohio. "Address to the Soldiers of Ohio, by the Democratic State Central Committee: 'The Union and the Constitution.' " Columbus, 1863.

Democratic Party, Pennsylvania. "Address of the Democratic State Central Committee. Letter of Major Geo. A. Woodward. Letter of Judge Woodward." Philadelphia, 1863.

——. "The Issues of the Hour: Negro Suffrage and Negro Equality." Philadelphia, 1865.

Dickson, William M. "The Absolute Equality of All Men before the Law, the Only True Basis of Reconstruction: An Address by William M. Dickson, Delivered at Oberlin, Ohio, October 3, 1865." Cincinnati, 1865.

"Facts for the People. Who are the Amalgamationists? Who Commenced the War?" Leaflet. N.p. [1863?].

Feeks, J. F. (pub.). "Abraham Africanus I: His Secret Life, as Revealed under the Mesmeric Influence. Mysteries of the White House." New York, 1861 [actually 1864?].

——. "Book of the Prophet Stephen, Son of Douglas, Wherein Marvelous Things Are Foretold of the Reign of Abraham." New York, 1863.

——. "Copperhead Minstrel: A Choice Collection of Democratic Poems and Songs, for the Use of Political Clubs and the Social Circle." New York, 1863.

——. "Democratic Presidential Campaign Songster No. 1: McClellan and Pendleton, Original Campaign Songs, Choruses, Etc." New York, 1864.

——. "The Lincoln Catechism, Wherein the Ecentrics & Beauties of Despotism Are Full Set Forth: A Guide to the Presidential Election of 1864." New York [1863].

——. "Revelations: A Companion to the 'New Gospel of Peace,' according to Abraham." New York, 1863.

——. "Songs and Ballads of Freedom. A Choice Selection: Inspired by the Incidents and Scenes of the Present War." New York, 1864.

Field, Stephen J. "The Chinese Question. Views of Judge Field of the United States Supreme Court. A Letter to General Miller." Washington, D. C., 1880.

——. "Power of the State to Exclude Foreigners from Its Limits, and to Prevent Their Landing, on Account of the Immorality of Their Past Lives, Considered." San Francisco, 1874.

"For Peace and Peaceable Separation: Citizen's Democratic Address, to the People of the State of Ohio, and the People of the Several States of the West and North." Cincinnati, 1863.

"The Freedmen's Bureau!" Broadside. [Philadelphia, 1868.]

Friese, Philip C. "Letter to the President and the People of the United States, Showing that the President Cannot Lawfully Execute an Unconstitutional Law, and that the So-Called Reconstruction Acts Are Both Unconstitutional and Repugnant to the Republican Party's Original Higher Law Policy." Baltimore, 1869.

Garfield, James A. "Can the Democratic Party Be Safely Intrusted with the Administration of the Government?: Speech of Hon. James A. Garfield of Ohio, in the House of Representatives, Friday, August 4, 1876." N.p., 1876.

Gilmer, John H. "War of Races. By Whom It Is Sought to Be Brought About. Considered in Two Letters, with Copious Extracts from the Recent Work of Hinton R. Helper." Richmond, Va., 1867.

"God Bless Abraham Lincoln!: A Solemn Discourse by a Local Preacher." N.p. [1863?].

"Greeley's Amnesty Record." Leaflet. [New York, 1872.]

Hager, John S. "Fifteenth Amendment to Constitution: Speech of Hon. John S. Hager of San Francisco in the Senate of California, January 28, 1870, on Senator Hager's Joint Resolution to Reject the Fifteenth Amendment to the Constitution of the United States." N.p., 1870.

Haight, Henry H. "Message of H. H. Haight, Governor of the State of California, Transmitting the Proposed Fifteenth Amendment to the Federal Constitution." Sacramento, 1870.

Harness, A. C. "The Genius of Democracy; or, The Fall of Babylon." Philadelphia, 1873.

Hartley, Thomas W. "Universal Suffrage-Female Suffrage." [New York?], 1867.

Hayes, J. R. "Negrophobia 'On the Brain,' in White Men, or an Essay upon the Origin and Progress, both Mental and Physical, of the Negro Race, and the Use to Be Made of Him by Politicians in the United States." Washington, D. C., 1869.

Hendricks, Thomas A. "Speech of Hon. T. A. Hendricks, of Indiana, in the Senate of the United States, February 16, 1866." Washington, D. C., 1866.

Hoar, George F. "Political Condition of the South: Speech of George F. Hoar of Massachusetts, in the House of Representatives, Wednesday, August 9, 1876." Washington, D. C., 1876.

Holcombe, William H. "The Alternative: A Separate Nationality, or the Africanization of the South." New Orleans, 1860.

Hopkins, John H. "Bible View of Slavery." No. 8 of Papers from the Society for the Diffusion of Political Knowledge. New York, 1863.

Horlacher, Jacob. "Is Slavery Condemned by the Bible or Prohibited by the Constitution of the United States?" N.p., 1862.

Hunt, James. "The Negro's Place in Nature: A Paper Read before the London Anthropological Society." New York, 1864.

[Johnson, Reverdy.] "The Dangerous Condition of the Country, the Causes Which Have Led to It, and the Duty of the People." Baltimore, 1867.

[———.] "A Further Consideration of the Dangerous Condition of the Country, the Causes Which Have Led to It, and the Duty of the People." Baltimore, 1867.

Johnston, James Hugo. "Miscegenation in the Ante-Bellum South." Chicago, 1937. Private edition, distributed by the University of Chicago Libraries, 1939.

Kedar, Obed (pseud.). "A Vision: The Cause and Progress of the Present War, and Its Final Termination, Foretold by Obed Kedar, July 4, 1861." Columbus, Ohio, 1862.

——. "Visions Concerning the Present War, Its Causes, Progress and Final Termination; Seen by Obed Kedar, July 4, 1861, and July 4, 1863." Columbus, Ohio, 1863.

Kendall, Amos. "Letters on Our Country's Crisis." Washington, D. C., 1864.

Lefler, Hugh Talmadge. "Hinton Rowan Helper: Advocate of a 'White America.' " No. 1 of Southern Sketches. Charlottesville, Va., 1935.

Mason, Charles. "The Election in Iowa." No. 11 of Papers from the Society for the Diffusion of Political Knowledge. New York, 1863.

McClellan Headquarters and Reading-Room Association, 21st Ward, New York City. "Songs for the People: McClellan Campaign Song." Leaflet. New York, 1864.

Miles, Thomas Jefferson. 'To All Whom It May Concern': The Conspiracy of the Leading Men of the Republican Party to Destroy the American Union, Proved by Their Words and Antecedent and Subsequent to the Rebellion." New York, 1864.

Mitchell, James. "A Letter on the Relation of the White and African Races in the United States, Showing the Necessity of the Colonization of the Latter. Addressed to the President of the U. S." Washington, D. C., 1862.

"Modern Philanthropy Illustrated: How They Tried to Make a White Man of a Negro Twenty-Five Hundred Years Ago. Will the Experiment Succeed Any Better Now?" N.p., n.d.

Morgan, George W. "Reform: Speech of Gen. Geo. W. Morgan, at Delaware, Ohio." Columbus, 1870.

Morrison, William R. "Speech Delivered by Col. W. R. Morrison, at Edwardsville, Madison County, Ill., October 13, 1863." St. Louis, 1863.

Morse, Samuel F. B. "An Argument on the Ethical Position of Slavery in the Social System, and Its Relation to the Politics of the Day." No. 12 of Papers from the Society for the Diffusion of Political Knowledge. New York, 1863.

——, George Ticknor Curtis, and Samuel J. Tilden. "The Constitution: Addresses of Prof. Morse, Mr. George Ticknor Curtis, and Mr. S. J. Tilden at the Organization." No. 1 of Papers from the Society for the Diffusion of Political Knowledge. New York, 1863.

Morton, Oliver P. "Speech of Hon. O. P. Morton, Delivered in the United States Senate, January 19, 1876, on the Mississippi Election." N.p., 1876.

National Union Executive Committee. "The Proceedings of the National Union Convention." Philadelphia, August 14, 1866.

"Negroes and Religion: The Episcopal Church of the South, Memorial to the General Convention of the Protestant Episcopal Church in the United States of America." Charleston S. C. [1863?].

"Notes on Colored Troops and Military Colonies on Southern Soil by an Officer of the 9th Army Corps." New York, 1863. [Stephen B. Brague, supposed author.]

Nott, Josiah Clark. "Instincts of Races." New Orleans, 1866.

"Only Authentic Life of Abraham Lincoln, Alias 'Old Abe,' also of Gen. Geo. B. McClellan, Alias 'Little Mac,' with an Account of His Numerous Victories, from Phillipi to Antietam." New York [1864].

"Only Authentic Life of Abraham Lincoln, Alias 'Old Abe,' with an Account of His Birth and Education, His Rail-Splitting and Flat-Boating, His Joke-Cutting and Soldiering, with Some Allusions to His Journeys from Springfield to Washington and Back Again." [New York, 1864?]

"Only Seven Millions!" Broadside. [Philadelphia, 1866.]

Patten, E. P. (pub.). "Little Mac Campaign Songster." New York, 1864.

[Payne, Buckner H.] "Ariel's Reply to the Rev. John [Joseph?] A. Seiss, D. D., of Philadelphia; also, His Reply to the Scientific Geologist and Other Learned Men, in Their Attacks on the Credibility of the Mosaic Account of the Creation and the Flood." Nashville, Tenn., 1876.

[——.] "The Negro: What Is His Ethnological Status; Is He a Progeny of Ham? Is He a Descendant of Adam and Eve? Has He a Soul? Or Is He a Beast in God's Nomenclature? What Is His Status as Fixed by God in Creation? What Is His Relation to the White Race?" Cincinnati, 1867.

[Philpot, Francis.] "Facts for White Americans, with a Plain Hint for Dupes, and a Bone to Pick for White Nigger Demagogues and Amalgamation Abolitionists, Including the Parentage, Brief Career, and Execution, of Amalgamation Abolitionism, Whose Funeral Sermon Was Preached at Washington on the 7th day of February, 1839." Philadelphia, 1839.

"A Plain Statement Addressed to All Honest Democrats." Boston, 1868.

Pollard, Edward A. "A Southern Historian's Appeal for Horace Greeley." Lynchburg, Va., 1872.

[Pomeroy, Marcus Mills.] "Condensed History of the War, Its Causes and Results: Plain Home-Told Facts for the Young Men and Working Men of the United States." N.p., 1868.

——. "Soliloquies of the Bondholder, the Poor Farmer, the Soldier's Widow, the Political Preacher, the Poor Mechanic, the Freed Negro, the Radical Congressman, the Returned Soldier, the Southerner, and Other Political Articles." New York, 1866.

Potts, William D. (ed.). "Campaign Songs for Christian Patriots and True Democrats." New York, 1864.

Prentiss, George L. "The Political Situation." New York, 1866. Reprinted from American Presbyterian and Theological Review, April 1866.

Prospero (pseud.). "Caliban: A Sequel to 'Ariel.' " New York, 1868.

Quinby, Watson F. "Mongrelism." Wilmington, Del., 1876.

"The Real Chicago Platform, as Expounded by the Democratic Orators at Chicago." Leaflet. [Chicago? 1864.]

Reed, Henry. "Southern Slavery and Its Relations to Northern Industry: A Lecture Delivered at the Catholic Institute, in Cincinnati, January 24, 1862." Cincinnati, 1862.

Robbins, William M. "Civil Rights: Speech of Hon. William M. Robbins, of North Carolina, in the House of Representatives, Saturday, January 24, 1874." N.p., 1874.

Robinson, John Bell. "An Address to the 'People' of the Several Sovereign States of the United States, on the Frauds Committed on Their Elective Franchise, under Official Orders, and the Danger of the People Being Reduced to Mere Serfs to a Tyrant Despot, under the Pretext of Negro Freedom, Military Necessity, Union, and Liberty." Philadelphia, 1864.

———. "Pictures of Slavery and Anti-Slavery: Advantages of Negro Slavery and the Benefits of Negro Freedom; Morally, Socially, and Politically Considered." Philadelphia, 1863.

———. "A Reply to the Resolutions Passed by the Late Philadelphia Annual Conference of the Methodist Episcopal Church in March, 1864, with a Slight Notice of the Acts of the Late General Conference of Said Church in the Following May." Philadelphia, 1864.

Rodman, William B., and George W. Gahagan. "To the People of North Carolina." N.p., 1868.

Rogers, Andrew Jackson. "A White Man's Government: Speech of Hon. Andrew J. Rogers, of New Jersey, Delivered in the House of Representatives, January 11, 1866." Washington, D. C., 1866.

Saulsbury, Willard. "Suffrage Constitution Amendment: Speech of Hon. Willard Saulsbury, of Delaware, Delivered in the Senate of the United States, February 8, 1869." Washington, D. C., 1869.

[Schmidt, George.] "The Guide Post for Patriots." Milwaukee, Wis., 1864.

Seaman, L. "What Miscegenation Is! and What We Are to Expect Now that Mr. Lincoln Is Re-Elected." New York [1864?].

Seymour, Horatio, and Samuel J. Tilden. "Speeches of Ex-Gov. Horatio Seymour & Samuel J. Tilden, before the Democratic State Convention at Albany, March 11, 1868." World Tracts No. 1. [New York], 1868.

Shiveley, J. W. "An Extra of the Sovereign People's Magna Carta: The White Man in Chains and the Nigger Reigns." Leaflet. N.p., 1864.

Sister Sallie (pseud.). "The Color Line. Devoted to the Restoration of Good Government, Putting an End to Negro Authority and Misrule, and Establishing a White Man's Government in the White Man's Country, by Organizing the White People of the South." N.p. [1868?].

Sitgreaves, Charles. "Speech of Hon. Charles Sitgreaves, of New Jersey, on Radicalism and Reconstruction; Saturday, June 16, 1866." Washington, D. C., 1866.

Stewart, James A. "A Campaign Document for 1868; to the People of the United States: Can't Ye See Where Ye Are Drifting? Must Ye Ever Be the Accomplice, or the Victim of Political Charlatans, Knaves, and Demagogues?" Atlanta, 1868.

Stinchfield, D. L. "Principle, Policy and Practice! or Democracy versus Passiveism and Sectionalism! or Truth as Opposed to Sacrificing Established

National Principles to Sectional Departing Expediency!! Also—What I Know about Farming-Out Political Parties." Cincinnati, 1872.

Tioga, Pennsylvania, Democratic Club. "Huzza for Seymour and Blair!!! The People Are Coming to the Rescue, with Equal Rights for All; Read and Circulate." New York, 1868.

"Uncivilized Races: Proving that Many Races of Men Are Incapable of Civilization, by an Appeal to the Most Eminent Scientific Naturalists, Explorers and Historians of All Ages, Being the Substance of a Paper Read before the Anthropological Society of America." New York, 1868.

Union League Club of New York. "Report of Special Committee on the Passage by the House of Representatives of the Constitutional Amendment for the Abolition of Slavery, January 31, 1865." New York, 1865.

Urbanus, Caius (pseud.). "Subjects for Thinkers: What Shall We Do with the Negro?" A Tract for the Times (First Paper). St. Louis, 1862.

Vallandigham, Clement Laird. "The Great Civil War in America: Speech of Hon. Clement Laird Vallandigham, of Ohio, in the House of Representatives, January 14, 1863." Washington, D. C., 1863.

[Van Evrie, John H.] "Emancipation and Its Results." No. 6 of Papers from the Society for the Diffusion of Political Knowledge. New York, 1863.

[———.] "Free Negroism: or, Results of Emancipation in the North and the West India Islands; with Statistics of the Decay of Commerce, Idleness of the Negro, His Return to Savageism, and the Effect of Emancipation upon the Farming, Mechanical, and Laboring Classes." Anti-Abolition Tract No. 2. New York, 1862.

[———.] "The Six Species of Men, with Cuts Representing the Types of the Caucasian, Mongul, Malay, Indian, Esquimaux and Negro, with Their General Physical and Mental Qualities, Laws of Organization, Relations to Civilization, Etc." Anti-Abolition Tract No. 5. New York, 1866.

———. "Subjenation: The Theory of the Normal Relation of the Races; An Answer to 'Miscegenation.' " New York, 1864.

"The Voice of the Clergy." Leaflet. [Philadelphia, 1863.]

Walter, J. (ed.). "The Vallandigham Song Book: Songs for the Times." Columbus, Ohio, 1863.

White, Chilton A. "Speech of Hon. Chilton A. White, of Ohio, on the Enlistment of Negro Soldiers; Delivered in the House of Representatives, February 2, 1863." Washington, D. C., 1863.

[Wilson, Montgomery.] "The Copperhead Catechism: For the Instruction of Such Politicians as Are of Tender Years, Carefully Compiled by Divers Learned and Designing Men, Authorized and with Admonitions by Fernando the Gothamite, High Priest of the Order of Copperheads." New York, 1864.

Young, Robert A. "The Negro: A Reply to Ariel. The Negro Belongs to the Genus Homo—He Is a Descendant of Adam and Eve—He Is the Offspring of Ham—He Is Not a Beast, but a Human Being—He Has an Immortal Soul—He May Be Civilized, Enlightened, and Converted to Christianity." Nashville, Tenn., 1867.

OTHER WORKS

Allen, William G. *The American Prejudice against Color: An Authentic Narrative, Showing How Easily the Nation Got into an Uproar.* London, 1853.

The American Annual Cyclopedia and Register of Important Events. 84 vols. New York, 1870–1903.

Andreano, Ralph (ed.). *The Economic Impact of the American Civil War.* Cambridge, Mass., 1962.

Andrews, Sidney. *The South since the War: As Shown by Fourteen Weeks of Travel and Observation in Georgia and the Carolinas.* Boston, 1866.

Aptheker, Herbert (ed.). *A Documentary History of the Negro People in the United States.* New York, 1951.

Avary, Myrta Lockett. *Dixie after the War: An Exposition of Social Conditions Existing in the South, during the Twelve Years Succeeding the Fall of Richmond.* New York, 1906.

Bailey, Hugh C. *Hinton Rowan Helper: Abolitionist-Racist.* University, Ala., 1965.

Baker, Ray Stannard. *Following the Color Line: American Negro Citizenship in the Progressive Era.* New York, 1964 [1908].

Basler, Roy P. (ed.). *The Collected Works of Abraham Lincoln.* 9 vols. New Brunswick, N. J., 1953.

Beale, Howard K. *The Critical Year: A Study of Andrew Johnson and Reconstruction.* New York, 1930.

Berger, Morroe. *Equality by Statute: Legal Controls over Group Discrimination.* New York, 1950.

Blair, Lewis H. *A Southern Prophecy: The Prosperity of the South Dependent upon the Elevation of the Negro.* Boston, 1964 [1889].

Boatner, Mark M. *The Civil War Dictionary.* New York, 1959.

Bowers, Claude G. *The Tragic Era: The Revolution after Lincoln.* Cambridge, Mass., 1929.

Brewster, James. *Sketches of Southern Mystery, Treason and Murder: The Secret Political Societies of the South, Their Methods and Manners. The Phagedenic Cancer on Our National Life.* Milwaukee, Wis., 1903.

Broca, Paul. *On the Phenomena of Hybridity in the Genus Homo.* London, 1864.

Brodie, Fawn. *Thaddeus Stevens: Scourge of the South.* New York, 1959.

Brown, Donald Norton. Southern Attitudes toward Negro Voting during the Bourbon Period, 1877–1890. Unpublished Ph.D. dissertation. University of Oklahoma, 1960.

Burton, Richard F. *Mission to Gelele, King of Dahome: With Notices of the So Called "Amazons," the Grand Customs, the Yearly Customs, the Human Sacrifices, the Present State of the Slave Trade, and the Negro's Place in Nature.* 2 vols. Second edition. London, 1864.

Cable, George W. *The Negro Question: A Selection of Writings on Civil Rights in the South.* Garden City, N. Y., 1958 [1889].

Campbell, Sir George. *White and Black: The Outcome of a Visit to the United States.* London, 1878.

Carter, Hodding. *The Angry Scar: The Story of Reconstruction.* New York, 1959.

Clemenceau, Georges. *American Reconstruction, 1865–1870: And the Impeachment of President Johnson.* New York, 1928. The letters in this volume were originally published as *Lettres des Etats-Unis,* in the daily *Paris Temps,* between 1865 and 1870.

Cochrane, William. Freedom without Equality: A Study of Northern Opinion and the Negro Issue, 1861–1870. Unpublished Ph.D. dissertation. University of Minnesota, 1957.

Coleman, Charles H. *The Election of 1868: The Democratic Effort to Regain Control.* New York, 1933.

Coulter, E. Merton. *The South during Reconstruction, 1865–1877.* Baton Rouge, La., 1947.

Cox, LaWanda and John H. *Politics, Principle, and Prejudice, 1865–1866: Dilemma of Reconstruction America.* New York, 1963.

Cox, Samuel Sullivan. *Eight Years in Congress, from 1857–1865: Memoirs and Speeches.* New York, 1865.

———. *Three Decades of Federal Legislation, 1855–1885.* San Francisco, 1885.

Croly, David G. *Seymour and Blair, Their Lives and Services: With an Appendix Containing a History of Reconstruction.* New York, 1868.

Dabney, Robert L. *A Defence of Virginia, and through Her, of the South, in Recent and Pending Contests against the Sectional Party.* New York, 1867.

Daniels, John. *In Freedom's Birthplace: A Study of Boston Negroes.* Boston, 1914.

Democratic Party, Pennsylvania. *Proceedings of the Nob Mountain Meeting, Held in Columbus County, Pa., on the Last Three Days of August, 1865.* Philadelphia, 1865.

Denison, John D. *Iowa Democracy: A History of Politics and Personalities of the Democratic Party, 1846–1938.* 4 vols. [Des Moines], Iowa, 1939.

Dickinson, Anna E. *What Answer?* Boston, 1868.

Dictionary of American Biography. 22 vols. New York, 1930–1936.

Dixon, William Hepworth. *New America.* 2 vols. Sixth edition. London, 1867.

———. *White Conquest.* 2 vols. London, 1876.

Downey, Matthew Thomas. The Rebirth of Reform: A Study of Liberal Reform Movements, 1865–1872. Unpublished Ph.D. dissertation. Princeton University, 1963.

Duberman, Martin (ed.). *The Antislavery Vanguard: New Essays on the Abolitionists.* Princeton, 1965.

Duke, Basil W. *Reminiscences of General Basil W. Duke.* New York, 1911.

Dunning, William Archibald. *Essays on the Civil War and Reconstruction and Related Topics.* New York, 1898.

Ezell, John Samuel. *The South since 1865.* New York, 1963.

Fleming, Walter L. (ed.). *The Constitution and Ritual of the Knights of the White Camelia.* No. 1 of *West Virginia University Documents Relating to Reconstruction.* Morgantown, West Va., 1904.

—— (ed.). *Documentary History of Reconstruction: Political, Military, Social, Religious, Educational & Industrial, 1865 to the Present Time.* 2 vols. Cleveland, 1907.

—— (ed.). *Laws Relating to Freedmen, 1865–6.* No. 8 of *West Virginia University Documents Relating to Reconstruction.* Morgantown, West Va., 1904.

Fortune, T. Thomas. *Black and White: Land Labor, and Politics in the South.* New York, 1884.

Franklin, John Hope. *From Slavery to Freedom: A History of the American Negroes.* Second edition. New York, 1956.

——. *Reconstruction: After the Civil War.* Chicago, 1961.

Fredrickson, George M. *The Inner Civil War: Northern Intellectuals and the Crisis of the Union.* New York, 1965.

Gilchrist, David T., and W. David Lewis (eds.). *Economic Change in the Civil War Era: Proceedings of the Conference on American Economic Institutional Change, 1850–1873, and the Impact of the Civil War.* Greenville, Del., 1964.

Gobineau, Count Joseph Arthur de. *The Moral and Intellectual Diversity of Races, with Particular Reference to Their Respective Influence in the Civil and Political History of Mankind.* Philadelphia, 1856.

Goldstein, Naomi Friedman. *The Roots of Prejudice against the Negro in the United States.* Boston, 1948.

Gossett, Thomas F. *Race: The History of an Idea in America.* Dallas, Tex., 1963.

Govan, Gilbert E., and James W. Livingood. *The Chattanooga Country, 1540–1951: From Tomahawks to TVA.* New York, 1952.

Gray, Wood. *The Hidden Civil War: The Story of the Copperheads.* New York, 1942.

Grayson, William J. *The Hireling and the Slave, Chicora, and Other Poems.* Charleston, S. C., 1856.

Green, Fletcher Melvin (ed.). *Essays in Southern History.* Vol. 31 of *James Sprunt Studies in History and Political Science.* Chapel Hill, N. C., 1949.

Gregory, Winifred (ed.). *American Newspapers, 1821–1936: A Union List of Files Available in the United States and Canada.* New York, 1937.

Grinnell, Josiah Bushnell. *Men and Events of Forty Years: Autobiographical Reminiscences of an Active Career from 1850 to 1890.* Boston, 1891.

[Halpine, Charles Graham] *The Life and Adventures, Songs, Services, and Speeches of Private Miles O'Reilly.* New York, 1864. First published in the New York *Herald* between Apr. 1863 and Jan. 1864.

Harness, A. C. *The Great Trial; or, The Genius of Civilization Brought to Judgement.* Philadelphia, 1873.

Harris, Robert J. *The Quest for Equality.* Baton Rouge, La., 1960.

Helper, Hinton Rowan. *The Impending Crisis of the South: How to Meet It.* New York, 1857.

—— (ed.). *The Negroes in Negroland; the Negroes in America; and Negroes Generally. Also, the Several Races of White Men, Considered as the Involuntary and Predestined Supplanters of the Black Races.* New York, 1868.

——. *Nojoque: A Question for a Continent.* New York, 1867.

——. *Noonday Exigencies in America.* New York, 1871.

Henry, G. Selden. Radical Republican Policy toward the Negro during Reconstruction. Unpublished Ph.D. dissertation. Yale University, 1963.

Henry, Ralph Selph. *The Story of Reconstruction.* New York, 1938.

Hernton, Calvin C. *Sex and Racism in America.* New York, 1965.

Hesseltine, William B. *Lincoln's Plan of Reconstruction.* Tuscaloosa, Ala., 1960.

—— (ed.). *The Tragic Conflict: The Civil War and Reconstruction.* New York. 1962.

Hickok, Charles Thomas. *The Negro in Ohio, 1802–1870.* Cleveland, 1896.

Hirshson, Stanley P. *Farewell to the Bloody Shirt: Northern Republicans & the Southern Negro, 1877–1893.* Bloomington, Ind., 1962.

Hofstadter, Richard (ed.). *Great Issues in American History: A Documentary Record.* 2 vols. New York, 1958.

Holden, William W. *Memoirs of W. W. Holden.* Durham, N. C., 1911.

An Inquiry into the Condition and Prospects of the African Race in the United States: And the Means of Bettering Its Fortunes. Philadelphia, 1839.

Jamaica Committee, London. *The Blue Books.* Jamaica Papers No. II. London, [1866].

——. *Facts and Documents Relating to the Alleged Rebellion in Jamaica, and the Measures of Repression; Including Notes of the Trial of Mr. Gordon.* Jamaica Papers No. I. London, 1866.

James, Joseph B. *The Framing of the Fourteenth Amendment.* Urbana, Ill., 1956.

Kendrick, Benjamin B. (ed.). *The Journal of the Joint Committee of Fifteen on Reconstruction, 39th Congress, 1865–1867.* New York, 1914.

Klement, Frank L. *The Copperheads in the Middle West.* Chicago, 1960.

Knox, Arbuthnot John Graham. Race Relations in Jamaica, 1833–1958: With Special Reference to British Colonial Policy. Unpublished Ph.D. dissertation. University of Florida, 1962.

Konvitz, Milton R. *A Century of Civil Rights.* New York, 1961.

Lewinson, Paul. *Race, Class, & Party: A History of Negro Suffrage and White Politics in the South.* New York, 1932.

Lindsey, David. *"Sunset" Cox: Irrepressible Democrat*. Detroit, 1959.

Litwack, Leon F. *North of Slavery: The Negro in the Free States, 1790–1860*. Chicago, 1961.

[Locke, David Ross.] *Ekkoes from Kentucky, Bein a Perfect Record uv the Ups, Downs, and Experiences uv the Dimocrisy, doorin the Eventful Year 1867, ez Seen by a Naturalized Kentuckian*. Boston, 1868.

Lowie, Robert H. *The History of Ethnological Theory*. New York, 1937.

Lunt, George. *The Origin of the Late War: Traced from the Beginning of the Constitution to the Revolt of the Southern States*. New York, 1867.

Lurie, Edward. *Louis Agassiz: A Life in Science*. Chicago, 1960.

Lynch, John R. *The Facts of Reconstruction*. New York, 1914.

Macrae, David. *The Americans at Home*. New York, 1952.

Mangum, Charles S., Jr. *The Legal Status of the Negro*. Chapel Hill, N. C., 1940.

Martin, Michael, and Leonard Gelber (eds.). *Dictionary of American History*. Paterson, N. J., 1959.

Massey, Mary Elizabeth. *Bonnet Brigades*. New York, 1966.

McCabe, James D., Jr. *The Life and Public Services of Horatio Seymour: Together with a Complete and Authentic Life of Francis P. Blair, Jr*. New York, 1868.

McClure, Alexander Kelly. *The South: Its Industrial, Financial, and Political Condition*. Philadelphia, 1886.

McKitrick, Eric L. *Andrew Johnson and Reconstruction*. Chicago, 1960.

McPherson, Edward (ed.). *The Political History of the United States of America during the Period of Reconstruction, from April 15, 1865 to July 15, 1870*. Washington, D. C., 1880.

McPherson, James M. *The Struggle for Equality: Abolitionists and the Negro in the Civil War and Reconstruction*. Princeton, N. J., 1964.

Melville, Herman. *Battle-Pieces and Aspects of the War*. Gainesville, Fla., 1960 [New York, 1866].

Miller, Marion Mills (ed.). *Great Debates in American History*. 14 vols. New York, 1913.

Milton, George Fort. *Abraham Lincoln and the Fifth Column*. New York, 1942.

Morgan, A. T. *Yazoo; or, On the Picket Line of Freedom in the South*. Washington, D. C., 1884.

Morrow, Ralph E. *Northern Methodism and Reconstruction*. East Lansing, Mich., 1956.

Mott, Frank Luther. *American Journalism: A History of Newspapers in the United States through 260 Years: 1690 to 1950*. Revised. New York, 1950.

Murphy, John C. *An Analysis of the Attitudes of American Catholics toward the Immigrant and the Negro, 1825–1925*. Washington, D. C., 1940.

Murray, Pauli. *Proud Shoes*. New York, 1956.

Myrdal, Gunnar. *An American Dilemma: The Negro Problem and Modern Democracy*. Revised. New York, 1962.

The Mystery Finished: The Negro Has a Soul; His Normal Relation Is that of a Servant of Tribute to Shem and Japheth; the Negro Is Not a Citizen of the State, but a Member of the Church by Divine Appointment. Memphis, Tenn., 1868.

Nicholas, S. S. *Conservative Essays, Legal and Political.* Second series. Philadelphia, 1865.

Nordhoff, Charles. *The Cotton States in the Spring and Summer of 1875.* New York, 1876.

Northend, William D. *Speeches and Essays upon Political Subjects from 1860 to 1869.* Salem, Mass., 1869.

Nott, Josiah Clark. *Indigenous Races of the Earth: or, New Chapters of Ethnological Inquiry.* Philadelphia, 1857.

———, and George R. Gliddon. *Types of Mankind: or, Ethnological Researches, Based upon the Ancient Monuments, Paintings, Sculptures, and Crania of Races, and upon Their Natural, Geographical, Philological and Biblical History.* Philadelphia, 1855.

Oberholtzer, Ellis Paxson. *A History of the United States since the Civil War.* 5 vols. New York, 1917.

[Payne, Buckner H.] *The Negro: What Is His Ethnological Status? Is He the Progeny of Ham? Is He a Descendant of Adam and Eve? Has He a Soul? Or Is He a Beast in God's Nomenclature? What Is His Status as Fixed by God in Creation? What Is His Relation to the White Race? Enlarged, with a Review of His Reviewers, Exhibiting the Learning of the "Learned."* Cincinnati, Ohio, 1872.

Pike, James S. *The Prostrate State: South Carolina under Negro Government.* New York, 1935 [1873].

Political Oats: A Kernel or Two for Everybody. New York, 1872.

Pollard, Edward A. *Black Diamonds Gathered in the Darkey Homes of the South.* New York, 1859.

———. *The Lost Cause Regained.* New York, 1868.

Pomeroy, Marcus Mills "Brick." *Democratic Campaign Song Book: A Red Hot One for the Boys.* New York, 1868.

Porter, Kirk H., and Donald Bruce Johnson (eds.). *National Party Platforms, 1840–1956.* Urbana, Ill., 1956.

Potts, William D. *Freemen's Guide to the Polls, and a Solemn Appeal to American Patriots.* New York, 1864.

Randall, James G., and David Donald. *The Civil War and Reconstruction.* Revised. Boston, 1961.

Read, Hollis. *The Negro Problem Solved: or, Africa as She Is, and as She Shall Be. Her Curse and Her Cure.* New York, 1864.

Reed, Emily Hazen. *Life of A. P. Dostie; or, the Conflict in New Orleans.* New York, 1868.

Reid, Whitelaw. *After the War: A Southern Tour, May 1, 1865, to May 1, 1866.* New York, 1866.

Ryan, Daniel J. (ed.). *The Civil War Literature of Ohio: A Bibliography with Explanatory and Historical Notes.* Cleveland, 1911.

Sabin, Joseph, and sons (eds.). *A Dictionary of Books Relating to America, from Its Discovery to the Present Time.* New York, 1868–1936.

Seabury, Samuel. *American Slavery Distinguished from the Slavery of English Theorists and Justified by the Law of Nature.* New York, 1861.

Sellers, Charles Grier, Jr. (ed.). *The Southerner as American.* Chapel Hill, N. C., 1960.

Seymour, Horatio. *Public Record: Including Speeches, Messages, Proclamations, Official Correspondence, and Other Public Utterances of Horatio Seymour; from the Campaign of 1856 to the Present Time.* New York, 1868.

Shenton, James P. (ed.). *The Reconstruction: A Documentary History of the South after the War, 1865–1877.* New York, 1963.

Sinclair, William A. *The Aftermath of Slavery: A Study of the Condition and Environment of the American Negro.* Boston, 1905.

Singletary, Otis A. *Negro Militia and Reconstruction.* Austin, Tex., 1957.

[Smith, Charles Henry.] *Bill Arp's Peace Papers.* New York, 1873.

Smith, George Winston, and Charles Judah (eds.). *Life in the North during the Civil War: A Source History.* Albuquerque, N. M., 1966.

Smith, William Ernest. *The Francis Preston Blair Family in Politics.* 2 vols. New York, 1933.

Somers, Robert. *The Southern States since the War, 1870–71.* London, 1871.

Spence, James. *The American Union: Its Effect on National Character and Policy, with an Inquiry into Secession as a Constitutional Right, and the Causes of the Disruption.* Third edition. London, 1862.

Spring, Lindley. *The Negro at Home: An Inquiry after His Capacity for Self-Government and the Government of Whites for Controlling, Leading, Directing or Co-operating in the Civilization of the Age.* New York, 1868.

Sproat, John Gerald. Party of the Center: The Politics of Liberal Reform in Post-Civil War America. Unpublished Ph.D. dissertation. University of California, Berkeley, 1960.

Stampp, Kenneth M. *The Era of Reconstruction, 1865–1877.* New York, 1965.

Stanton, William. *The Leopard's Spots: Scientific Attitudes toward Race in America, 1815–59.* Chicago, 1960.

Steiner, Bernard C. *Life of Reverdy Johnson.* Baltimore, 1914.

Stephenson, Gilbert Thomas. *Race Distinctions in American Law.* New York, 1910.

Tarbox Increase N. *The Curse; or, The Position in the World's History Occupied by the Race of Ham.* Boston, 1864.

Thorpe, Earl E. *The Mind of the Negro: An Intellectual History of Afro-Americans.* Baton Rouge, La., 1961.

Throop, Montgomery E. *The Future: A Political Essay.* New York, 1864.

Trefousse, Hans L. *Benjamin Franklin Wade: Radical Republican from Ohio.* New York, 1963.

United States Bureau of the Census, Department of Commerce. *Negro Population, 1790–1915*. Washington, D. C., 1918.

———. *The Statistical History of the United States from Colonial Times to the Present*. Stamford, Conn., 1965.

———. *Ku Klux Report*. 13 vols. 42 Cong., 2 Sess., Senate Reports No. 41, House Reports No. 22. Washington, D. C., 1872.

United States Senate. *Report of the Committee on Outrages in Mississippi*. Washington, D. C., 1876.

Vallandigham, Clement Laird. *The Record of Hon. C. L. Vallandigham on Abolition, the Union, and the Civil War*. Cincinnati, Ohio, 1863.

Van Evrie, John H. *Negroes and Negro "Slavery": The First an Inferior Race: The Latter Its Normal Condition*. New York, 1861. The title of the 1870 edition was *White Supremacy and Negro Subordination*.

Weatherford, Willis D., and Charles S. Johnson. *Race Relations: Adjustment of Whites and Negroes in the United States*. Boston, 1934.

Welles, Gideon. *Diary of Gideon Welles*. 3 vols. Boston, 1911.

Weyl, Nathaniel. *The Negro in American Civilization*. Washington, D. C., 1960.

Wharton, Vernon Lane. *The Negro in Mississippi, 1865–1890*. Chapel Hill, N. C., 1947.

Wheat, Marvin T. *The Progress and Intelligence of Americans; Collateral Proof of Slavery, from the First to the Eleventh Chapter of Genesis, as Founded on Organic Law; and from the Fact of Christ Being a Caucasian, Owing to His Peculiar Parentage*. Second edition. Louisville, Ky., 1862. In 1865, the popular binder's title was changed to *Normal Group Servitude*.

[White, Richard Grant.] *The New Gospel of Peace According to St. Benjamin*. New York, 1866.

Wilson, Edmund. *Patriotic Gore: Studies in the Literature of the American Civil War*. New York, 1962.

Wish, Harvey (ed.). *Ante-Bellum: Writings of George Fitzhugh and Hinton Rowan Helper on Slavery*. New York, 1960.

Woodson, Carter G. *The Negro in Our History*. Seventh edition. Washington, D. C., 1941.

Woodward, Comer Vann. *The Burden of Southern History*. New York, 1961.

———. *Origins of the New South*. Baton Rouge, La., 1951.

———. *The Strange Career of Jim Crow*. Revised. New York, 1957.

Workers of the Writers' Program (eds.). *Nebraska and Reconstruction, 1865–1873: Editorial Opinions*. Omaha, Neb., 1941.

Young, Wayland. *Eros Denied*. Studies in Exclusion I. London, 1965.

Index